JOHN LOCKE

Two Treatises of Government

JOHN LOCKE

Two Treatises of Government

Edited, with Introduction and Notes,

by Lee Ward

focus an imprint of
Hackett Publishing Company, Inc
Indianapolis/Cambridge

A Focus book

Focus an imprint of
   Hackett Publishing Company

Copyright © 2016 by Hackett Publishing Company, Inc.

19 18 17 16   1 2 3 4 5 6 7

For further information, please address
Hackett Publishing Company, Inc.
P.O. Box 44937
Indianapolis, Indiana 46244-0937

www.hackettpublishing.com

Composition by Aptara, Inc.

Library of Congress Cataloging-in-Publication Data

Names: Locke, John, 1632–1704. | Ward, Lee, 1970– editor.
Title: Two treatises of government / John Locke ; edited with introduction
   and notes, by Lee Ward.
Description: Indianapolis, Indiana : Focus, 2016.
Identifiers: LCCN 2015041306 | ISBN 9781585107971 (paperback)
Subjects: LCSH: Locke, John, 1632–1704. Two treatises of government. |
   BISAC: POLITICAL SCIENCE / History & Theory. | PHILOSOPHY /
   Political. | PHILOSOPHY / History & Surveys / Modern.
Classification: LCC JC153 .L8 2016 | DDC 320—dc23
LC record available at http://lccn.loc.gov/2015041306

CONTENTS

Editor's Introduction to Locke's Two Treatises of Government

John Locke (1632–1704) is celebrated as one of the philosophical founders of modern liberal democracy. But this intellectual forbearer of modernity came forth into a world still very much dominated by the premodern authority of throne and altar. Locke was born in 1632 into West Country English gentry with small but prosperous estates in Somerset, near Bristol, into a family whose loyalties were decidedly on the Parliamentary side in England's civil wars of the 1640s. In 1646 Locke was admitted to the prestigious Westminster School in London before entering Christ Church College at Oxford University in 1652 and graduating with a master of arts in 1658. He studied medicine and taught philosophy at Oxford for much of the next four decades. His interest and achievements in the study of natural science brought him considerable attention, and in 1668 he was admitted as a Fellow of The Royal Society of London for Improving Natural Knowledge, joining such scientific luminaries as Robert Boyle, Robert Hooke, and Richard Lower.

Locke's political involvement began with his personal relationship with Anthony Ashley Cooper, 1st Lord of Shaftesbury, who was the leader of the Whig movement in Parliament that opposed the absolutist pretensions of Stuart King Charles II during the 1670s and early 1680s. In time, Locke became a trusted advisor to the Whig leadership. After the death of Shaftesbury (in 1683) and the scattering of the Whig leaders following the Exclusion Crisis of 1679–1681, Locke fled to Holland, where he lived for four years incognito, out of fear of arrest and extradition back to England. During his sojourn in Holland, Locke became a confidante of the Orangists surrounding future King William and Queen Mary, returning with them to England in the Glorious Revolution of 1688–1689 that removed from the throne the last Stuart king,

Charles' brother, James II. It was in the decade following the Glorious Revolution that Locke published his most important works, including the *Letters Concerning Toleration* (1690, 1692), *Some Thoughts Concerning Education* (1693), and the work for which he was most famous during his lifetime, the *Essay Concerning Human Understanding* (1689), which, when he died in 1704, firmly established his reputation as one of the most influential philosophers of the era.

The Context of the *Two Treatises*

Locke's most significant contribution to the development of modern political philosophy was, however, *Two Treatises of Government*, published anonymously in 1690. Together the treatises were a *pièce d'occasion* justification for the Whig-inspired Glorious Revolution as well as a statement of sophisticated political theory in their own right. In order to understand the context of the *Two Treatises* it is important to recognize that while they were published in the wake of the Glorious Revolution, Locke actually composed practically all of this work nearly a decade earlier, during the Exclusion Crisis of 1679–1681. The issue at that time was whether Parliament had the right to exclude from the succession James II, the Catholic brother of King Charles II, who was without a legitimate successor of his own. The Exclusion Crisis pitted the monarch's supporters, known as Tories, against the Whig supporters of Parliament, led by Locke's friend Shaftesbury. The outcome of this confrontation was defeat for the Parliamentary cause as Charles succeeded in mobilizing Tory support in the House of Lords and among the leaders of the Church of England. This powerful Royalist alliance allowed the king to dissolve the Exclusion Parliament in 1681 and gradually drive the Whig leadership into exile.

In some respects, the Glorious Revolution was the exact opposite of what transpired during the Exclusion Crisis, inasmuch as in removing James II from the throne in 1688 the Parliamentary forces achieved the practical success that eluded them in their efforts to exclude him from the succession a decade earlier. Yet in another sense, the fundamental issue in both events was essentially the same, namely, whether Parliament had the right to determine who would occupy the English throne. Another link between the

Exclusion Crisis and the Glorious Revolution was a set of writings that framed many of the great constitutional, philosophical, and religious questions raised by these conflicts. In particular, Locke's *Two Treatises*, as well as works by other Whigs, including James Tyrrell and Algernon Sidney, were composed as a critical response to the writings of a long-dead English Royalist named Sir Robert Filmer, whose works had been republished by the Tories at the height of the Exclusion Crisis. Filmer's *Patriarcha* and other writings supplied the intellectual thread running through the Royalist position in both the Exclusion Crisis and the Glorious Revolution. Indeed, Locke identified Filmer, who died in 1653, as his chief interlocutor, whose ideas had been put forth by leading Anglican clergy, such as Archbishop Sancroft (the "pulpit" and the "Drum Ecclesiastic" identified in Locke's preface to the *Two Treatises*), as the core of the Royalist position on the English Constitution and the duty of political obedience. But who was Robert Filmer, and why are his ideas central to understanding the *Two Treatises*?

Filmer and Patriarchal Divine Right

Robert Filmer was a Kentshire gentleman born in 1588 who had connections both to the higher clergy in the Church of England, by marrying the daughter of the Bishop of Ely, and to the royal court from which he secured a knighthood from James I in 1619. Filmer was an arch-Royalist who was horrified to witness the rebellion against Charles I and his execution at the end of England's civil wars in 1649. Why did Filmer become the intellectual doyen of English Toryism three decades after his death? Principally it was because he wrote several works including his commentaries on Hugo Grotius, Thomas Hobbes, and John Milton in which he extolled the moral and religious duty of subjects to obey monarchical authority. Filmer was hardly unique in putting forth the case for political obedience, but the real strength of his argument, and what set it apart from other Royalist tracts, was the extreme political conclusions he drew from widely accepted cultural beliefs and attitudes toward the patriarchal family and the authority of the Bible. In particular, Filmer's *Patriarcha*, written in the 1630s, relied on the biblical account of Adam's creation in the book of Genesis to ground a potent combination of patriarchalism and the divine-right political theology that produced what was for many readers in the seventeenth century a compelling argument for absolute monarchy.

Filmer's Adamite thesis rested on the claim that the "lordship which Adam by creation had over the whole world, and by right descending from him the patriarchs did enjoy, was as large and ample as the absolutest dominion of any monarch which hath been since creation."[1] Filmer built upon the sociological fact represented by the ubiquity of the patriarchal family and seen in the official endorsement of the fifth commandment to honor parents by the Church of England as the basis of political obligation. From this material Filmer constructed an *ontology of creatureliness*, according to which every human being is defined by their obligation to the source of one's being. Adam was the first father and all subsequent rulers derive their authority to govern from Adam's original right such that in all "kingdoms or commonwealths in the world" the ruler is the "supreme father of the people" (Filmer 1991: 11). The divine source of this right to rule meant that the consent of the people played no role whatsoever in the formation of governments. The political implications of Filmer's essentially theological conception of sovereignty were profoundly authoritarian as Filmer rejected any idea of a popular right of resistance and dismissed any form of government apart from absolute monarchy as fundamentally flawed claimants to be heirs of Adam's original rule over creation. In Filmer's writings, English Royalists in the turbulent 1680s found the most uncompromising and biblically grounded case for sweeping monarchical power available to them in their polemical war with the Whigs.

The Exclusion Tracts

Identifying Locke's most direct divine-right ideological foe in the *Two Treatises* is only part of the task of revealing the context of this work. It is also important to recognize that the *Two Treatises* represent one distinct strand among several variants of Whig political thought at the time. Indeed, Locke's offering was written more or less contemporaneously with two other significant refutations

---

1.   Robert Filmer, *Patriarcha and Other Writings*, Johann Somerville, ed. (Cambridge: Cambridge University Press, 1991), p. 7.

of Filmer. The first, and the only one actually published during the Exclusion Crisis, was James Tyrrell's *Patriarcha non monarcha* (1680). At this time Tyrrell was a personal friend of Locke, although there is no evidence that they collaborated in their political writings. Tyrrell wrote a detailed response to Filmer that is heavily influenced by Aristotle-inspired ideas about the "ancient mixed constitution" and by the natural-law theory of German legal thinker Samuel Pufendorf. *Patriarcha non monarcha* appealed to moderate Whig opponents of Charles II who believed that the actions and policies of the Stuarts threatened to overturn England's national church and the country's balanced constitution comprising the king, lords, and commons. These socially and politically conservative Whig-landed elites defended a limited right of resistance to the Crown and supported Parliament's right to alter the succession. However, they rejected Locke's radical principle of popular sovereignty and individual natural rights derived from a theoretical state of nature. For Tyrrell and like-minded moderate Whigs, nothing in scripture supported the absolutist model of monarchy advanced by Filmer. Rather, both the Bible and unassisted reason leave human beings free to form compacts and institutions designed to protect their historic rights.

Another important Exclusion-era Whig tract was Algernon Sidney's *Discourses Concerning Government*. Sidney was the firebrand martyr to the Whig cause, whose unpublished *Discourses* were used as evidence in the trial that condemned him as a traitor to the Crown and led to his execution in 1683. In this lengthy point-by-point response to Filmer's republished work, Sidney advanced an argument for republicanism based on popular sovereignty and the right of revolution. In Sidney, we see the radical democratic wing of the Whig movement, a small group of hardened revolutionaries who shared the political ideals of the Civil War–era commonwealth's-men, and for whom the parliamentary republic of the 1640s and early 1650s prior to Oliver Cromwell's protectorate was the best government that England had ever enjoyed. Sidney excoriated Filmer's divine-right monarchy and his putative biblical supports, and extolled the republican ideals of civic virtue and government by large representative assemblies chosen through frequent elections and regular rotation in office. Locke, then, represents a distinctly liberal strain of Whiggism that shares features of both the moderate and radical democratic strains but also departs from both in crucial ways. That is to say, Locke's liberal political doctrine both advanced a radical theory of natural rights and, at the same time, expressed reservations about direct democracy. In the *Two Treatises* Locke developed a philosophy of government with radical features, such as a state of nature, individual natural rights, and a right of revolution, yet he also eschewed republican ideas of civic virtue and endorsed the traditional English constitutional separation of powers. But before we can fully grasp the unique features of Locke's liberal arguments in their historical context, it is necessary to analyse the relationship between the *First Treatise* and the *Second Treatise*.

The Relation between the *First* and *Second Treatises*

In order to grasp the complex relation between the *First* and *Second Treatises*, we must confront the divergent legacies of the two works. The *First Treatise* is rarely read or studied today except by specialists, whereas the *Second Treatise* is widely regarded as a classic text in political philosophy, routinely read in political theory and intellectual history courses. How can we explain this discrepancy? And why should we read the *First Treatise* today? The prevailing impression is that the *First Treatise* is simply a *pièce d'occasion* offered as a detailed, often tedious, response to the obsolete and at times absurd arguments of the supporters of divine-right monarchy, such as Robert Filmer. In contrast, the *Second Treatise* is typically regarded as a path-breaking work of political philosophy that reframed the parameters of modern thinking about individual rights and constitutional government. This stark contrast is, however, very misleading and unfair, as it understates the significance of the *First Treatise* and it isolates the *Second Treatise* from its proper intellectual context. The connection between these two discourses is much closer and, I would argue, much more important than is normally supposed. Many of the distinctively Lockean teachings on natural rights, property, and constitutional government that we associate with the *Second Treatise* are foreshadowed by Locke's discussion of these topics in the *First Treatise*. More importantly, the *First Treatise* assumes a kind of logical priority over the *Second*, as it was in the *First Treatise* that Locke first took it upon himself to make natural liberty the central focus of his political philosophy. This premise of natural liberty would ground Locke's theory of government in the *Second Treatise*. Thus it is difficult to truly understand the *Second Treatise* without a sense of Locke's argument in the *First*.

Admittedly, the *Two Treatises* themselves are very different kinds of works. At one time it was commonly thought that Locke had written them in different periods of time, many years apart. Several decades ago Peter Laslett demonstrated that these treatises were composed at the same time, during the Exclusion Crisis rather than in the later Glorious Revolution period. Though both treatises were written in the same period, the reader is struck by the difference in style and tone of the two separate works. The *First Treatise* is sharply polemical, comprising a detailed refutation of Filmer's entire argument. In the *First Treatise* Locke frequently refers the reader back to passages in Filmer's text, upon which he directs his scathing commentary. Whereas the *First Treatise* revolves around rebutting Filmer's idea of patriarchal divine-right monarchy, the *Second Treatise* is less polemical and more theoretical. It is in the *Second Treatise* that Locke presented his most original arguments about natural rights, property, and limited government. The unifying thread between the two works is the doctrine of natural liberty. The treatises reflect both Locke's defense of the natural-liberty school of early modern political philosophy—which maintained that human beings are naturally free and must therefore consent to government—and his own unique contribution to that venerable philosophical school. By rebutting Filmer, Locke cast himself as an ally of thinkers as varied as Thomas Hobbes, Hugo Grotius, Richard Hooker, as well as the Jesuit scholastics Roberto Bellarmine and Francisco Suarez, who all began from the premise of consent even if they often reached different conclusions about the political and constitutional implications of natural liberty. Filmer's scripture-based ontology of obedience and creatureliness denied the very possibility of consent having any formative role in government.

Thus we can understand the rhetorical structure and plan of the *Two Treatises* in the following manner. By challenging Filmer in the *First Treatise*, Locke took the opportunity to defend the well-established doctrine of natural liberty associated with many respectable philosophical sources and intellectual authorities.

With this gesture toward philosophical tradition delivered in the *First Treatise*, Locke then used the *Second Treatise* to put forth his own distinctive version of the natural-liberty doctrine, one that departs in critical ways from earlier thinkers and even from the position of most his Whig comrades.

The *First Treatise*

The central question guiding Locke's analysis in the *First Treatise* is; What is the status of the Bible as a guide for political life? Early on in the *First Treatise* Locke focused on the scriptural basis of what he calls "the sum of all" of Filmer's arguments against natural liberty, those being:

> If God created only Adam, and of a piece of him made the woman, and if by generation from them two, as parts of them, all Mankind be propagated . . . as long as Adam lived, no man could claim or enjoy anything but by donation, assignation, or permission from him. (I: 14)[2]

If Filmer's claims about the political implications of Adam's means of creation are false, as Locke contends they are, then we are left with the long-held doctrine of natural liberty, which means that "governments must be left again to the old way of being made by contrivance, and the consent of men (*anthropine ktisis*) making use of their reason to unite together into society" (I: 6). Either Filmer is correct and no one is born free or, Locke argues, the proponents of the natural-liberty doctrine are right, and everyone is, in some sense, born free.

Locke's argument in the *First Treatise* develops in response to four separate claims advanced by Filmer with respect to the divine source of Adam's rule—that is, Adam's title by virtue of his creation; God's donation; the subjection of Eve; and the rights of fatherhood. First, with respect to creation, Filmer argued that all of Adam's progeny, and by extension every human being since, is bound in obedience to the source of one's being. In Filmer's patriarchal world view, of course, the male is the source of generation. Locke tried to refute this claim in terms of Filmer's own great authority—namely,

2. In this book Roman numerals refer to either the *First* or the *Second Treatise*, and the Arabic numerals that follow indicate the sections in the specified treatise.

scripture—by arguing that in the Genesis account, the lion was created prior to Adam (I: 15) and would thus by Filmer's logic have a better claim to universal sovereignty. Moreover, Locke ridiculed the suggestion that Genesis intended to confer regal power on Adam, given that for a long time he was alone and therefore "he could not de facto be by providence constituted the governor of the world, at a time when there was actually no government, no subjects to be governed" (I: 16). According to Locke, Genesis meant to convey that Adam's children were as free to consent to rule as their father before them. The bare act of sexual generation thus does not carry with it a form of political obligation.

Next, Locke turns to Filmer's claim that the Bible gives ownership of all of creation to Adam and to all kings who rule as his heirs. In this view, no one has a right to property without permission of their ruler. To this Locke responds that both scripture and natural reason agree that God originally gave the world in common to all human beings, not to any specific individual through a special donation. In response to Filmer's use of the famous passage in Genesis in which God gave Adam "dominion" over "every living thing that moveth upon the earth" (I: 23), Locke replies that this grant was given not to Adam alone, but rather to "the whole species of man" (I: 31). Instead of a fantastic donation from God directly to Adam, Locke argues that reason indicates that God implanted in human beings "a strong desire of self-preservation, and furnished the world with things fit for food and raiment, and other necessaries of life, subservient to his design, that man should live and abide for some time upon the face of the earth" (I: 86). It is this basic consciousness of self-preservation that would supply the basis for Locke's theory of individual natural rights in the *Second Treatise*.

The third feature of Filmer's patriarchal divine right ontology of obedience derives from the scriptural passage enjoining the subjection of Eve to Adam, "thy desire shall be to thy husband, and he shall rule over thee" (Gen. 3:16 [KJV]). For Filmer, this biblical command indicates that as Adam ruled over his wife and family, so too by analogy does a king assume rightful authority over his subjects. To this, Locke responds that the subjection of Eve was not meant to suggest any grant of government to Adam but rather the subjection that "the female sex . . . should ordinarily be in to their husbands" (I: 47). But this concession to the ubiquitous patriarchal family and marriage does not provide a model for government, nor does the biblical injunction even bind all married women at all times, as Locke insists that there is no more natural reason that a woman may not improve her married lot by "contract with her husband" than that "she should bring forth her children in sorrow and pain" (I: 47). Clearly, for Locke undeniable inequalities in the traditional family have to be strictly separated conceptually and legally from our understanding of the origins of government. At the very least, Locke insists that the apparent biblical support for patriarchy with the subjection of Eve in Genesis 3:16 has no bearing whatsoever on matters of political right.

The final aspect of Filmer's Adamite thesis was his claim that Adam derived political rule in part from his status as the first father of humankind. Just as all fathers must be obeyed by their offspring as honor to the source of their being, so too does the political ruler, Adam's heir, assume this natural power of fathers to compel obedience. Locke countered in characteristic fashion by arguing that Filmer has badly misinterpreted key biblical passages. For example, the injunction in Exodus to honor one's father is, Locke reminds the reader, invariably paired with the requirement to honor one's mother as well (Exod. 20:12). Locke insists that each time the Bible calls for obedience and honor for fathers, it always must include honor and obedience for mothers too. Thus this parental, as opposed to paternal, authority will hardly suit the purposes of the patriarchists who seek to buttress divine-right monarchy with scriptural support. Far from having any mystical claim over the obedience of children, as their source, fathers, in Locke's view, have by nature little more to do with it than the bare act of procreation: "What father of a thousand, when he begets a child, thinks farther than the satisfying his present appetite!" (I: 54). Besides, given the shared parental character of the Bible's repeated calls for obedience of children, Locke insists the "mother too hath her title, which destroys the sovereignty of one supreme monarch" (I: 65). Once again, Locke concludes that neither reason nor revelation support the radically absolutist political implications that Filmer tried to derive from the Bible.

After having systematically dismantled Filmer's argument for divine-right monarchy based upon Adam's creation, donation, the subjection of Eve, and fatherhood, Locke turns in the concluding chapters of the *First Treatise* to the vexing question of how, according to Filmer, this original title of Adam could be transmitted throughout history and conveyed upon rulers in the present. In other words, how could Filmer's Adamite thesis have any political meaning today? Filmer's account is twofold. First, he insisted that the descent of Adam's title can be traced for centuries through the several genealogies in the Old Testament, at least until the dispersal at Babel. After Babel, Filmer concedes that the direct descent from Adam became harder to determine. However, the second strand of Filmer's argument blithely dismissed any qualms his readers may have about Adam's bequest, by asserting that any ruler in the present should simply be assumed to have inherited Adam's title through an act of divine providence. Locke countered that Filmer's providentialism simply reduces to an injunction to maintain total obedience to any existing government. As Locke observes, Filmer's argument for obedience collapses under the arbitrariness of his account of providence, for by Filmer's logic the subject must obey any usurper or brigand who is lucky enough or ruthless enough to seize power. For Locke, the implications of Filmer's putative absolutism is, ironically, anarchism, for it would mean that God's original grant of power to Adam gives "a right to government in the hands of a Cade, or a Cromwell, and so all obedience . . . of subjects will be due to them, by the same right" (I: 121). Not only is it impossible to determine Adam's heirs now, but once we accept Filmer's claim that Adam's title is transferable in completely unaccountable ways through providence, then practically anyone can be, or at least plausibly claim to be, Adam's heirs if they have enough force to seize power. Such absurdity, Locke claims, is where you inevitably wind up once you reject the long-established natural-liberty principle that all government originates in consent.

Natural Rights in the *Second Treatise*

As we have seen, the central thrust of Locke's argument in the *First Treatise* is to refute the divine-right monarchist claim of Filmer that the Bible provides an absolutist blueprint for political life. In the *Second Treatise* Locke continued the movement begun in the *First* to replace scripture with nature and reason as the authoritative guide for politics. While the idea of nature providing a normative standard is certainly present in the *First Treatise*, it is in the *Second Treatise* that Locke developed his most theoretical, constructive, and innovative formulation of natural rights.

What the account of Adam's creation in Genesis was for Filmer, the theoretical abstraction that is the "state of nature" is for Locke, namely, the foundation of his entire philosophy of government. The discussion of the state of nature in Chapters II–IV of the *Second Treatise* lays out what Locke refers to as "what state all men are naturally in" (II: 4). This natural human condition is a state without government in which all human beings are free and equal. By this, Locke means that no individual has a right to rule another without their consent. There are four main features of Locke's state of nature theory: individual natural rights, the law of nature, the natural executive power of the law of nature, and the concept of the state of war.

The chief moral fact in the state of nature is that every individual has a natural right to "his own preservation" (II: 6). It is on the basis of this primordial right of self-preservation that Locke builds the broader rights theory that includes the right to life, liberty, and estate (or property) (II: 123), the preservation of which he sees as the primary purpose of government. These are rights or powers that every individual possesses irrespective of civil law or personal characteristics because these rights derive from the indefeasible human passion to preserve oneself from death and harm. But Locke insists that the individual's natural right to do what is required for self-preservation does not mean that there are no natural moral obligations. As Locke reveals, while the state of nature has no law, properly speaking (that is, no government), this does not mean that it is a "state of license" (II: 6). There is a law of nature that enjoins us to do no harm to any other human being. The law of nature compels us to recognize that other human beings are as much the "workmanship of one omnipotent, and infinitely wise maker" as we are, and thus we should not only not harm others, but we should also actively "preserve the rest of mankind" (II: 6). It is important to note, however, that the command to do no harm and to preserve all others does not diminish the primary natural right of self-preservation. Indeed, Locke claims that the right each has to "preserve himself" means that the duty to preserve others is only fully operational when one's "own preservation comes not in competition" with the more altruistic goal (II: 6).

There are two major issues of which Locke's treatment of the law of nature invites further analysis. First, Locke raises the hypothetical objection: "Where are, or ever were there any men in such a state of nature?" (II: 14). To this, Locke responds that there are several conditions in real life that prove the state of nature is not purely a theoretical abstraction. These conditions or situations include the rulers of independent governments in relation to each other (II: 14), individuals from different communities who meet in a remote location (II: 14) and resident aliens in relation to the government of the land in which they temporarily reside (II: 9), and finally Locke concludes that "all men are naturally" in the state of nature until "by their own consents they make themselves members of some politic society" (II: 15). The common thread running through these four examples is the idea that the parties in question have neither agreed nor consented to form a formal association, and thus the only sort of law binding them equally is the moral code apprehensible and applicable to all rational creatures. The second important issue raised by Locke's state of nature account relates to the executive power of the law of nature. This is the right, Locke argues, that every individual has, to enforce the law of nature in the state of nature, for otherwise the law of nature would "be in vain, if there were nobody that in the state of nature had a power to execute that law" (II: 7). Does the execution of the law of nature not require punishment and, hence, harming others? Would executing the law of nature not, then, violate the no-harm principle of that very same law of nature? Locke's response to both of these questions is yes, albeit in a qualified sense. The only time that the individual in the state of nature is permitted to harm another person is when the individual to be punished has already harmed and is thus a violator of the law of nature himself. That is to say, one can harm an aggressor who has harmed another without cause. The extent of the punishment permissible under the law of nature is that which is required for purposes of "reparation and restraint" (II: 8). Locke is clear, however, that the natural-punishment right includes capital punishment, the fullest departure from the no-harm principle imaginable. When is a person authorized to take a human life in service of the law of nature?

This question constitutes the central issue in Locke's account of the state of war. The state of war differs from the state of nature inasmuch as the former relates to any use of force without right, whereas the latter simply means "men living together according to reason, without a common superior on earth" (II: 19). The legitimate use of lethal force in response to harm extends to four situations. First, one can kill an aggressor who threatens one's life as "I should have a right to destroy that which threatens me with destruction" (II: 16). Second, an individual may kill anyone in the state of nature who has expressed an "enmity" to one's being through a "sedate settled design upon another man's life" (II: 16). Third, the executive power of the law of nature authorizes any individual to "kill a thief," who does no other harm than try to place an individual under his control for anyone who will take away my liberty may "when he had me in his power, take away everything else" (II: 18). Finally, Locke insists that the law of nature permits a third-party punishment right by which anyone may join in defense of another and espouse his quarrel (II: 16).

Locke's treatment of the exercise of the executive power of the law of nature in the state of nature/state of war is a demonstration of the radical character of his individualistic rights theory for several reasons. First, Locke attributes complex reasoning with respect to criminal justice to individuals in the state of nature rather than solely to the legal systems in civil society. This capital-punishment right was completely absent in earlier natural-law thinkers such as Hooker, Suarez, and Bellarmine, all of whom insisted that only the legitimate authorities of the political community have a right to punish with death (or to punish at all, in the strict sense). Second, Locke claims that the individual's punishment right is the basis for government's right to punish criminals for it is the "magistrate [who] has the common right of punishing put into his hands" (II: 11). That is to say, there is no significant normative difference between the right that government exercises in punishing criminals and the right every individual has to execute the law of nature. Indeed, government's right presupposes the prior authorization of individuals. Third, the individualistic basis of the state of nature contains within itself the need for government, because in Locke's estimation there cannot but be serious "inconveniencies" in the state of nature when every individual is judge in their own case (II:

13). Hasty, ill-informed, and passionate judgments and actions are practically inevitable without a common legislative power that is recognized by all. To Locke, the insecurity of individual rights in the state of nature points toward the need for the establishment of government.

Locke's Teaching on Property

Chapter V of the *Second Treatise*, titled "Of Property," is perhaps the single most influential element of Locke's political philosophy. It is in this discussion of the nature and origin of property rights that Locke revolutionized the modern world's understanding of what it means to claim ownership of anything. In this respect Locke departed from previous thinking on the subject in three main ways. First, practically all political philosophers since Plato and Aristotle had stressed the prudential character of any presumable right to own property. That is to say, the heavy preponderance among past thinkers was to identify the knowledge of the correct use of something as the basis of a putative right of possession. In this traditional view, the means of acquiring a thing, especially through labor, was seen as having little consequence in determining to whom something belongs. For Locke, on the other hand, acquisition and labor became the central consideration in regard to property rights. Second, as we have seen from our discussion of the *First Treatise*, the natural-liberty school of the seventeenth century believed that the earth was originally given in common to all human beings; as a result, the introduction of private property rights was interpreted as an addition to, or modification of, the natural law. While Locke defends the basic idea of an original common, against Filmer, he adds a more individualistic interpretation of the right to appropriate than do his predecessors in the natural-liberty tradition. For Locke, not only does the individual not need the consent of others to use a thing once held in common, but also, Locke insists, the source of the right to exclude others from the use of a thing one has appropriated lies in the moral fact that one has ownership over one's body and actions. Third, in keeping with Locke's individualistic interpretation of acquisition, we see in Chapter V the argument for the presence of rudimentary market relations in the state of nature, including even the invention of money, which Locke insists does not depend on the existence of government.

The structure of Locke's argument in Chapter V bears a familiar rhetorical feature in which his initial argument sticks closely to that of the traditional natural-liberty school and only gradually becomes more radical and distinctively Lockean. For instance, Locke began his discussion of property by following the tracks laid previously in the *First Treatise*, as he emphasized that God gave the earth to all humankind, not simply to Adam (II: 26). Not only is God's donation universal, it is also bountiful for, as Locke affirms, paraphrasing 1 *Timothy* 6:17, "God has given all things richly" (II: 31). The obvious question confronting any argument about the original common is: How does any individual assume the right to make a thing originally belonging to no one the property of oneself? Locke's answer is labor:

> He that is nourished by the acorns he picked up under an oak, or the apples he gathered from the trees in the wood, has certainly appropriated them to himself. Nobody can deny but the nourishment is his. I ask then, when did they begin to be his? When he digested? Or when he ate? Or when he boiled? Or when he brought them home? Or when he picked them up? And it is plain, if the first gathering made them not his, nothing else could. That labor put a distinction between them and the common: that added something to them more than nature, the common mother of all, had done; and so they became his private right. (II: 28)

Locke, however, presupposed the even more fundamental moral fact that "every man has a property in his own person: this nobody has right to but himself. The labor of his body, and the work of his hands, we may say are properly his" (II: 27). It is this concept of self-ownership that provides the individualistic core of Locke's rights theory. The exclusive character of property, what makes it an intrinsically private right, derives from the natural right of self-preservation. This does not mean, however, that Locke entirely disregards natural-law reasoning in his account of property. Indeed, he insisted that the law of nature imposes two moral restrictions on the individual's capacity to acquire property. One can only acquire as much as one can use (II: 33). However, Locke's primary point is not that taking more than one can use involves stealing from others but rather that it is folly to waste one's time on an activity such as this that does not advance the goal of self-preservation. An individual is also forbidden to let anything one appropriates spoil, for that too is both foolish and a kind of theft from those who could have used what was left to rot (II: 31). These natural-law limits are rooted in traditional Christian and classical moral strictures against greed. But as we now come to anticipate, Locke gradually overturns these limits and makes them largely redundant in his later treatment of agriculture and money.

One of the striking features of Locke's treatment of property is that he locates the origins of agriculture and the invention of money in the precivil state of nature. In fact, Locke insisted that the "chief matter of property" is not perishable goods, but rather the "earth itself" (II: 32). The main thrust of Locke's account of agriculture is his labor theory of value and his claims about the potential for massive expansion of humanity's acquisitive capacities. First, with respect to the value of labor, Locke radically reconsidered the human relation to God and nature. We recall that initially in Chapter V Locke assured the reader about God's gift of natural bounty. Through the course of this chapter Locke revalued what portion of the necessities of life is given by the "spontaneous hand of nature" and what proportion is due to human labor and toil. In the span of a few sections, the proportion of value owing to labor as opposed to nature goes from 10:1 to 100:1 (II: 37) and finally to 1000:1 (II: 43). In the final analysis, Locke claims that nature itself, uncultivated by human labor, is worth "little more than nothing" (II: 42). Thus all that nature and God actually provide is the natural right to acquire property rooted in self-ownership.

The massive increase of human acquisitive capacities is tied to the invention of money. Locke argued that given the penury of nature, labor alone faces enormous obstacles in the struggle to secure preservation. The liberating potential of money lies in its capacity to incentivize economic expansion. Agriculture produces scarcity of available land, for, as Locke observes, "waste land" (II: 36) disappears among any people who have consented to the use of money (II: 45). How does money facilitate enclosure of what was once common land and thus in principle accessible to all? Simply put, money gives an incentive for an individual to labor on more land than one needs for bare subsistence inasmuch as the surplus product can be sold or traded for some recognizable currency: "What would a man value ten thousand, or a hundred thousand acres of excellent land, . . . where he had no hopes of commerce with other parts of the world, to draw money to him by the sale of his product? It would not be worth the enclosing." (II: 48). Money, Locke claims, is the nonperishable item, "a sparkling pebble or a diamond" (II: 46), that is introduced by mutual consent to be used in exchange "for the truly useful" perishable things (II: 47).

Money does two things. Not only does it provide an incentive for expansion of agriculture so that individuals have the "opportunity to continue and enlarge" their holdings (II: 48), money also signifies consent to "disproportionate and unequal possession" (II: 50). How can Locke justify this potentially enormous material inequality in the state of nature in which all individuals are, at least in principle, free and equal? Locke's response is that inequality serves the larger natural-law goal of preserving humankind, because the increased productive capacities, frankly enflamed by greed, lead to the production of more things useful to the support of human life. Thus, those with more property do not take anything away from those with less because "he who appropriates land to himself by his labor, does not lessen, but increases the common stock of mankind" (II: 37). The difference between the quality of life among people in a monetized economic system and those in a land left entirely to human labor is stark. As Locke declares "a king of a large and fruitful territory" in precolonial America "feeds, lodges, and is clad worse than a day-laborer in England" (II: 41). Inequality is, then, justified by its positive socioeconomic consequences for society as a whole. In addition to this utilitarian argument to justify material inequality, Locke also presents a moral case that stresses the intrinsic goodness of work and the evils of vanity and sloth, for God gave the world "to the use of the industrious and rational, . . . not to the fancy or covetousness of the quarrelsome and contentious" (II: 34).

Locke's individualistic theory of property rights pervades his later account of both the family and civil government. In contrast to Filmer's religiously sanctioned model of the patriarchal family,

Locke conceives of the family in Chapters VII and VIII of the *Second Treatise* as an association based on consent in which every member is a rights-bearing individual who assesses their relationships within the family not in terms of natural paternal authority but rather in light of the family's capacity to acquire the property required for preservation of the family members. The logical complement to Locke's reformulated liberal family is a new conception of government as a product of human reason and consent designed principally to protect the private property rights of the individual members of society.

Constitutional Government

Natural-liberty theorists prior to Locke, such as Hobbes, Grotius, and Pufendorf, tended to draw authoritarian, and even absolutist, political conclusions from the concept of a state of nature. That is to say, naturally free individuals are free to form any kind of government they choose, and often the best way to end the chaotic state of nature is to produce a sovereign power with sweeping authority. Locke, however, believed that only limited government is compatible with natural freedom and equality. In this respect, Locke helped lay the foundation of the liberal idea of constitutional government. There are four main features of Locke's constitutional theory.

First, Locke affirmed the contractual origins of civil government. People agree to leave the state of nature by unanimously consenting to form one body politic and further agreeing to let the majority decide upon the actual system of government (II: 96, 97). The legislative power is the first and most fundamental institution of government that the people create (II: 134). A common system of legislation was the institution most seriously lacking in the state of nature. While Locke accepts that the formation of society requires individuals to surrender to civil government the natural punishment right that they possessed in the state of nature, this laying down of right is neither absolute nor irrevocable. Locke sees the contractual relationship as a transfer of power by which individuals give up some of their freedom for the sake of the benefits of civil government. The chief benefit of civil government is the "preservation of their lives, liberties and estates, which I call by the general name, property" (II: 123). The contractual origin of government confirms that for Locke the protection of property is central to the basic idea of government. The purpose of government is not to allow for only self-preservation but rather to establish conditions for *comfortable* self-preservation, which is only possible in a polity with solid legal protection for private property.

Second, Locke insists that only limited government is consistent with the protection of natural rights. He assumes that individuals would be better off staying in a state of nature than submitting to an absolute government: "This is to think, that men are so foolish, that they take care to avoid what mischiefs may be done them by pole-cats, or foxes; but are content, nay, think it safety, to be devoured by lions" (II: 93). Thus, the delegation of power from individuals in the state of nature to civil government rests on a notion of trust that government will only use this power to protect the people's rights. Locke identifies four limits to what can be considered legitimate government action. First, the government can have no arbitrary power over the lives and property of the people (II: 135). Second, the government must rule by promulgated standing laws as opposed to extemporary decrees (II: 136). Third, the government cannot take from anyone their property without that individual's consent (II: 138). This limitation extends to a general constitutional principle that no community may be taxed by government without representation in the assembly that levies the taxes (II: 140). Finally, Locke declares that the legislature cannot transfer the right to make laws to any other hands, for the legislative power can only reside where the people have originally placed it (II: 141). Any government that acts contrary to these limits is, in Locke's view, prima facie illegitimate.

Third, Locke outlines a version of the separation of powers theory. Given the dangers of concentrated power, Locke argues that in all "well-ordered commonwealths" the legislative and executive power is "put into the hands of diverse persons" (II: 143). While the legislature is the supreme institutional power, Locke is at pains to ensure that sovereignty is difficult to locate. Sovereignty does not reside in any particular institution but rather in the community as a whole. An independent executive power provides a double advantage insofar as it means the law will apply to those who make it and the executive can counteract, and in some sense counterbalance, the legislature. An important way that the executive can do this is through prerogative, which Locke defines as the "power to act according to discretion, for the public good, without the prescription of the law, and sometimes even against it" (II: 160). Executive prerogative, no less than legislative power, is limited ultimately by the consent or support of the people. Thus, Locke's separation of powers argument is meant to show that popular sovereignty cannot be contained by any institutional or purely legal expression or instrument.

Fourth, the logical outcome of Locke's popular-sovereignty doctrine is a natural right of revolution, which he describes in terms of "dissolution of government" (II: 211). When a government violates its trust in a sustained and systematic manner its power reverts back to the principals in society. Locke's right of revolution extends much further than the resistance right one sees among some of his predecessors and more moderate Whig contemporaries. As Locke describes it, when the government is dissolved, the people are "at liberty to provide for themselves, by erecting a new legislative, differing from the other, by the change of persons, or form, or both, as they shall find it most for their safety and good" (II: 220). The people's "supreme power to remove or alter" the government (II: 149) finds expression in Locke's use of the phrase "[an] appeal . . . to heaven" to describe the people's right to resist an oppressive government (II: 240–42). While Locke acknowledged that the legislative power can violate its trust, he argued that the most probable cause for a dissolution of government is tyrannical actions on the part of the executive (i.e., the king). The actions that would reasonably produce popular hostility would include any attempt to alter or interfere with the legislature, as well as any attempt to subject the people to a foreign power (II: 212, 215, 216, 217). In these situations, the people need no further justification to defend their resistance. Thus, for Locke, the ultimate guarantee of limited government is the extra-constitutional device of popular resistance.

Locke's Political Legacy

It is difficult to think of a political theorist who had a greater impact on the modern world than John Locke. Our ideas of constitutional government, capitalist economics, and the liberal conception of individual rights all bear the indelible impression of Locke. Of course, Locke's most immediate impact was in his role as chief Whig apologist for the Glorious Revolution of 1688–1689, which established the doctrine of parliamentary sovereignty in England and, later in the United Kingdom, the British Empire and beyond. While there would continue to be tension between the Crown and the Commons for many years, following the Glorious Revolution justified by Locke the principle of legislative supremacy was never again in any real doubt in the British Constitution. The reformed parliamentary system that Locke outlined in the *Second Treatise* would become in effect the model for parliamentary democracy around the globe.

Locke's political teaching also had a far-reaching but complex legacy in terms of colonialism. On the one hand, Locke's teaching on the need for representation in any legislature that imposes taxes became the famous battle cry of American patriots ("No taxation without representation!") in arguably the first anticolonial war of national liberation in the modern era. However, Locke's argument for private property rights was also employed cynically by European colonial powers who justified the expropriation of indigenous peoples' traditional lands on the self-serving grounds that these lands were supposedly uncultivated waste subject to any foreign power that can claim them. Behind this story of revolution and dispossession lay the distinctively Lockean idea of the subjective individual right of appropriation that grounds his teaching on property. Arguably Locke made the notion of protecting property a higher-order priority for civil government than did practically any previous thinker. In this respect, Locke's conception of private property laid the philosophical foundation for the liberal capitalist economic and political order that triumphed in the post–Cold War era and today dominates the global system with support of the Group of Twenty (G-20) great economic powers and of global financial institutions, such as the World Bank and International Monetary Fund.

Finally, it is impossible to exaggerate the impact Locke had on the modern conception of rights. It is to Locke more than to any other political philosopher that we owe the idea of a right as a possession inhering in individuals. Rights, in this sense, are inseparable from the primary moral and intellectual material out of which the individual constructs a self that is recognized by government and other selves as a rights-bearing individual. From the Lockean premise of the natural right to "life, liberty, and estate," contemporary liberal democratic societies have drawn a commitment to human rights that extends to freedom of speech and expression, religious toleration, political participation, and the separation of church and state. The battle that Locke fought in the *First Treatise* to eliminate the theological justifications for political power was a vital early step on the road to the secular idea of political life that is taken for granted in liberal societies today. While contemporary liberal democrats generally eschew the discourse of "natural rights" out of a distrust of a reified notion of nature, our "rights talk," from the Universal Declaration of Human Rights adopted by the United Nations to the various charters, codes, and bills-of-rights that are practically de rigueur in every liberal democracy today, still carries a recognizably Lockean flavor. Reading Locke's *Two Treatises* serves, then, to place a mirror before the eyes of modern peoples so that we can better learn more about ourselves.

Bibliography

A. Other Political Works by Locke

Locke, John. *A Letter Concerning Toleration*. Edited by James H. Tully. Indianapolis: Hackett Publishing Company, 1983.

———. *Political Essays*. Edited by Mark Goldie. Cambridge: Cambridge University Press, 1997.

———. *Some Thoughts Concerning Education and the Conduct of the Understanding*. Edited by Ruth Grant and Nathan Tarcov. Indianapolis: Hackett Publishing Company, 1996.

B. Biographies

Cranston, Maurice. *John Locke: A Biography*. London: MacMillan, 1957.

Woolhouse, Roger. *Locke: A Biography*. Cambridge: Cambridge University Press, 2007.

C. Robert Filmer's Political Thought

Filmer, Robert. *Patriarcha and Other Writings*. Edited by Johann Somerville. Cambridge: Cambridge University Press, 1991.

Daly, James. *Sir Robert Filmer and English Political Thought*. Toronto: University of Toronto Press, 1979.

Schochet, Gordon. *Patriarchalism in Political Thought*. Oxford: Oxford University Press, 1975.

Ward, Lee. *The Politics of Liberty in England and Revolutionary America*. Cambridge: Cambridge University Press, 2004. See esp. Part One.

D. Studies of Locke's Political Theory

Arneil, Barbara. *John Locke and America: The Defence of English Colonialism.* Oxford: Clarendon Press, 1996.

Ashcraft, Richard. *Revolutionary Politics and Locke's "Two Treatises."* Princeton, NJ: Princeton University Press, 1986.

Ashcraft, Richard. *Locke's "Two Treatises of Government."* London: Allen and Unwin, 1987.

Butler, Melissa. "Early Liberal Roots of Feminism: Locke and His Attack on Patriarchy." *American Political Science Review,* vol. 72, no. 1 (March 1978): 135–50.

Corbett, Ross. *The Lockean Commonwealth.* Albany: State University of New York Press, 2009.

Dunn, John. *The Political Thought of John Locke.* Cambridge: Cambridge University Press, 1969.

Franklin, Julian. *John Locke and the Theory of Sovereignty.* Cambridge: Cambridge University Press, 1978.

Grant, Ruth. *John Locke's Liberalism.* Chicago: University of Chicago Press, 1987.

Josephson, Peter. *The Great Art of Government: Locke's Use of Consent.* Lawrence: University Press of Kansas, 2002.

Kramer, Matthew. *John Locke and the Origins of Private Property.* Cambridge: Cambridge University Press, 1997.

MacPherson, C. B. *The Political Theory of Possessive Individualism.* Oxford: Oxford University Press, 1962.

Myers, Peter C. *Our Only Star and Compass: Locke and the Struggle for Political Rationality.* Lanham, MD: Rowman & Littlefield, 1998.

Pangle, Thomas L. *The Spirit of Modern Republicanism: The Moral Vision of the American Founders and the Philosophy of Locke.* Chicago: University of Chicago Press, 1988.

Parker, Kim Ian. *The Biblical Politics of John Locke.* Waterloo, ON: Wilfrid Laurier University Press, 2004.

Simmons, John. *The Lockean Theory of Rights.* Princeton, NJ: Princeton University Press, 1992.

———. *The Edge of Anarchy*. Princeton, NJ: Princeton University Press, 1993.

Seliger, Martin. *The Liberal Politics of John Locke*. London: Allen & Unwin, 1969.

Tuckness, Alex. *Locke and the Legislative Point of View*. Princeton, NJ: Princeton University Press, 2002.

Tully, James. *A Discourse on Property: Locke and His Adversaries*. Cambridge: Cambridge University Press, 1980.

———. *An Approach to Political Philosophy: Locke in Contexts*. Cambridge: Cambridge University Press, 1993.

Waldron, Jeremy. *God, Locke and Equality: Christian Foundations in Locke's Political Thought*. Cambridge: Cambridge University Press, 2002.

Ward, Lee. *John Locke and Modern Life*. Cambridge: Cambridge University Press, 2010.

Wood, Neal. *The Politics of Locke's Philosophy*. Berkeley: University of California Press, 1983.

Zuckert, Michael. *Launching Liberalism: On Lockean Political Philosophy*. Lawrence: University of Kansas Press, 2002.

A Note on the Text and Acknowledgments

This edition of the *Two Treatises* is based upon a reproduction from a digitized version of the 1821 edition printed for Whitmore and Fenn, Charing Cross, London, which was corrected and amended to bring it into conformity with the 1764 Hollis edition (the sixth edition, which corrected many errors present in the earlier editions published during Locke's lifetime). The aim of this new edition is to offer a faithful version of Locke's text that is accessible to contemporary undergraduate students. As such, in the present edition a number of typographical errors have been corrected, and, where appropriate throughout Locke's text (but not in his quotations from other authors), the spelling and punctuation has been modernized. In addition, spelling has been Americanized (e.g., color, labor). The general rule is that all of the quotations from other texts that appeared in Locke's original (primarily from the Bible, but also from the works of Robert Filmer, Richard Hooker, and other authors) have kept their original (often archaic) spelling and are italicized as they are in the 1764 edition. For purposes of clarity, most other italics from the body of Locke's text contained in the 1764 edition have been removed with the exception of book titles, some foreign words, and Locke's occasional highlighting of words as words. Some quotations from Hooker in the *Second Treatise* are marked by °.

I would like to acknowledge the generous funding for the original digitization of this text by York University Libraries of Toronto, Canada, and the Clara Thomas Archives and Special Collections there, and thank them for allowing me to use their digitized version of the 1821 edition contained in the Yolton Library Rare Book Collection as the basis for this edition. I would also like to thank Andrea Kosavic and Anna St. Onge, librarians at the York University Libraries, and Elaina St. Onge, librarian at the Campion

College Library, for their helpful and timely advice. As well, I thank my colleagues at Campion College at the University of Regina: Dr. Jackie Kuikman for helping me with Hebrew translations, and Dr. Jan Purnis for introducing me to the wonders of the online Oxford English Dictionary in my search for understanding Locke's sometimes archaic words and terms. I am especially grateful to Brian Rak of Hackett Publishing for his support of this project, and to Paul Rahe and Peter Josephson, whose careful reading of earlier versions of the text improved this edition in countless ways. Any remaining errors are, of course, entirely my responsibility.

This edition of Locke's *Two Treatises of Government* is dedicated to the people of Saskatchewan, Canada, who have supported my research for more than a decade. I trust that Locke's teaching on popular sovereignty from the seventeenth century will remain an inspiration to them well into the twenty-first.

Two Treatises of Government

by John Locke

TWO TREATISES OF GOVERNMENT. IN
THE FORMER THE FALSE PRINCIPLES AND
FOUNDATION OF SIR ROBERT FILMER
AND HIS FOLLOWERS ARE DETECTED AND
OVERTHROWN. THE LATTER IS AN ESSAY
CONCERNING THE TRUE ORIGINAL, EXTENT,
AND END OF CIVIL GOVERNMENT.

PREFACE

Reader, you have here the beginning and end of a discourse concerning government; what fate has otherwise disposed of the papers that should have filled up the middle, and were more than all the rest, it is not worthwhile to tell you. These, which remain, I hope are sufficient to establish the throne of our great restorer, our present King William; to make good his title, in the consent of the people, which being the only one of all lawful governments, he has more fully and clearly, than any prince in Christendom; and to justify to the world the people of England, whose love of their just and natural rights, with their resolution to preserve them, saved the nation when it was on the very brink of slavery and ruin. If these papers have that evidence, I flatter myself is to be found in them, there will be no great miss of those which are lost, and my reader may be satisfied without them: for I imagine, I shall have neither the time, nor inclination to repeat my pains, and fill up the wanting part of my answer, by tracing Sir Robert again, through all the windings and obscurities, which are to be met with in the several branches of his wonderful system. The king, and body of the nation, have since so thoroughly confuted his hypothesis, that I suppose nobody hereafter will have either the confidence to appear against our common safety, and be again an advocate for slavery; or the weakness to be deceived with contradictions dressed up in a popular style, and well-turned periods: for if anyone will be at the pains, himself, in those parts, which are here untouched, to strip Sir Robert's discourses of the flourish of doubtful expressions, and endeavor to reduce his words to direct, positive, intelligible propositions, and then compare them one with another, he will quickly be satisfied, there was never so much glib nonsense put together in well-sounding English. If he think it not worthwhile to examine his works all through, let him make an experiment in that part, where he treats of usurpation; and let him try, whether he can, with all his skill, make Sir Robert intelligible, and consistent with himself, or common sense. I should not speak so plainly of a gentleman, long since past answering, had not the pulpit, of late years, publicly owned his doctrine, and made it the current divinity of the times. It is necessary those men, who taking on them to be teachers, have so dangerously misled others, should be openly shown of what authority this their Patriarch is, whom they have so blindly followed, that so they may either retract what upon so ill grounds they have vented, and cannot be maintained; or else justify those principles which they preached up for gospel; though they had no better an author than an English courtier: for I should not have writ against Sir Robert, or taken the pains to show his mistakes, inconsistencies, and want of (what he so much boasts of, and pretends wholly to build on) scripture-proofs, were there not men among us, who, by crying up his books, and espousing his doctrine, save me from the reproach of writing against a dead adversary. They have been so zealous in this point, that, if I have done him any wrong, I cannot hope they should spare me. I wish, where they have done the truth and the public wrong, they would be as ready to redress it, and allow its just weight to this reflection, viz. that there cannot be done a greater mischief to prince and people, than the propagating wrong notions concerning government; that so at last all times might not have reason to complain of the Drum Ecclesiastic. If anyone, concerned really for truth, undertake the confutation of my hypothesis, I promise him either to recant my mistake, upon fair conviction; or to answer his difficulties. But he must remember two things.

First, that cavilling here and there, at some expression, or little incident of my discourse, is not an answer to my book.

Secondly, that I shall not take railing for arguments, nor think either of these worth my notice, though I shall always look on myself as bound to give satisfaction to anyone, who shall appear to be conscientiously scrupulous in the point, and shall show any just grounds for his scruples.

I have nothing more, but to advertise the reader, that *Observations* stands for *Observations on Hobbs, Milton, &c.** and that a bare quotation of pages always means pages of his *Patriarcha,* Edition 1680.

*Locke is here referring to Filmer's work *Observations Concerning the Originall of Government, upon Mr Hobs 'Leviathan', Mr Milton against Salamasius, H. Grotius 'De Jure Belli'* published in 1652.

Contents of Book I

Contents of Book II

Book I

CHAPTER I
The Introduction

§. 1. Slavery is so vile and miserable an estate of man, and so directly opposite to the generous temper and courage of our nation; that it is hardly to be conceived, that an Englishman, much less a gentleman, should plead for it. And truly I should have taken Sir Robert Filmer's *Patriarcha*, as any other treatise, which would persuade all men, that they are slaves, and ought to be so, for such another exercise of wit, as was his who wrote the *Encomium of Nero*;[1] rather than for a serious discourse meant in earnest, had not the gravity of the title and epistle, the picture in the front of the book, and the applause that followed it, required me to believe, that the author and publisher were both in earnest. I therefore took it into my hands with all the expectation, and read it through with all the attention due to a treatise that made such a noise at its coming abroad, and cannot but confess myself mightily surprised that in a book, which was to provide chains for all mankind, I should find nothing but a rope of sand, useful perhaps to such, whose skill and business it is to raise a dust, and would blind the people, the better to mislead them; but in truth not of any force to draw those into bondage who have their eyes open, and so much sense about them as to consider, that chains are but an ill wearing, how much care soever has been taken to file and polish them.

§. 2. If anyone think I take too much liberty in speaking so freely of a man, who is the great champion of absolute power, and the idol of those who worship it; I beseech him to make this small allowance

---

1. Satirical work about the infamous Roman emperor Nero (37–68 CE), published in 1546 by Milanese thinker Girolamo Cardono (1501–1576).

for once, to one, who, even after the reading of Sir Robert's book, cannot but think himself, as the laws allow him, a freeman: and I know no fault it is to do so, unless anyone better skilled in the fate of it, than I, should have it revealed to him, that this treatise, which has lain dormant so long, was, when it appeared in the world, to carry, by strength of its arguments, all liberty out of it; and that thenceforth our author's short model was to be the pattern in the mount, and the perfect standard of politics for the future. His system lies in a little compass, it is no more but this,

That all government is absolute monarchy.

And the ground he builds on, is this,

That no man is born free.

§. 3. In this last age a generation of men has sprung up among us, that would flatter princes with an opinion, that they have a divine right to absolute power, let the laws by which they are constituted, and are to govern, and the conditions under which they enter upon their authority, be what they will, and their engagements to observe them never so well ratified by solemn oaths and promises. To make way for this doctrine, they have denied mankind a right to natural freedom; whereby they have not only, as much as in them lies, exposed all subjects to the utmost misery of tyranny and oppression, but have also unsettled the titles, and shaken the thrones of princes: (for they too by these men's system, except only one, are all born slaves, and by divine right are subjects to Adam's right heir) as if they had designed to make war upon all government, and subvert the very foundation of human society, to serve their present turn.

§. 4. However we must believe them upon their own bare words, when they tell us, we are all born slaves, and we must continue so, there is no remedy for it; life and thraldom we entered into together, and can never be quit of the one, till we part with the other. Scripture or reason I am sure do not anywhere say so, notwithstanding the noise of divine right, as if divine authority has subjected us to the unlimited will of another. An admirable state of mankind, and that which they have not had wit enough to find out till this latter age. For, however Sir Robert Filmer seems to condemn the novelty of the contrary opinion, *Patr.* p. 3. yet I believe it will be hard for him to find any other age, or country of the world, but this, which has asserted monarchy to be *jure divino*. And he confesses, *Patr.* p. 4. That Heyward, Blackwood, Barclay,[2] and others, that have bravely vindicated the right of kings in most points, never thought of this, but with one consent admitted the natural liberty and equality of mankind.

§. 5. By whom this doctrine came at first to be broached, and brought in fashion among us, and what sad effects it gave rise to, I leave to historians to relate, or to the memory of those, who were contemporaries with Sibthorp and Manwering,[3] to recollect. My business at present is only to consider what Sir Robert Filmer, who is allowed to have carried this argument farthest, and is supposed to have brought it to perfection, has said in it; for from him everyone, who would be as fashionable as French was at court, has learned, and runs away with this short system of politics, viz. *Men are not born free, and therefore could never have the liberty to choose either governors, or forms of government. Princes have their power absolute, and by divine right; for slaves could never have a right to compact or consent. Adam was an absolute monarch, and so are all princes ever since.*

CHAPTER II
Of Paternal and Regal Power

§. 6. Sir Robert Filmer's great position is that men are not naturally free. This is the foundation on which his absolute monarchy stands, and from which it erects itself to such an height, that its power is above every power, *caput inter nubila,*[4] so high above all earthly and human things, that thought can scarce reach it; that promises and oaths, which tie the infinite Deity, cannot confine it. But if this foundation fails, all his fabric falls with it, and governments must be left again to the old way of being made by

2. John Hayward (1560–1627) was an English champion of the divine right of kings. Adam Blackwood (1539–1613) and William Barclay (1546–1608) were Scottish supporters of the idea of absolute monarchical power.

3. Robert Sibthorpe (d. 1662) and Roger Manwaring (1590–1653), English clergymen and outspoken defenders of the divine right of kings.

4. Latin for "head in the clouds."

contrivance, and the consent of men (Ἀνθρωπινη κτισις)[5] making use of their reason to unite together into society. To prove this grand position of his, he tells us, p. 12. men are born in subjection to their parents, and therefore cannot be free. And this authority of parents he calls royal authority, p. 12, 14. Fatherly authority, right of fatherhood, p. 12, 20. One would have thought he would, in the beginning of such a work as this, on which was to depend the authority of princes, and the obedience of subjects, have told us expressly, what that fatherly authority is, have defined it, though not limited it, because in some other treatises of his he tells us, it is unlimited and unlimitable;* he should at least have given us such an account of it, that we might have had an entire notion of this fatherhood, or fatherly authority, whenever it came in our way in his writings: this I expected to have found in the first chapter of his *Patriarcha*. But instead thereof, having, (1) en passant, made his obeisance to the *arcana imperii*, p. 5., (2) made his compliment to the rights and liberties of this or any other nation, p. 6. which he is going presently to null and destroy; and (3) made his leg to those learned men, who did not see so far into the matter as himself, p. 7. He comes to fall on Bellarmine,[6] p. 8. and, by a victory over him, establishes his fatherly authority beyond any question. Bellarmine being routed by his own confession, p. 11., the day is clear got, and there is no more need of any forces: for having done that, I observe not that he states the question, or rallies up any arguments to make good his opinion, but rather tells us the story, as he thinks fit, of this strange kind of domineering phantom, called the fatherhood, which whoever could catch, presently got empire, and unlimited absolute power. He assures us how this fatherhood began in Adam continued its course, and kept the world in order all the time of the patriarchs till the flood, got out of the ark with Noah and his sons, made and supported all the kings of the earth till the captivity of the Israelites in Egypt, and then the poor fatherhood was under hatches, till God, by giving the Israelites kings,

---

5. Locke translates the Greek as "consent of men," but the original in 1 Peter 2:13 is translated, with more authoritarian implications, as "submit yourselves to every ordinance of men" (*anthropinē ktisei*).

6. Roberto Bellarmine (1542–1621), a Jesuit cardinal and the author of *De potestate summi pontifici*, engaged in famous polemical exchange with James I of England about the limits of royal power.

re-established the ancient and prime right of the lineal succession in paternal government. This is his business from p. 12. to p. 19. And then obviating an objection, and clearing a difficulty or two, with one half reason, p. 23., to confirm the natural right of regal power, he ends the first chapter. I hope it is no injury to call an half quotation an half reason; for God says, *Honour thy father and mother*; but our author contents himself with half, leaves out thy mother quite, as little serviceable to his purpose. But of that more in another place.

*In grants and gifts that have their original from God or nature, as the power of the father hath, no inferior power of man can limit, nor make any law of prescription against them. Observations, 158. The scripture teaches, that supreme power was originally in the father, without any limitation. Observations, 245.

§. 7. I do not think our author so little skilled in the way of writing discourses of this nature, nor so careless of the point in hand, that he by oversight commits the fault, that he himself, in his *Anarchy of a Mixed Monarchy*, p. 239. objects to Mr. Hunton[7] in these words: *Where first I charge the author, that he hath not given us any definition, or description of Monarchy in general; for by the rules of method he should have first defined.* And by the like rule of method Sir Robert should have told us, what his fatherhood or fatherly authority is, before he had told us, in whom it was to be found, and talked so much of it. But perhaps Sir Robert found, that this fatherly authority, this power of fathers, and of kings, for he makes them both the same, p. 24. would make a very odd and frightful figure, and very disagreeing with what either children imagine of their parents, or subjects of their kings, if he should have given us the whole draught together in that gigantic form, he had painted it in his own fancy; and therefore, like a wary physician, when he would have his patient swallow some harsh or corrosive liquor, he mingles it with a large quantity of that which may dilute it; that the scattered parts may go down with less feeling, and cause less aversion.

---

7. Philip Hunton (1600–1682) was a Puritan divine and a supporter of the Parliamentary cause in the English Civil War (1642–1651). He argued for limits on royal power in *A Treatise of Monarchie* (1643).

§. 8. Let us then endeavor to find what account he gives us of this fatherly authority, as it lies scattered in the several parts of his writings. And first, as it was vested in Adam, he says, *Not only Adam, but the succeeding patriarchs, had, by right of fatherhood, royal authority over their children*, p. 12. *This lordship which Adam by command had over the whole world, and by right descending from him the patriarchs did enjoy, was as large and ample as the absolute dominion of any monarch, which hath been since the creation*, p. 13. *Dominion of life and death, making war, and concluding peace*, p. 13. *Adam and the patriarchs had absolute power of life and death*, p. 35. *Kings, in the right of parents, succeed to the exercise of supreme jurisdiction*, p. 19. *As kingly power is by the law of God, so it hath no inferior law to limit it; Adam was lord of all*, p. 40. *The father of a family governs by no other law, than by his own will*, p. 78. *The superiority of princes is above laws*, p. 79. *The unlimited jurisdiction of kings is so amply described by Samuel*, p. 80. *Kings are above the laws*, p. 93. And to this purpose see a great deal more which our author delivers in Bodin's[8] words: *It is certain, that all laws, privileges, and grants of princes, have no force, but during their life; if they be not ratified by the express consent, or by sufferance of the prince following, especially privileges, Observations*, p. 279. *The reason, why laws have been also made by kings, was this; when kings were either busied with wars, or distracted with public cares, so that every private man could not have access to their persons, to learn their wills and pleasure, then were laws of necessity invented, that so every particular subject might find his prince's pleasure deciphered unto him in the tables of his laws*, p. 92. *In a monarchy, the king must by necessity be above the laws*, p. 100. *A perfect kingdom is that, wherein the king rules all things according to his own will*, p. 100. *Neither common nor statute laws are, or can be, any diminution of that general power, which kings have over their people by right of fatherhood*, p. 115. *Adam was the father, king, and lord over his family; a son, a subject, and a servant or slave, were one and the same thing at first. The father had power to dispose or sell his children or servants; whence we find, that the first reckoning up of goods*

---

8. French *Politique* Jean Bodin (1530–1596) was a supporter of royal power during the French religious wars of the 1560s and 1570s. His most famous work, *Les Six livres de la République* (1576), was a sophisticated defense of absolute sovereignty. Filmer admired Bodin and quoted him often.

in scripture, the man-servant and the maid-servant, are numbered among the possessions and substance of the owner, as other goods were, Observations Pref. *God also hath given to the father a right or liberty, to alien his power over his children to any other; whence we find the sale and gift of children to have been much in use in the beginning of the world, when men had their servants for a possession and an inheritance, as well as other goods; whereupon we find the power of castrating and making eunuchs much in use in old times, Observations,* p. 155. *Law is nothing else but the will of him that hath the power of the supreme father, Observations,* p. 223. *It was God's ordinance that the supremacy should be unlimited in Adam, and as large as all the acts of his will; and as in him so in all others that have supreme power, Observations,* p. 245.

§. 9. I have been fain to trouble my reader with these several quotations in our author's own words, that in them might be seen his own description of his fatherly authority, as it lies scattered up and down in his writings, which he supposes was first vested in Adam, and by right belongs to all princes ever since. This fatherly authority then, or right of fatherhood, in our author's sense, is a divine unalterable right of sovereignty, whereby a father or a prince has an absolute, arbitrary, unlimited, and unlimitable power over the lives, liberties, and estates of his children and subjects; so that he may take or alienate their estates, sell, castrate, or use their persons as he pleases, they being all his slaves, and he lord or proprietor of everything, and his unbounded will their law.

§. 10. Our author having placed such a mighty power in Adam, and upon that supposition founded all government, and all power of princes, it is reasonable to expect, that he should have proved this with arguments clear and evident, suitable to the weightiness of the cause; that since men had nothing else left them, they might in slavery have such undeniable proofs of its necessity, that their consciences might be convinced, and oblige them to submit peaceably to that absolute dominion, which their governors had a right to exercise over them. Without this, what good could our author do, or pretend to do, by erecting such an unlimited power, but flatter the natural vanity and ambition of men, too apt of itself to grow and increase with the possession of any power? And by persuading

those, who, by the consent of their fellow men, are advanced to
great, but limited degrees of it, that by that part which is given
them, they have a right to all, that was not so; and therefore may
do what they please, because they have authority to do more than
others, and so tempt them to do what is neither for their own, nor
the good of those under their care; whereby great mischiefs cannot
but follow.

§. 11. The sovereignty of Adam, being that on which, as a sure
basis, our author builds his mighty absolute monarchy, I expected,
that in his *Patriarcha*, this his main supposition would have been
proved, and established with all that evidence of arguments, that
such a fundamental tenet required; and that this, on which the
great stress of the business depends, would have been made out
with reasons sufficient to justify the confidence with which it was
assumed. But in all that treatise, I could find very little tending that
way; the thing is there so taken for granted, without proof, that
I could scarce believe myself, when, upon attentive reading that
treatise, I found there so mighty a structure raised upon the bare
supposition of this foundation. For it is scarce credible, that in a
discourse, where he pretends to confute the erroneous principle
of man's natural freedom, he should do it by a bare supposition
of Adam's authority, without offering any proof for that authority.
Indeed he confidently says, that *Adam had royal authority*, p. 12.,
and 13. *absolute lordship and dominion of life and death*, p. 13. *an
universal monarchy*, p. 33. *absolute power of life and death*, p. 35.
He is very frequent in such assertions; but, what is strange, in all
his whole *Patriarcha* I find not one pretence of a reason to establish
this his great foundation of government; not anything that looks
like an argument, but these words: *To confirm this natural right of
regal power, we find in the Decalogue, that the law which enjoins
obedience to kings, is delivered in the terms, Honour thy father, as
if all power were originally in the father.* And why may I not add
as well, that in the Decalogue, the law that enjoins obedience to
queens, is delivered in the terms of *Honour thy mother*, as if all
power were originally in the mother? The argument, as Sir Robert
puts it, will hold as well for one as the other. But of this, more in
its due place.

§. 12. All that I take notice of here is that this is all our author says in his first, or any of the following chapters, to prove the absolute power of Adam, which is his great principle; and yet, as if he had there settled it upon sure demonstration, he begins his second chapter with these words, *By conferring these proofs and reasons, drawn from the authority of the scripture.* Where those proofs and reasons for Adam's sovereignty are, bating that of *Honour thy father,*[9] above mentioned, I confess, I cannot find, unless what he says, p. 11. *In these words we have an evident confession, viz. of Bellarmine, that creation made man prince of his posterity,* must be taken for proofs and reasons drawn from scripture, or for any sort of proof at all: though from thence by a new way of inference, in the words immediately following, he concludes, the royal authority of Adam sufficiently settled in him.

§. 13. If he has in that chapter, or anywhere in the whole treatise, given any other proofs of Adam's royal authority, other than by often repeating it, which among some men, goes for argument, I desire anybody for him to show me the place and page, that I may be convinced of my mistake, and acknowledge my oversight. If no such arguments are to be found, I beseech those men, who have so much cried up this book, to consider, whether they do not give the world cause to suspect, that it is not the force of reason and argument, that makes them for absolute monarchy, but some other by interest, and therefore are resolved to applaud any author, that writes in favor of this doctrine, whether he support it with reason or no. But I hope they do not expect, that rational and indifferent men should be brought over to their opinion, because this their great doctor of it, in a discourse made on purpose, to set up the absolute monarchical power of Adam, in opposition to the natural freedom of mankind, has said so little to prove it, from whence it is rather naturally to be concluded, that there is little to be said.

§. 14. But that I might omit no care to inform myself in our author's full sense, I consulted his, *Observations on Aristotle, Hobbes, &c.* to see whether in disputing with others he made use of any

---

9. The verb "to bate," now obsolete, was used in Locke's time to mean "to lower in amount, weight, estimation, to reduce" (Oxford English Dictionary, Second Edition, *s.v.* "bate.").

arguments for this his darling tenet of Adams sovereignty; since in his treatise of the Natural power of Kings, he has been so sparing of them. In his *Observations on Hobbes' Leviathan*,[10] I think he has put, in short, all those arguments for it together, which in his writings I find him anywhere to make use of: his words are these: *If God created only Adam, and of a piece of him made the woman, and if by generation from them two, as parts of them, all mankind be propagated: if also God gave to Adam, not only the dominion over the woman and the children that should issue from them, but also over all the earth to subdue it, and over all the creatures on it, so that as long as Adam lived, no man could claim or enjoy anything but by donation, assignation or permission from Him, I wonder, &c. Observations*, 165. Here we have the sum of all his arguments, for Adam's sovereignty, and against natural freedom, which I find up and down in his other treatises; and they are these following; God's creation of Adam, the dominion he gave him over Eve, and the dominion he had as father over his children, all which I shall particularly consider.

CHAPTER III
Of Adam's Title to Sovereignty by Creation

§. 15. Sir Robert, in his preface to his *Observations on Aristotle's Politics*, tells us, a natural freedom of mankind cannot be supposed without the denial of the creation of Adam: but how Adam's being created, which was nothing but his receiving a being immediately from omnipotence and the hand of God, gave Adam a sovereignty over anything, I cannot see, nor consequently understand, how a supposition of natural freedom is a denial of Adam's creation, and would be glad anybody else (since our author did not vouchsafe us the favor) would make it out for him. For I find no difficulty to suppose the freedom of mankind, though I have always believed the creation of Adam. He was created, or began to exist by God's immediate power, without the intervention of parents or the pre-existence of any of the same species to beget him, when it pleased

---

10. The most important work by English political philosopher Thomas Hobbes (1588–1679). *Leviathan* (1651) advanced a case for absolute monarchy based on contractualist grounds and on the natural liberty of a state of nature.

God he should; and so did the lion, the king of beasts, before him, by the same creating power of God: and if bare existence by that power, and in that way, will give dominion without any more ado, our author, by this argument, will make the lion have as good a title to it, as he, and certainly the ancienter. No! for Adam had his title by the appointment of God, says our author in another place. Then bare creation gave him not dominion, and one might have supposed mankind free without the denying the creation of Adam, since it was God's appointment made him monarch.

§. 16. But let us see, how he puts his creation and this appointment together. By the appointment of God, says Sir Robert, as soon as Adam *was created, he was monarch of the world, though he had no subjects; for though there could not be actual government till there were subjects, yet by the right of nature it was due to Adam to be governor of his posterity: though not in act, yet at least in habit, Adam was a king from his creation.* I wish he had told us here, what he meant by God's appointment. For whatsoever providence orders, or the law of nature directs, or positive revelation declares, may be said to be by God's appointment: but I suppose it cannot be meant here in the first sense, i.e. by providence; because that would be to say no more, but that as soon as Adam was created he was de facto monarch, because by right of nature it was due to Adam, to be governor of his posterity. But he could not de facto be by providence constituted the governor of the world, at a time when there was actually no government, no subjects to be governed, which our author here confesses. Monarch of the world is also differently used by our author; for sometimes he means by it a proprietor of all the world exclusive of the rest of mankind, and thus he does in the same page of his preface before cited, *Adam,* says he, *being commanded to multiply and people the earth, and to subdue it, and having dominion given him over all creatures, was thereby the monarch of the whole world; none of his posterity had any right to possess anything but by his grant or permission, or by succession from him.*

2. Let us understand then by monarch proprietor of the world, and by appointment God's actual donation, and revealed positive grant made to Adam, Gen. 1. 28. as we see Sir Robert himself does in this parallel place, and then his argument will stand thus *by the positive grant of God, as soon as Adam was created, he was*

proprietor of the world, because by the right of nature it was due to Adam to be governor of his posterity. In which way of arguing there are two manifest falsehoods. First, it is false, that God made that grant to Adam, as soon as he was created, since, though it stands in the text immediately after his creation, yet it is plain it could not be spoken to Adam, till after Eve was made and brought to him, and how then could he be monarch by appointment as soon as created, especially since he calls, if I mistake not, that which God says to Eve, Gen. 3. 16, the original grant of government, which not being till after the fall, when Adam was somewhat, at least in time, and very much distant in condition, from his creation, I cannot see, how our author can say in this sense, that by *God's appointment, as soon as Adam was created, he was monarch of the world.* Secondly, were it true that God's actual donation appointed Adam monarch of the world as soon as he was created, yet the reason here given for it, would not prove it, but it would always be a false inference, that God, by a positive donation, appointed Adam *monarch of the world, because by right of nature it was due to Adam to be governor of his posterity*: for having given him the right of government by nature, there was no need of a positive donation, at least it will never be a proof of such a donation.

§. 17. On the other side the matter will not be much mended, if we understand by God's appointment the law of nature, (though it be a pretty harsh expression for it in this place) and by monarch of the world, sovereign ruler of mankind; for then the sentence under consideration must run thus: By the law of nature, as soon as Adam was created he was governor of mankind, for by right of nature it was due to Adam to be governor of his posterity; which amounts to this, he was governor by right of nature, because he was governor by right of nature. But supposing we should grant, that a man is by nature governor of his children, Adam could not hereby be a monarch as soon as created; for this right of nature being founded in his being their father, how Adam could have a natural right to be governor, before he was a father, when by being a father only he had that right, is methinks, hard to conceive, unless he will have him to be a father before he was a father, and to have a title before he had it.

§. 18. To this foreseen objection, our author answers very logically, he was governor in habit, and not in act: a very pretty way of being a governor without government, a father without children, and a king without subjects. And thus Sir Robert was an author before he wrote his book, not in act, it is true, but in habit, for when he had once published it, it was due to him by the right of nature, to be an author, as much as it was to Adam to be governor of his children, when he had begot them. And if to be such a monarch of the world, an absolute monarch in habit, but not in act, will serve the turn, I should not much envy it to any of Sir Robert's friends, that he thought fit graciously to bestow it upon, though even this of act and habit, if it signified anything but our author's skill in distinctions, be not to his purpose in this place. For the question is not here about Adam's actual exercise of government, but actually having a title to be governor. Government, says our author, was due to Adam by the right of nature. What is this right of nature? A right fathers have over their children by begetting them; *generatione jus acquiritur parentibus in liberos*, says our author out of Grotius,[11] *Observations*, 223. The right then follows the begetting as arising from it, so that, according to this way of reasoning or distinguishing of our author, Adam, as soon as he was created, had a title only in habit, and not in act, which in plain English is, he had actually no title at all.

§. 19. To speak less learnedly, and more intelligibly, one may say of Adam, he was in a possibility of being governor, since it was possible he might beget children, and thereby acquire that right of nature, be it what it will, to govern them, that accrues from thence, but what connection has this with Adam's creation, to make him say, that, as soon as he was created, he was monarch of the world? For it may be as well said of Noah, that as soon as he was born, he was monarch of the world, since he was in possibility (which in our author's sense is enough to make a monarch, a monarch in habit) to outlive all mankind, but his own posterity. What such necessary

11. Hugo Grotius (1583–1645) was a Dutch political thinker and the author of *De jure belli ac pacis* (1625), which advanced an argument for the contractual origins of government based on an idea of subjective rights that foreshadowed Locke's later natural rights argument in some respects but did not require limited government.

connection there is between Adam's creation and his right to government, so that a natural freedom of mankind cannot be supposed
without the denial of the creation of Adam, I confess for my part I
do not see; nor how those words, *by the appointment, etc. Observations*, 254. however explained, can be put together, to make any tolerable sense, at least to establish this position, with which they end,
viz. Adam was a king from his creation; a king, says our author, not
in act but in habit, i.e. actually no king at all.

§. 20. I fear I have tired my reader's patience, by dwelling longer on
this passage, than the weightiness of any argument in it seems to
require; but I have unavoidably been engaged in it by our author's
way of writing, who, huddling several suppositions together, and
that in doubtful and general terms, makes such a medley and
confusion, that it is impossible to show his mistakes, without examining the several senses wherein his words may be taken, and without seeing how, in any of these various meanings, they will consist
together, and have any truth in them; for in this present passage
before us, how can anyone argue against this position of his, that
Adam was a king from his creation, unless one examine, whether
the words, from his creation, be to be taken, as they may, for the
time of the commencement of his government, as the foregoing
words import, *as soon as he was created he was monarch*, or, for the
cause of it, as he says, p. 11. *Creation made man prince of his posterity?* How farther can one judge of the truth of his being thus king,
till one has examined whether king be to be taken, as the words in
the beginning of this passage would persuade, on supposition of
his private dominion, which was, by God's positive grant, monarch of the world by appointment; or king on supposition of his
fatherly power over his offspring, which was by nature, due by the
right of nature, whether, I say, king be to be taken in both, or one
only of these two senses, or in neither of them, but only this, that
creation made him prince, in a way different from both the other?
For though this assertion, that *Adam was king from his creation*, be
true in no sense, yet it stands here as an evident conclusion drawn
from the preceding words, though in truth it be but a bare assertion joined to other assertions of the same kind, which confidently
put together in words of undetermined and dubious meaning,
look like a sort of arguing, when there is indeed neither proof nor

connection: a way very familiar with our author, of which having given the reader a taste here, I shall, as much as the argument will permit me, avoid touching on hereafter; and should not have done it here, were it not to let the world see, how incoherencies in matter, and suppositions without proofs put handsomely together in good words and a plausible style, are apt to pass for strong reason and good sense, till they come to be looked into with attention.

CHAPTER IV
Of Adam's Title to Sovereignty by Donation, Gen. 1. 28

§. 21. Having at last got through the foregoing passage, where we have been so long detained, not by the force of arguments and opposition, but the intricacy of the words, and the doubtfulness of the meaning; let us go on to his next argument for Adam's sovereignty. Our author tells us in the words of Mr. Selden,[12] that *Adam by donation from God, Gen. 1. 28. was made the general lord of all things, not without such a private dominion to himself, as without his grant did exclude his children. This determination of Mr. Selden,* says our author, *is consonant to the history of the Bible, and natural reason, Observations,* 210. And in his Pref. to his *Observations on Aristotle,* he says thus, *The first government in the world was monarchical in the father of all flesh, Adam being commanded to people and multiply the earth, and to subdue it, and having dominion given him over all creatures, was thereby the monarch of the whole world: none of his posterity had any right to possess anything, but by his grant or permission, or by succession from him. The earth, saith the Psalmist, hath he given to the children of men, which show the title comes from fatherhood.*

§. 22. Before I examine this argument, and the text on which it is founded, it is necessary to desire the reader to observe, that our author, according to his usual method, begins in one sense, and concludes in another; he begins here with Adam's propriety, or

---

12. John Selden (1584–1654) was an important English jurist and a supporter of the Parliamentary side in the English Civil War. He advanced natural-law thinking in England, and his *Mare clausum* (1635) became an important work in the emerging field of international law.

private dominion, by donation; and his conclusion is, *which shows the title comes from fatherhood.*

§. 23. But let us see the argument. The words of the text are these; *and God blessed them, and God said unto them, be fruitful and multiply, and replenish the earth and subdue it, and have dominion over the fish of the sea, and over the fowl of the air, and over every living thing that moveth upon the earth,* Gen. 1. 28. From whence our author concludes, *that Adam, having here dominion given him over all creatures, was thereby the monarch of the whole world.* Whereby must be meant, that either this grant of God gave Adam property, or as our author calls it, private dominion over the earth, and all inferior or irrational creatures, and so consequently that he was thereby monarch: or secondly, that it gave him rule and dominion over all earthly creatures whatsoever, and thereby over his children, and so he was monarch: for, as Mr. Selden has properly worded it, *Adam was made general lord of all things,* one may very clearly understand him, that he means nothing to be granted to Adam here but property, and therefore he says not one word of Adam's monarchy. But our author says, Adam was hereby monarch of the world, which, properly speaking, signifies sovereign ruler of all the men in the world, and so Adam, by this grant, must be constituted such a ruler. If our author means otherwise, he might with much more clearness have said, that Adam was hereby proprietor of the whole world. But he begs your pardon in that point, clear distinct speaking not serving everywhere to his purpose, you must not expect it in him, as in Mr. Selden, or other such writers.

§. 24. In opposition therefore to our author's doctrine, that Adam was monarch of the whole world, founded on this place, I shall show,

1. That by this grant, Gen. 1. 28. God gave no immediate power to Adam over men, over his children, over those of his own species; and so he was not made ruler, or monarch, by this charter.

2. That by this grant God gave him not private dominion over the inferior creatures, but right in common with all mankind; so neither was he monarch, upon the account of the property here given him.

§ 25. 1. That this donation, Gen. 1. 28. gave Adam no power over men, will appear if we consider the words of it. For since all positive grants convey no more than the express words they are made in will carry, let us see which of them here will comprehend mankind, or Adam's posterity; and those, I imagine, if any, must be these, *every living thing that moveth* the words in Hebrew[13] are, חיה הרמשה of which words the scripture itself is the best interpreter. God having created the fishes and fowls the fifth day, the beginning of the sixth, he creates the irrational inhabitants of the dry land, which, ver. 24, are described in these words, *Let the earth bring forth the living creature after his kind; cattle and creeping things, and beasts of the earth, after his kind, and, ver. 25. and God made the beasts of the earth after his kind, and cattle after their kind, and everything that creepeth on the earth after his kind.* Here, in the creation of the brute inhabitants of the earth, he first speaks of them all under one general name, of living creatures, and then afterwards divides them into three ranks. 1. Cattle or such creatures as were or might be tame, and so be the private possession of particular men; 2. חיה which, ver. 24, 25. in our Bible, is translated beasts, and by the Septuagint[14] θηρία, wild beasts, and is the same word, that here in our text, ver. 28, where we have this great charter to Adam, is translated living thing, and is also the same word used, Gen. ix. 2. where this grant is renewed to Noah, and there likewise translated beast. 3. The third rank were the creeping animals, which ver. 24, 25. are comprised under the word, הרמשת the same that is used here, ver. 28, and is translated moving, but in the former verses, creeping, and by the Septuagint in all these places, ἑρπετὰ, or reptiles, from whence it appears that the words which we translate here in God's donation, ver. 28. *living creatures moving*, are the same, which in the history of the creation, ver. 24,

---

13. Throughout sections 25–27 of the *First Treatise* Locke employed several Hebrew terms (and a few Greek words) in order to dispute arcane points of translation against Filmer. Most versions of the *Two Treatises* published during Locke's lifetime failed to use the correct words and translations. Dr. Jacuba Kuikman, professor of religious studies at Campion College at the University of Regina, reasons that Locke's use of the Hebrew in the original adds little to illuminate his argument.

14. The authoritative translation of the Hebrew Bible into Greek, redacted in the late second century BCE.

25. signify two ranks of terrestrial creatures, viz. wild beasts and reptiles, and are so understood by the Septuagint.

§ 26. When God had made the irrational animals of the world, divided into three kinds, from the places of their habitation, viz. fishes of the sea, fowls of the air, and living creatures of the earth; and these again into cattle, wild beasts, and reptiles; he considers of making man, and the dominion he should have over the terrestrial world, ver. 26. and then he reckons up the inhabitants of these three kingdoms, but in the terrestrial leaves out the second rank, חיה or wild beasts: but here, ver. 28. where he actually executes this design, and gives him this dominion, the text mentions the fishes of the sea, and fowls of the air, and the terrestrial creatures in the words that signify the wild beasts and reptiles, though translated *living thing that moveth*, leaving out cattle. In both which places, though the word which signifies wild beasts, be omitted in one, and that which signifies cattle in the other, yet, since God certainly executed in one place, what he declares he designed in the other, we cannot but understand the same in both places, and have here only an account how the terrestrial irrational animals, which were already created, and reckoned up at their creation, in three distinct ranks of cattle, wild beasts, and reptiles, were here, ver. 28. actually put under the dominion of man, as they were designed, ver. 26. nor do these words contain in them the least appearance of anything that can be wrested to signify God's giving to one man dominion over another, Adam over his posterity.

§ 27. And this further appears from Gen. 9. 2. where God renewing this charter to Noah and his sons, he gives them dominion over the fowls of the air, and the fishes of the sea, and the terrestrial creatures, expressed by חיה and הרמש wild beasts and reptiles, the same words that in the text before us, Gen. 1. 28. are translated *every moving thing, that moveth on the earth*, which by no means can comprehend man, the grant being made to Noah and his sons, all the men then living, and not to one part of men over another: which is yet more evident from the very next words, ver. 3. where God gives every רמש *every moving thing*, the very words used, ch. 1. 28. to them for food. By all which it is plain, that God's donation to Adam, ch. 1. 28. and his designation, ver. 26. and his grant again to

Noah and his sons; refer to, and contain in them, neither more nor less than the works of the creation the fifth day, and the beginning of the sixth, as they are set down from the 20th to 26th ver. inclusively of the 1st ch. and so comprehend all the species of irrational animals of the terraqueous globe, though all the words, whereby they are expressed in the history of their creation, are nowhere used in any of the following grants, but some of them omitted in one, and some in another. From whence I think it is past all doubt that man cannot be comprehended in this grant, nor any dominion over those of his own species be conveyed to Adam. All the terrestrial irrational creatures are enumerated at their creation, ver. 25. under the names *beasts of the earth, cattle, and creeping things*, but man, being not then created, was not contained under any of those names; and therefore, whether we understand the Hebrew words right or no, they cannot be supposed to comprehend man in the very same history, and the very next verses following, especially since that Hebrew word רמש which, if any in this donation to Adam, ch. 1. 28. must comprehend man, is so plainly used in contradistinction to him, as Gen. 6. 20; 7. 14, 21, 23; Gen. 8. 17, 19. And if God made all mankind slaves to Adam and his heirs, by giving Adam dominion over *every living thing that moveth on the earth*, ch. 1. 28. as our author would have it, methinks sir Robert should have carried his monarchical power one step higher, and satisfied the world, that princes might eat their subjects too, since God gave as full power to Noah and his heirs, ch. 9. 2. to eat *every living thing that moveth*, as he did to Adam to have dominion over them: the Hebrew words in both places being the same.

§. 28. David, who might be supposed to understand the donation of God in this text, and the right of kings too, as well as our author in his comment on this place, as the learned and judicious Ainsworth[15] calls it, in the 8th Psalm, finds here no such charter of monarchical power, his words are, *Thou hast made him*, i.e. man, the son of man, *a little lower than the angels; thou madest him to have dominion over the works of thy hands, thou hast put all things under his feet, all sheep and oxen, and the beasts of the field, and the fowl of the air, and fish of the sea, and whatsoever passeth through*

---

15. Henry Ainsworth (1571–1622) was an English Puritan clergyman and the author of *Annotations upon the Five Books of Moses* (1616–1619).

the paths of the sea. In which words, if anyone can find out, that there is meant any monarchical power of one man over another, but only the dominion of the whole species of mankind, over the inferior species of creatures, he may, for aught I know, deserve to be one of Sir Robert's monarchs in habit, for the rareness of the discovery. And by this time, I hope it is evident, that he that gave dominion over *every living thing that moveth on the earth*, gave Adam no monarchical power over those of his own species, which will yet appear more fully in the next thing I am to show.

§. 29. 2. Whatever God gave by the words of this grant, Gen. 1. 28. it was not to Adam in particular, exclusive of all other men: whatever dominion he had thereby, it was not a private dominion, but a dominion in common with the rest of mankind. That this donation was not made in particular to Adam, appears evidently from the words of the text, it being made to more than one, for it was spoken in the plural number, God blessed *them*, and said unto them, Have dominion. God says unto Adam and Eve, Have dominion; thereby, says our author, *Adam was monarch of the world*: but the grant being to them, i.e. spoke to Eve also, as many interpreters think with reason, that these words were not spoken till Adam had his wife, must not she thereby be lady, as well as he lord of the world? If it be said, that Eve was subjected to Adam, it seems she was not so subjected to him, as to hinder her dominion over the creatures, or property in them: for shall we say that God ever made a joint grant to two, and one only was to have the benefit of it?

§. 30. But perhaps it will be said, Eve was not made till afterward: grant it so, what advantage will our author get by it? The text will be only the more directly against him, and show that God, in this donation, gave the world to mankind in common, and not to Adam in particular. The word *them* in the text must include the species of man, for it is certain *them* can by no means signify Adam alone. In the 26th verse, where God declares his intention to give this dominion, it is plain he meant, that he would make a species of creatures, that should have dominion over the other species of this terrestrial globe: the words are, *And God said, Let us make man in our image, after our likeness, and let them have dominion over the fish*, &c. They then were to have dominion. Who? Even those who were to have the image of God, the individuals of that species of man, that he was going to make, for that *them* should signify Adam singly, exclusive of the rest that should be in the world with him, is against both scripture and all reason: and it cannot possibly be made sense, if man in the former part of the verse do not signify the same with them in the latter, only man there, as is usual, is taken for the species, and them the individuals of that species: and we have a reason in the very text. God makes him in his own image, after His own likeness, makes him an intellectual creature, and so capable of dominion. For wherein soever else the image of God consisted, the intellectual nature was certainly a part of it, and belonged to the whole species, and enabled them to have dominion over the inferior creatures; and therefore David says in the 8th Psalm above cited, *Thou hast made him little lower than the angels, thou hast made him to have dominion.* It is not of Adam King David speaks here, for verse 4 it is plain, it is of man, and the son of man, of the species of mankind.

§. 31. And that this grant spoken to Adam was made to him, and the whole species of man, is clear from our author's own proof out of the Psalmist. *The earth*, says the Psalmist, *hath he given to the children of men; which shows the title comes from fatherhood.* These are Sir Robert's words in the preface before cited, and a strange inference it is he makes, God hath given the earth to the children of men, ergo the title comes from fatherhood. It is pity the propriety of the Hebrew tongue had not used fathers of men, instead of children of men, to express mankind, then indeed our author might have had the countenance of the sound of words, to have placed the title in the fatherhood. But to conclude, that the fatherhood had the right to the earth, because God gave it to the children of men, is a way of arguing peculiar to our author. And a man must have a great mind to go contrary to the sound as well as the sense of the words before he could light on it. But the sense is yet harder, and more remote from our author's purpose: for as it stands in his preface, it is to prove Adam's being monarch, and his reasoning is thus, *God gave the earth to the children of men*, ergo *Adam was monarch of the world.* I defy any man to make a more pleasant conclusion than this, which cannot be excused from the most obvious absurdity, till it can be shown, that by children of men, he who had no father, Adam alone is signified; but whatever our author does, the scripture speaks not nonsense.

§. 32. To maintain this property and private dominion of Adam, our author labors in the following page to destroy the community granted to Noah and his sons, in that parallel place, Gen. 9. 1, 2, 3, and he endeavors to do it two ways.

1. Sir Robert would persuade us against the express words of the scripture, that what was here granted to Noah, was not granted to his sons in common with him. His words are, *As for the general community between Noah and his sons, which Mr. Selden will have to be granted to them, Gen. 9. 2. the text does not warrant it.* What warrant our author would have, when the plain express words of scripture, not capable of another meaning, will not satisfy him, who pretends to build wholly on scripture, is not easy to imagine. The text says, *God blessed Noah and his sons, and said unto them,* i.e. as our author would have it, *unto him: for, saith he, although the sons are there mentioned with Noah in the blessing, yet it may best be understood, with a subordination or benediction in succession,* Observations, 211. That indeed is best, for our author to be understood, which best serves to his purpose, but that truly may best be understood by anybody else, which best agrees with the plain construction of the words, and arises from the obvious meaning of the place, and then with subordination and in succession, will not be best understood, in a grant of God, where he himself put them not, nor mentions any such limitation. But yet, our author has reasons, why it may *best be understood so. The blessing, says he in the following words, might truly be fulfilled, if the sons, either under or after their father, enjoyed a private dominion,* Observations, 211. which is to say, that a grant, whose express words give a joint title in present (for the text says, into your hands they are delivered) *may best be understood with a subordination, or succession;* because it is possible, that in subordination, or in succession, it may be enjoyed. Which is all one as to say, that a grant of anything in present possession, may best be understood of reversion: because it is possible one may live to enjoy it in reversion. If the grant be indeed to a father and to his sons after him, who is so kind as to let his children enjoy it presently in common with him, one may truly say, as to the

event one will be as good as the other: but it can never be true, that what the express words grant in possession, and in common, *may best be understood*, to be in reversion. The sum of all his reasoning amounts to this: God did not give to the sons of Noah the world in common with their father, because it was possible they might enjoy it under, or after him. A very good sort of argument against an express text of scripture: but God must not be believed, though he speaks it himself, when he says he does anything, which will not consist with Sir Robert's hypothesis.

§. 33. For it is plain, however he would exclude them, that part of this benediction, as he would have it in succession, must needs be meant to the sons, and not to Noah himself at all. *Be fruitful, and multiply, and replenish the earth*, says God, in this blessing. This part of the benediction, as appears by the sequel, concerned not Noah himself at all, for we read not of any children he had after the flood; and in the following chapter, where his posterity is reckoned up, there is no mention of any, and so this benediction in succession was not to take place till three hundred and fifty years after, and to save our author's imaginary monarchy, the peopling of the world must be deferred three hundred and fifty years; for this part of the benediction cannot be understood with subordination, unless our author will say, that they must ask leave of their father Noah to lie with their wives. But in this one point our author is constant to himself in all his discourses, he takes great care there should be monarchs in the world, but very little that there should be people: and indeed his way of government is not the way to people the world. For how much absolute monarchy helps to fulfill this great and primary blessing of God Almighty, *Be fruitful, and multiply, and replenish the earth*, which contains in it the improvement too of arts and sciences, and the conveniences of life, may be seen in those large and rich countries which are happy under the Turkish government, where are not now to be found one third, nay, in many, if not most parts of them one thirtieth, perhaps I might say not one hundredth of the people, that were formerly, as will easily appear to anyone, who will compare the accounts we have of it at this time, with ancient history. But this by the by.

§. 34. The other parts of this benediction, or grant, are so expressed, that they must needs be understood to belong to Noah and his

sons, to them as much as to him, and not to his sons *with a subordination, or in succession. The fear of you, and the dread of you, says
God, shall be upon every beast,* &c. Will anybody but our author
say, that the creatures feared and stood in awe of Noah only, and
not of his sons without his leave, or till after his death? And the
following words, *into your hands they are delivered,* are they to
be understood as our author says, if your father please, or they
shall be delivered into your hands hereafter? If this be to argue
from scripture, I know not what may not be proved by it, and I
can scarce see how much this differs from that fiction and fancy,
or how much a surer foundation it will prove, than the opinions
of philosophers and poets, which our author so much condemns
in his preface.

§. 35. But our author goes on to prove, that it *may best be understood with a subordination, or a benediction in succession,* for, says
he, *it is not probable that the private dominion which God gave to
Adam, and by his donation, assignation, or cession to his children,
was abrogated, and a community of all things instituted between
Noah and his sons—Noah was left the sole heir of the world; why
should it be thought that God would disinherit him of his birth right,
and make him of all men in the world the only tenant in common
with his children? Observations,* 211.

§. 36. The prejudices of our own ill-grounded opinions, however
by us called probable, cannot authorize us to understand scripture
contrary to the direct and plain meaning of the words. I grant, it
is not probable, that Adam's private dominion was here abrogated;
because it is more than improbable, (for it will never be proved)
that ever Adam had any such private dominion: and since parallel places of scripture are most probable to make us know how
they may be best understood, there needs but the comparing this
blessing here to Noah and his sons after the flood, with that to
Adam after the creation, Gen. 1. 28. to assure anyone that God
gave Adam no such private dominion. It is probable, I confess, that
Noah should have the same title, the same property and dominion
after the flood, that Adam had before it. But since private dominion cannot consist with the blessing and grant God gave to him
and his sons in common, it is a sufficient reason to conclude, that

Adam had none, especially since in the donation made to him, there are no words that express it, or do in the least favor it; and then let my reader judge whether it may best be understood, when in the one place there is not one word for it, not to say what has been above proved, that the text itself proves the contrary, and in the other, the words and sense are directly against it.

§. 37. But our author says, *Noah was the sole heir of the world, why should it be thought that God would disinherit him of his birth right?* Heir, indeed, in England, signifies the eldest son, who is by the law of England to have all his father's land, but where God ever appointed any such heir of the world, our author would have done well to have shown us, and how God disinherited him of his birth-right, or what harm was done him if God gave his sons a right to make use of a part of the earth for the support of themselves and families, when the whole was not only more than Noah himself, but infinitely more than they all could make use of, and the possessions of one could not at all prejudice, or as to any use straighten that of the other.

§. 38. Our author probably foreseeing he might not be very successful in persuading people out of their senses, and, say what he could, men would be apt to believe the plain words of scripture, and think, as they saw, that the grant was spoken to Noah and his sons jointly. He endeavors to insinuate, as if this grant to Noah conveyed no property, no dominion; because, *subduing the earth and dominion over the creatures are therein omitted, nor the earth once named. And therefore,* says he, *there is a considerable difference between these two texts, the first blessing gave Adam a dominion over the earth and all creatures, the latter allows Noah liberty to use the living creatures for food, here is no alteration or diminishing of his title to a property of all things, but an enlargement only of his commons, Observations,* 211. So that in our author's sense, all that was said here to Noah and his sons, gave them no dominion, no property, but only enlarged the commons; their commons, I should say, since God says, *To you are they given*, though our author says *his*, for as for Noah's sons, they, it seems, by Sir Robert's appointment, during their father's lifetime, were to keep fasting days.

§. 39. Anyone but our author would be mightily suspected to be blinded with prejudice, that in all this blessing to Noah and his sons, could see nothing but only an enlargement of commons: for as to dominion which our author thinks omitted, *the fear of you, and the dread of you, says God, shall be upon every beast,* which I suppose expresses the dominion or superiority was designed man over the living creatures, as fully as may be. For in that fear and dread seems chiefly to consist what was given to Adam over the inferior animals, who, as absolute a monarch as he was, could not make bold with a lark or rabbit to satisfy his hunger, and had the herbs but in common with the beasts, as is plain from Gen. 1. 2, 9, and 30. In the next place, it is manifest that in this blessing to Noah and his sons, property is not only given in clear words, but in a larger extent than it was to Adam. *Into your hands they are given,* says God to Noah and his sons; which words, if they give not property, nay, property in possession, it will be hard to find words that can, since there is not a way to express a man's being possessed of anything more natural, nor more certain, than to say, it is delivered into his hands. And ver. 3. to show, that they had then given them the utmost property man is capable of, which is to have a right to destroy anything by using it, *Every moving thing that liveth,* says God, *shall be meat for you,* which was not allowed to Adam in his charter. This our author calls *a liberty of using them for food, and only an enlargement of commons, but no alteration of property, Observations,* 211. What other property man can have in the creatures, but the liberty of using them, is hard to be understood, so that if the first blessing, as our author says, gave *Adam dominion over the creatures,* and the blessing to Noah and his sons, gave them *such a liberty to use them,* as Adam had not; it must needs give them something that Adam with all his sovereignty wanted, something that one would be apt to take for a greater property; for certainly he has no absolute dominion over even the brutal part of the creatures, and the property he has in them is very narrow and scanty, who cannot make that use of them, which is permitted to another. Should anyone who is absolute lord of a country, have bidden our author subdue the earth, and given him dominion over the creatures in it, but not have permitted him to have taken a kid or a lamb out of the flock, to satisfy his hunger, I guess, he would scarce have thought himself lord or proprietor of that land, or the cattle on it: but would have found the difference between having dominion, which a shepherd may have, and having full property as an owner. So that, had it been his own case, Sir Robert, I believe, would have thought here was an alteration, nay, an enlarging of property, and that Noah and his children had by this grant, not only property given them, but such a property given them in the creatures, as Adam had not; for however, in respect of one another, men may be allowed to have propriety in their distinct portions of the creatures; yet in respect of God the maker of heaven and earth, who is sole lord and proprietor of the whole world, man's propriety in the creatures is nothing but that liberty to use them, which God has permitted, and so man's property may be altered and enlarged, as we see it was here, after the flood, when other uses of them are allowed, which before were not. From all which I suppose it is clear, that neither Adam, nor Noah, had any private dominion, any property in the creatures, exclusive of his posterity, as they should successively grow up into need of them, and come to be able to make use of them.

§. 40. Thus we have examined our author's argument for Adam's monarchy, founded on the blessing pronounced, Gen. 1. 28. wherein I think it is impossible for any sober reader, to find any other but the setting of mankind above the other kinds of creatures, in this habitable earth of ours. It is nothing but the giving to man, the whole species of man, as the chief inhabitant, who is the image of his maker, the dominion over the other creatures. This lies so obvious in the plain words, that anyone, but our author, would have thought it necessary to have shown, how these words, that seemed to say quite the contrary, *gave Adam monarchical absolute power* over other men, or the sole property in all the creatures, and it seems to me in a business of this moment, and that whereon he builds all that follows, he should have done something more than barely cite words, which apparently make against him. For I confess, I cannot see anything in them, tending to *Adam's monarchy, or private dominion*, but quite the contrary. And I the less deplore the dullness of my apprehension herein, since I find the apostle seems to have as little notion of any such private dominion of Adam as I, when he says, *God gives us all things richly to enjoy*, which he could not do, if it were all given away already, to monarch Adam, and the monarchs his heirs and successors. To conclude, this text is so far from proving Adam sole proprietor, that, on the contrary, it is a confirmation of the original community of all things among the sons of men, which appearing from this donation of God, as well as other places of scripture, the sovereignty of Adam, built upon his private dominion, must fall, not having any foundation to support it.

§. 41. But yet, if after all, anyone will needs have it so, that by this donation of God, Adam was made sole proprietor of the whole earth, what will this be to his sovereignty? And how will it appear, that property in land gives a man power over the life of another? Or how will the possession even of the whole earth, give anyone a sovereign arbitrary authority over the persons of men? The most specious thing to be said, is, that he that is proprietor of the whole world, may deny all the rest of mankind food, and so at his pleasure starve them, if they will not acknowledge his sovereignty, and obey his will. If this were true, it would be a good argument to prove, that there was never any such property, that God never gave any such private dominion; since it is more reasonable to think, that God, who bid mankind increase and multiply, should rather himself give them all a right to make use of the food and raiment, and other conveniences of life, the materials whereof he had so plentifully provided for them, than to make them depend upon the will of a man for their subsistence, who should have power to destroy them all when he pleased, and who, being no better than other men, was in succession likelier, by want and the dependence of a scanty fortune, to tie them to hard service, than by liberal allowance of the conveniences of life to promote the great design of God, increase and multiply. He that doubts this, let him look into the absolute monarchies of the world, and see what becomes of the conveniences of life, and the multitudes of people.

§. 42. But we know God has not left one man so to the mercy of another, that he may starve him if he please: God the Lord and Father of all, has given no one of his children such a property in his peculiar portion of the things of this world, but that he has given his needy brother a right to the surplus of his goods; so that it cannot justly be denied him, when his pressing wants call for it. And therefore no man could ever have a just power over the life of another by right of property in land or possessions, since it would always be a sin, in any man of estate, to let his brother perish for want of affording him relief out of his plenty. As justice gives every man a title to the product of his honest industry, and the fair acquisitions of his ancestors descended to him; so charity gives every man a title to so much out of another's plenty, as will keep him from extreme want, where he has no means to subsist otherwise; and a man can no more justly make use of another's necessity, to force him to become his vassal, by withholding that relief, God requires him to afford to the wants of his brother, than he that has more strength can seize upon a weaker, master him to his obedience, and with a dagger at his throat offer him death or slavery.

§. 43. Should anyone make so perverse an use of God's blessings poured on him with a liberal hand; should anyone be cruel and uncharitable to that extremity, yet all this would not prove that propriety in land, even in this case, gave any authority over the persons of men, but only that compact might; since the authority of the rich proprietor, and the subjection of the needy beggar, began not from the possession of the lord, but the consent of the poor man, who preferred being his subject to starving. And the man he thus submits to, can pretend to no more power over him, than he has consented to, upon compact. Upon this ground a man's having his stores filled in a time of scarcity, having money in his pocket, being in a vessel at sea, being able to swim, etc. may as well be the foundation of rule and dominion, as being possessor of all the land in the world, any of these being sufficient to enable me to save a man's life, who would perish if such assistance were denied him; and anything, by this rule, that may be an occasion of working upon another's necessity, to save his life, or anything dear to him, at the rate of his freedom, may be made a foundation of sovereignty, as well as property. From all which it is clear, that though God should have given Adam private dominion, yet that private dominion could give him no sovereignty; but we have already sufficiently proved, that God gave him no private dominion.

CHAPTER V
Of Adam's Title to Sovereignty by the Subjection of Eve

§. 44. The next place of scripture we find our author builds his monarchy of Adam on, is, Gen. 3. 16. *And thy desire shall be to thy husband, and he shall rule over thee. Here we have* (says he) *the original grant of government,* from whence he concludes, in the following part of the page, *Observations,* 244. *That the supreme power is settled in the fatherhood, and limited to one kind of government, that is, to monarchy.* For let his premises be what they will, this is always the conclusion, let rule, in any text, be but once named, and presently absolute monarchy is by divine right established. If anyone will but carefully read our author's own reasoning from these words, *Observations,* 244. and consider, among other things, the line and posterity of Adam, as he there brings them in, he will find some difficulty to make sense of what he says; but we will allow this at present to his peculiar way of writing, and consider the force of the text in hand. The words are the curse of God upon the woman for having been the first and most forward in the disobedience; and if we will consider the occasion of what God says here to our first parents, that he was denouncing judgment, and declaring his wrath against them both, for their disobedience, we cannot suppose that this was the time, wherein God was granting Adam prerogatives and privileges, investing him with dignity and authority, elevating him to dominion and monarchy: for though, as a helper in the temptation, as well as a partner in the transgression, Eve was laid below him, and so he had accidentally a superiority over her, for her greater punishment; yet he too had his share in the fall, as well as the sin, and was laid lower, as may be seen in the following verses; and it would be hard to imagine, that God, in the same breath, should make him universal monarch over all mankind, and a day-laborer for his life; turn him out of paradise to till the ground, ver. 23. and at the same time advance him to a throne, and all the privileges and ease of absolute power.

§. 45. This was not a time, when Adam could expect any favors, any grant of privileges from his offended Maker. If this be the original grant of government, as our author tells us, and Adam was now made monarch, whatever Sir Robert would have him, it

is plain, God made him but a very poor monarch, such an one, as
our author himself would have counted it no great privilege to be.
God sets him to work for his living, and seems rather to give him
a spade into his hand, to subdue the earth, than a sceptre to rule
over its inhabitants. *In the sweat of thy face, thou shalt eat thy bread*,
says God to him, ver. 19. This was unavoidable, may it perhaps be
answered, because he was yet without subjects, and had nobody
to work for him; but afterwards, living as he did above 900 years,
he might have people enough, whom he might command to work
for him; no, says God, not only whilst thou art without other help,
save thy wife, but as long thou lives, shalt thou live by thy labor, *In
the sweat of thy face, shalt thou eat thy bread, till thou return unto
the ground, for out of it was thou taken, for dust thou art, and unto
dust shalt thou return*, v. 19. It will perhaps be answered again in
favor of our author, that these words are not spoken personally
to Adam, but in him, as their representative, to all mankind, this
being a curse upon mankind, because of the fall.

§. 46. God, I believe, speaks differently from men, because he
speaks with more truth, more certainty: but when he vouchsafes
to speak to men, I do not think he speaks differently from them,
in crossing the rules of language in use among them. This would
not be to condescend to their capacities, when he humbles himself
to speak to them, but to lose his design in speaking what, thus
spoken, they could not understand. And yet thus must we think
of God, if the interpretations of scripture, necessary to maintain
our author's doctrine, must be received for good: for by the ordinary rules of language, it will be very hard to understand what
God says, if what he speaks here, in the singular number, to Adam,
must be understood to be spoken to all mankind, and what he
says in the plural number, Gen. 1. 26, 28. must be understood of
Adam alone, exclusive of all others, and what he says to Noah and
his sons jointly, must be understood to be meant to Noah alone,
Gen. 9.

§. 47. Farther it is to be noted, that these words here of Gen. 3. 10.
which our author calls the original grant of government, were not
spoken to Adam, neither indeed was there any grant in them made
to Adam, but a punishment laid upon Eve: and if we will take them

as they were directed in particular to her, or in her, as their representative to all other women, they will at most concern the female
sex only, and import no more, but that subjection they should
ordinarily be in to their husbands: but there is here no more law
to oblige a woman to such subjection, if the circumstances either
of her condition, or contract with her husband, should exempt her
from it, than there is, that she should bring forth her children in
sorrow and pain, if there could be found a remedy for it, which is
also a part of the same curse upon her: for the whole verse runs
thus, *Unto the woman he said, I will greatly multiply thy sorrow and
thy conception; in sorrow thou shalt bring forth children, and thy
desire shall be to thy husband, and he shall rule over thee.* It would,
I think, have been a hard matter for anybody, but our author, to
have found out a grant of monarchical government to Adam in
these words, which were neither spoke to, nor of him: neither will
anyone, I suppose, by these words, think the weaker sex, as by a
law, so subjected to the curse contained in them, that it is their
duty not to endeavor to avoid it. And will anyone say, that Eve, or
any other woman, sinned, if she were brought to bed without those
multiplied pains God threatens her here with? Or that either of our
queens, Mary or Elizabeth,[16] had they married any of their subjects, had been by this text, put into a political subjection to him?
Or that he thereby should have had monarchical rule over her?
God, in this text, gives not, that I see, any authority to Adam over
Eve, or to men over their wives, but only foretells what should be
the woman's lot, how by his providence he would order it so, that
she should be subject to her husband, as we see that generally the
laws of mankind and customs of nations have ordered it so; and
there is, I grant, a foundation in nature for it.

§. 48. Thus when God says of Jacob and Esau, that *the elder should
serve the younger,* Gen. 25. 23. nobody supposes that God hereby
made Jacob Esau's sovereign, but foretold what should de facto
come to pass. But if these words here spoke to Eve must needs
be understood as a law to bind her and all other women to subjection, it can be no other subjection than what every wife owes

---

16. English queens Mary I (1516–1558; reigned 1553–1558) and Elizabeth I
(1533–1603; reigned 1558–1603) were daughters of Henry VIII (1491–1547;
reigned 1509–1547).

her husband: and then if this be the original grant of government and the foundation of monarchical power, there will be as many monarchs as there are husbands. If therefore these words give any power to Adam, it can be only a conjugal power, not political; the power that every husband has to order the things of private concernment in his family, as proprietor of the goods and land there, and to have his will take place before that of his wife in all things of their common concernment; but not a political power of life and death over her, much less over anybody else.

§. 49. This I am sure: if our author will have this text to be a *grant, the original grant of government,* political government, he ought to have proved it by some better arguments than by barely saying, that *thy desire shall be unto thy husband,* was a law whereby Eve, and all that should come of her, were subjected to the absolute monarchical power of Adam and his heirs. *Thy desire shall be to thy husband,* is too doubtful an expression, of whose signification interpreters are not agreed, to build so confidently on, and in a matter of such moment, and so great and general concernment: but our author, according to his way of writing, having once named the text, concludes presently without any more ado, that the meaning is as he would have it. Let the words *rule* and *subject* be but found in the text or margin, and it immediately signifies the duty of a subject to his prince; the relation is changed, and though God says husband, Sir Robert will have it king; Adam has presently absolute monarchical power over Eve, and not only over Eve, but all that should come of her, though the scripture says not a word of it, nor our author a word to prove it. But Adam must for all that be an absolute monarch, and so down to the end of the chapter. And here I leave my reader to consider, whether my bare saying, without offering any reasons to evince it, that this text gave not Adam that absolute monarchical power, our author supposes, be not sufficient to destroy that power, as his bare assertion is to establish it, since the text mentions neither prince nor people, speaks nothing of absolute or monarchical power, but the subjection of Eve to Adam, a wife to her husband. And he that would trace our author so all through, would make a short and sufficient answer to the greatest part of the grounds he proceeds on, and abundantly confute them by barely denying; it being a sufficient answer to assertions without proof, to deny them without giving a reason. And therefore should I have said nothing but barely denied, that by this text *the supreme power was settled and founded by God himself, in the fatherhood, limited to monarchy, and that to Adam's person and heirs*, all which our author notably concludes from these words, as may be seen in the same page, *Observations*, 244. it had been a sufficient answer; should I have desired any sober man only to have read the text, and considered to whom, and on what occasion it was spoken, he would no doubt have wondered how our author found out monarchical absolute power in it, had he not had an exceeding good faculty to find it himself, where he could not show it others. And thus we have examined the two places of scripture, all that I remember our author brings to prove Adam's sovereignty, that supremacy, which he says, *it was God's ordinance should be unlimited in Adam, and as large as all the acts of his will, Observations*, 254. viz. Gen. 1. 28. and Gen. 3. 16. one whereof signifies only the subjection of the inferior ranks of creatures to mankind, and the other the subjection that is due from a wife to her husband, both far enough from that which subjects owe the governors of political societies.

CHAPTER VI
Of Adam's Title to Sovereignty by Fatherhood

§. 50. There is one thing more, and then I think I have given you all that our author brings for proof of Adam's sovereignty, and that is a supposition of a natural right of dominion over his children, by being their father: and this title of fatherhood he is so pleased with, that you will find it brought in almost in every page; particularly he says, not only Adam, *but the succeeding patriarchs had by right of fatherhood royal authority over their children*, p. 12. And in the same page, *this subjection of children being the fountain of all regal authority, &c.* This being, as one would think by his so frequent mentioning it, the main basis of all his frame, we may well expect clear and evident reason for it, since he lays it down as a position necessary to his purpose, *that every man that is born is so far from being free, that by his very birth he becomes a subject of him that begets him, Observations*, 156. So that Adam being the only man created, and all ever since being begotten, nobody has been born free. If we ask how Adam comes by this power over his children, he tells us here it is by begetting them: and so again, *Observations*, 223. *this natural dominion of Adam,* says he, *may be proved out of Grotius, himself, who teaches, that generatione jus acquiritur parentibus in liberos.*[17] And indeed the act of begetting being that which makes a man a father, his right of a father over his children can naturally arise from nothing else.

§. 51. Grotius tells us not here how far this *jus in liberos*, this power of parents over their children extends; but our author, always very clear in the point, assures us, it is supreme power and like that of absolute monarchs over their slaves, absolute power of life and death. He that should demand of him, how, or for what reason it is, that begetting a child gives the father such an absolute power over him, will find him answer nothing: we are to take his word for this, as well as several other things; and by that the laws of nature and the constitutions of government must stand or fall. Had he been an absolute monarch, this way of talking might have suited well enough; *pro ratione voluntas*[18] might have been of force in his mouth; but in the way of proof or argument is very unbecoming, and will little advantage his plea for absolute monarchy. Sir Robert has too much lessened a subject's authority to leave himself the hopes of establishing anything by his bare saying it; one slave's opinion without proof is not of weight enough to dispose of the liberty and fortunes of all mankind. If all men are not, as I think they are, naturally equal, I am sure all slaves are; and then I may without presumption oppose my single opinion to his; and be confident that my saying, that begetting of children makes them not slaves to their fathers as certainly sets all mankind free, as his affirming the contrary makes them all slaves. But that this position, which is the foundation of all their doctrine, who would have monarchy to be jure divino may have all fair play, let us hear what reasons others give for it, since our author offers none.

17. Filmer quoted the Latin phrase from Grotius, which reads "by generation a right over children is acquired by the parents."

18. The line from Juvenal is "*est pro ratione voluntas*" (his will is held to be reason).

§. 52. The argument, I have heard others make use of, to prove that fathers, by begetting them, come by an absolute power over their children, is this; that fathers have a power over the lives of their children, because they give them life and being; which is the only proof it is capable of, since there can be no reason, why naturally one man should have any claim or pretence of right over that in another, which was never his, which he bestowed not, but was received from the bounty of another. 1. I answer, that everyone who gives another anything, has not always thereby a right to take it away again. But, 2. They who say the father gives life to his children, are so dazzled with the thoughts of monarchy, that they do not, as they ought, remember God, who is *the author and giver of life: it is in Him alone we live, move, and have our being.* How can he be thought to give life to another, that knows not wherein his own life consists? Philosophers are at a loss about it after their most diligent enquiries; and anatomists, after their whole lives and studies spent in dissections, and diligent examining the bodies of men, confess their ignorance in the structure and use of many parts of man's body, and in that operation wherein life consists in the whole. And does the rude ploughman, or the more ignorant voluptuary, frame or fashion such an admirable engine as this is, and then put life and sense into it? Can any man say, he formed the parts that are necessary to the life of his child? Or can he suppose himself to give the life, and yet not know what subject is fit to receive it, nor what actions or organs are necessary for its reception or preservation?

§. 53. To give life to that which has yet no being, is to frame and make a living creature, fashion the parts, and mould and suit them to their uses, and having proportioned and fitted them together, to put into them a living soul. He that could do this, might indeed have some pretence to destroy his own workmanship. But is there anyone so bold, that dares thus far arrogate to himself, the incomprehensible works of the Almighty? Who alone did at first, and continues still to make a living soul, he alone can breathe in the breath of life. If anyone thinks himself an artist at this, let him number up the parts of his child's body which he has made, tell me their uses and operations, and when the living and rational soul began to inhabit this curious structure, when sense began, and how this engine, which he has framed, thinks and reasons: if he made it, let him, when it is out of order, mend it, at least tell wherein the defects lie. *Shall he that made the eye not see?* says the Psalmist, Psalm 94. 9. See these men's vanities: the structure of that one part is sufficient to convince us of an all-wise contriver, and he has so visible a claim to us as his workmanship, that one of the ordinary appellations of God in scripture is, *God our Maker*, and *the Lord our Maker*. And therefore though our author, for the magnifying his fatherhood, be pleased to say, *Observations*, 159. *That even the power which God himself exercises over mankind is by right of fatherhood*, yet this fatherhood is such an one as utterly excludes all pretence of title in earthly parents; for he is king, because he is indeed maker of us all, which no parents can pretend to be of their children.

§. 54. But had men skill and power to make their children, it is not so slight a piece of workmanship, that it can be imagined, they could make them without designing it. What father of a thousand, when he begets a child, thinks farther than the satisfying his present appetite! God in his infinite wisdom has put strong desires of copulation into the constitution of men, thereby to continue the race of mankind, which he does most commonly without the intention, and often against the consent and will of the begetter. And indeed those who desire and design children, are but the occasions of their being, and when they design and wish to beget them, do little more toward their making, than Deucalion[19] and his wife in the fable did toward the making of mankind, by throwing pebbles over their heads.

§. 55. But grant that the parents made their children, gave them life and being, and that hence there followed an absolute power. This would give the father but a joint dominion with the mother over them: for nobody can deny but that the woman has an equal share, if not the greater, as nourishing the child a long time in her own body out of her own substance; there it is fashioned, and from

---

19. In Greek mythology, Deucalion, son of Prometheus, is analogous to Noah; Deucalion and his wife, Pyrrha, built a boat to survive a catastrophic flood and then they repopulated the world by throwing stones over their shoulders. The stones from Deucalion's hand produced males, and those from Pyrrha's hand produced females.

her it receives the materials and principles of its constitution: and it is so hard to imagine the rational soul should presently inhabit the yet unformed embryo, as soon as the father has done his part in the act of generation, that if it must be supposed to derive anything from the parents, it must certainly owe most to the mother. But be that as it will, the mother cannot be denied an equal share in begetting of the child, and so the absolute authority of the father will not arise from hence. Our author indeed is of another mind; for he says, *We know that God at the creation gave the sovereignty to the man over the woman, as being the nobler and principal agent in generation, Observations*, 172. I remember not this in my Bible, and when the place is brought where God at the creation gave the sovereignty to man over the woman, and that for this reason, because he is the nobler and principal agent in generation, it will be time enough to consider, and answer it. But it is no new thing for our author to tell us his own fancies for certain and divine truths, though there be often a great deal of difference between his and divine revelations; for God in scripture says, *his father and his mother that begot him.*

§. 56. They who allege the practice of mankind, for exposing or selling their children, as a proof of their power over them, are with Sir Robert happy arguers; and cannot but recommend their opinion, by founding it on the most shameful action, and most unnatural murder, human nature is capable of. The dens of lions and nurseries of wolves know no such cruelty as this: these savage inhabitants of the desert obey God and nature in being tender and careful of their offspring: they will hunt, watch, fight, and almost starve for the preservation of their young; never part with them; never forsake them, till they are able to shift for themselves. And is it the privilege of man alone to act more contrary to nature than the wild and most untamed part of the creation? Does God forbid us under the severest penalty, that of death, to take away the life of any man, a stranger, and upon provocation? And does he permit us to destroy those, he has given us the charge and care of, and by the dictates of nature and reason, as well as his revealed command, requires us to preserve? He has in all the parts of the creation taken a peculiar care to propagate and continue the several species of creatures, and make the individuals act so strongly to this end, that they sometimes neglect their own private good for it, and seem to forget that general rule, which nature teaches all things, of self-preservation; and the preservation of their young, as the strongest principle in them, overrules the constitution of their particular natures. Thus we see, when their young stand in need of it, the timorous become valiant, the fierce and savage kind, and the ravenous tender and liberal.

§. 57. But if the example of what has been done, be the rule of what ought to be, history would have furnished our author with instances of this absolute fatherly power in its height and perfection, and he might have shown us in Peru, people that begot children on purpose to fatten and eat them. The story is so remarkable that I cannot but set it down in the author's words. "*In some provinces,*" says he, "*they were so liquorish after man's flesh, that they would not have the patience to stay till the breath was out of the body, but would suck the blood as it ran from the wounds of the dying man; they had public shambles of man's flesh, and their madness herein was to that degree, that they spared not their own children, which they had begot on strangers taken in war: for they made their captives their mistresses, and choicely nourished the children they had by them, till about thirteen years old they butchered and eat them; and they served the mothers after the same fashion, when they grew past childbearing, and ceased to bring them any more roasters.* Garcilasso de la Vega *Hist, des Yncas de Peru*, 1. i. c. 12."[20]

§. 58. Thus far can the busy mind of man carry him to a brutality below the level of beasts, when he quits his reason, which places him almost equal to angels. Nor can it be otherwise in a creature, whose thoughts are more than the sands, and wider than the ocean, where fancy and passion must needs run him into strange courses, if reason, which is his only star and compass be not that he steers by. The imagination is always restless, and suggests variety of thoughts, and the will, reason being laid aside, is ready for every extravagant project; and in this state, he that goes farthest out of the way, is thought fittest to lead, and is sure of most followers: and when fashion has once established what folly or craft

---

20. Garcilasso de la Vega (1539–1616) was a Spanish-Peruvian historian who chronicled the history of the Inca civilization of South America.

began, custom makes it sacred, and it will be thought impudence, or madness, to contradict or question it. He that will impartially survey the nations of the world, will find so much of their governments, religions, and manners, brought in and continued among them by these means, that he will have but little reverence for the practices which are in use and credit among men, and will have reason to think, that the woods and forests, where the irrational untaught inhabitants keep right by following nature, are fitter to give us rules, than cities and palaces, where those that call themselves civil and rational, go out of their way, by the authority of example. If precedents are sufficient to establish a rule in this case, our author might have found in holy writ children sacrificed by their parents, and this among the people of God themselves: the Psalmist tells us, Psal. 106. 38. *They shed innocent blood, even the blood of their sons and of their daughters, whom they sacrificed unto the idols of Canaan.* But God judged not of this by our author's rule, nor allowed of the authority of practice against his righteous law, but as it follows there, *the land was polluted with blood; therefore was the wrath of the Lord kindled against his people, insomuch that he abhorred his own inheritance.* The killing of their children, though it were fashionable, was charged on them as innocent blood, and so had in the account of God the guilt of murder, as the offering them to idols had the guilt of idolatry.

§. 59. Be it then, as Sir Robert says, *that anciently it was usual for men to sell and castrate their children, Observations,* 155. Let it be, that they exposed them; add to it, if you please, for this is still greater power, that they begat them for their tables, to fat and eat them: if this proves a right to do so, we may, by the same argument, justify adultery, incest and sodomy, for there are examples of these too, both ancient and modern; sins, which I suppose have their principal aggravation from this, that they cross the main intention of nature, which wills the increase of mankind, and the continuation of the species in the highest perfection, and the distinction of families, with the security of the marriage bed, as necessary thereunto.

§. 60. In confirmation of this natural authority of the father, our author brings a lame proof from the positive command of God in

scripture: his words are, *To confirm the natural right of regal power,*
we find in the Decalogue, that the law which enjoins obedience to
kings, is delivered in the terms, Honour thy father, p. 23. *Whereas*
many confess, that government only in the abstract, is the ordinance
of God, they are not able to prove any such ordinance in the scrip-
ture, but only in the fatherly power; and therefore we find the com-
mandment, that enjoins obedience to superiors, given in the terms,
Honour thy father; so that not only the power and right of govern-
ment, but the form of the power governing, and the person having
the power, are all the ordinances of God. The first father had not only
simply power, but power monarchical, as he was father immediately
from God, Observations, 254. To the same purpose, the same law
is cited by our author in several other places, and just after the
same fashion; that is, *and mother,* as apocryphal words, are always
left out; a great argument of our author's ingenuity, and the goodness of his cause, which required in its defender zeal to a degree of
warmth, able to warp the sacred rule of the word of God, to make it
comply with his present occasion; a way of proceeding not unusual
to those, who embrace not truths, because reason and revelation
offer them, but espouse tenets and parties for ends different from
truth, and then resolve at any rate to defend them; and so do with
the words and sense of authors, they would fit to their purpose,
just as Procrustes[21] did with his guests, lop or stretch them, as may
best fit them to the size of their notions: and they always prove like
those so served, deformed, lame, and useless.

§. 61. For had our author set down this command without garbling,
as God gave it, and joined mother to father, every reader would
have seen, that it had made directly against him; and that it was so
far from establishing the monarchical power of the father, that it
set up the mother equal with him, and enjoined nothing but what
was due in common, to both father and mother: for that is the
constant tenor of the scripture, *Honour thy father and thy mother,*
Exod. 20. *He that smiteth his father or mother, shall surely he put*
to death, 21. 15. *He that curseth his father or mother, shall surely*
be put to death, ver. 17. Repeated, *Lev. 20. 9.* and by our Saviour,
Matth. 15. 4. *Ye shall fear every man his mother and his father,* Lev.

---

21. In Greek legend, Procrustes was the highway robber who cut and trimmed
his victims to fit his bed.

19. 3. *If a man have a rebellious son, which will not obey the voice of his father, or the voice of his mother; then shall his father and his mother lay hold on him, and say, This our son is stubborn and rebellious, he will not obey our voice*, Deut. 21. 18, 19, 20, 21. *Cursed be he that setteth light by his father or his mother*, 28. 16. *My son, hear the instructions of thy father, and forsake not the law of thy mother*, are the words of Solomon, a king who was not ignorant of what belonged to him as a father or a king; and yet he joins father and mother together, in all the instruction he gives children quite through his book of Proverbs. *Woe unto him, that sayeth unto his father. What begettest thou? Or to the woman, What hast thou brought forth?* Isa. 45. ver. 10. *In thee have they set light by father or mother*, Ezek. 22. 2. *And it shall come to pass, that when any shall yet prophesy, then his father and his mother that begat him, shall say unto him, thou shall not live; and his father and his mother that begat him, shall thrust him through when he prophesied*, Zech. 13. 3. Here not the father only, but the father and mother jointly, had power in this case of life and death. Thus ran the law of the Old Testament, and in the New they are likewise joined, in the obedience of their children, Eph. 6. The rule is, *Children, obey your parents*; and I do not remember, that I anywhere read, *Children, obey your father*, and no more: the scripture joins mother too in that homage, which is due from children; and had there been any text, where the honor or obedience of children had been directed to the father alone, it is not likely that our author, who pretends to build all upon scripture, would have omitted it: nay, the scripture makes the authority of father and mother, in respect of those they have begot, so equal, that in some places it neglects even the priority of order, which is thought due to the father, and the *mother* is put first, as Lev. 19. 3. From which so constantly joining father and mother together, as is found quite through the scripture, we may conclude that the honor they have a title to from their children, is one common right belonging so equally to them both, that neither can claim it wholly, neither can be excluded.

§. 62. One would wonder then how our author infers from the fifth commandment, that *all power was originally in the father*. How he finds *monarchical power of government settled and fixed by the commandment, Honour thy father and thy mother*. If all the honor due by the commandment, be it what it will, be only the right of the father because he, as our author says, *has the sovereignty over the woman, as being the nobler and principal agent in generation,* why did God afterwards all along join the mother with him, to share in his honor? Can the father, by this sovereignty of his, discharge the child from paying this honor to his mother? The scripture gave no such license to the Jews, and yet there were often breaches wide enough between husband and wife, even to divorce and separation, and, I think, nobody will say a child may withhold honor from his mother, or, as the scripture terms it, set light by her, though his father should command him to do so, no more than the mother could dispense with him for neglecting to honor his father, whereby it is plain, that this command of God gives the father no sovereignty, no supremacy.

§. 63. I agree with our author that the title to this honor is vested in the parents by nature, and is a right which accrues to them by their having begotten their children, and God by many positive declarations has confirmed it to them. I also allow our author's rule, *that in grants and gifts, that have their original from God and nature, as the power of the father,* (let me add *and mother,* for whom God has joined together, let no man put asunder) *no inferior power of men can limit, nor make any law of prescription against them, Observations,* 158. So that the mother having, by this law of God, a right to honor from her children, which is not subject to the will of her husband, we see this absolute monarchical power of the father can neither be founded on it, nor consist with it; and he has a power very far from monarchical, very far from that absoluteness our author contends for, when another has over his subjects the same power he has, and by the same title: and therefore he cannot forbear saying himself that *he cannot see how any man's children can be free from subjection to their parents,* p. 12. Which, in common speech, I think, signifies mother as well as father; or if parents here signifies only father, it is the first time I ever yet knew it to do so, and by such an use of words, one may say anything.

§. 64. By our author's doctrine, the father, having absolute jurisdiction over his children, has also the same over their issue; and the consequence is good, were it true, that the father had such a power: and yet I ask our author whether the grandfather, by his sovereignty, could discharge the grandchild from paying to his father the honor due to him by the fifth commandment. If the grandfather has, by right of fatherhood, sole sovereign power in him, and that obedience which is due to the supreme magistrate, be commanded in these words, *Honour thy father*, it is certain the grandfather might dispense with the grandson's honoring his father, which since it is evident in common sense he cannot, it follows from hence, that *Honour thy father and mother*, cannot mean an absolute subjection to a sovereign power, but something else. The right therefore which parents have by nature, and which is confirmed to them by the fifth commandment, cannot be that political dominion which our author would derive from it: for that being in every civil society supreme somewhere, can discharge any subject from any political obedience to any one of his fellow subjects. But what law of the magistrate can give a child liberty, not to *Honour his father and mother*? It is an eternal law, annexed purely to the relation of parents and children, and so contains nothing of the magistrate's power in it, nor is subjected to it.

§. 65. Our author says, *God hath given, to a father a right or liberty to alien his power over his children to any other*, Observations, 155. I doubt whether he can alien wholly the right of honor that is due from them: but be that as it will, this I am sure, he cannot alien, and retain the same power. If therefore the magistrate's sovereignty be, as our author would have it, *nothing but the authority of a supreme father*, p. 23. It is unavoidable, that if the magistrate has all this paternal right, as he must have if fatherhood be the fountain of all authority, then the subjects, though fathers, can have no power over their children, no right to honor from them: for it cannot be all in another's hands, and a part remain with the parents. So that, according to our author's own doctrine, *Honour thy father and mother* cannot possibly be understood of political subjection and obedience; since the laws both in the Old and New Testament, that commanded children to *honour and obey their parents*, were given to such, whose fathers were under civil government, and fellow subjects with them in political societies; and to have bid them honor and obey their parents, in our author's sense, had been to bid them be subjects to those who had no title to it, the right to obedience from subjects, being all vested in another: and instead of teaching obedience, this had been to foment sedition, by setting up powers that were not. If therefore this command, *Honour thy father and mother*, concern political dominion, it directly overthrows our author's monarchy; since it being to be paid by every child to his father, even in society, every father must necessarily have political dominion, and there will be as many sovereigns as there are fathers: besides that the mother too has her title, which destroys the sovereignty of one supreme monarch. But if *Honour thy father and mother* means something distinct from political power, as necessarily it must, it is besides our author's business, and serves nothing to his purpose.

§. 66. *The law that enjoins obedience to kings is delivered,* says our author*, in the terms, Honour thy father, as if all power were originally in the father, Observations,* 254. And that law is also delivered, say I, in the terms, *Honour thy mother,* as if all power were originally in the mother. I appeal whether the argument be not as good on one side as the other, father and mother being joined all along in the Old and New Testament wherever honor or obedience is enjoined children. Again our author tells us, *Observations,* 254. *that this command, Honour thy father gives the right, to govern, and makes the form of government monarchical.* To which I answer, that if by *Honour thy father* be meant obedience to the political power of the magistrate, it concerns not any duty we owe to our natural fathers, who are subjects; because they, by our author's doctrine, are divested of all that power, it being placed wholly in the prince, and so being equally subjects and slaves with their children, can have no right, by that title, to any such honor or obedience, as contains in it political subjection. If *Honour thy father and mother* signifies the duty we owe our natural parents, as by our Saviour's interpretation, Matt. 15. 4. and all the other mentioned places, it is plain it does, then it cannot concern political obedience, but a duty that is owing to persons, who have no title to sovereignty, nor any political authority as magistrates over subjects. For the person of a private father, and a title to obedience, due to the supreme magistrate, are things inconsistent; and therefore this command, which must necessarily comprehend the persons of our natural fathers, must mean a duty we owe them distinct from our obedience to the magistrate, and from which the most absolute power of princes cannot absolve us. What this duty is, we shall in its due place examine.

§. 67. And thus we have at last got through all, that in our author looks like an argument for that absolute unlimited sovereignty described, Sect. 8. Which he supposes in Adam, so that mankind ever since have been all born slaves, without any title to freedom. But if creation, which gave nothing but a being, made not Adam prince of his posterity: if Adam, Gen. 1. 28. was not constituted lord of mankind, nor had a private dominion given him exclusive of his children, but only a right and power over the earth, and inferior creatures in common with the children of men: if also Gen. 3. 16. God gave not any political power to Adam over his wife and children, but only subjected Eve to Adam, as a punishment, or foretold the subjection of the weaker sex, in the ordering the common concernments of their families, but gave not thereby to Adam, as to the husband, power of life and death, which necessarily belongs to the magistrate: if fathers by begetting their children acquire no such power over them, and if the command, *Honour thy father and mother*, give it not, but only enjoins a duty owing to parents equally, whether subjects or not, and to the mother as well as the father; if all this be so, as I think, by what has been said, is very evident, then man has a natural freedom, notwithstanding all our author confidently says to the contrary, since all that share in the same common nature, faculties and powers, are in nature equal, and ought to partake in the same common rights and privileges, till the manifest appointment of God, who is Lord over all, blessed forever, can be produced to show any particular person's supremacy, or a man's own consent subjects him to a superior. This is so plain, that our author confesses, that Sir John Hayward, Blackwood, and Barclay, the great vindicators of the right of kings, could not deny it, *but admit with one consent the natural liberty and equality of mankind*, for a truth unquestionable. And our author has been so far from producing anything, that may make good his great position, that Adam was absolute monarch, and so men are not naturally free, that even his own proofs make against him; so that to use his own way of arguing, *This first erroneous principle failing, the whole fabric of this vast engine of absolute power and tyranny drops down of itself* and there needs no more to be said in answer to all that he builds upon so false and frail a foundation.

§. 68. But to save others the pains, were there any need, he is not sparing himself to show, by his own contradictions, the weakness of his own doctrine. Adam's absolute and sole dominion is that, which he is everywhere full of, and all along builds on, and yet he tells us, p. 12. *That as Adam was lord of his children, so his children under him had a command and power over their own children.* The unlimited and undivided sovereignty of Adam's fatherhood, by our author's computation, stood but a little while, only during the first generation, but as soon as he had grandchildren, Sir Robert could give but a very ill account of it. *Adam, as father of his children*, says he, *hath an absolute, unlimited royal power over them, and by virtue thereof over those that they begot, and so to all generations*; and yet his children, viz. Cain and Seth, have a paternal power over their children at the same time; so that they are at the same time absolute lords, and yet vassals and slaves; Adam has all the authority, as grandfather of the people, and they have a part of it as fathers of a part of them. He is absolute over them and their posterity, by having begotten them, and yet they are absolute over their children by the same title. No, says our author, *Adam's children under him had power over their own children, but still with subordination to the first parent.* A good distinction that sounds well, and it is pity it signifies nothing, nor can be reconciled with our author's words. I readily grant, that supposing Adam's absolute power over his posterity, any of his children might have from him a delegated, and so a subordinate power over a part, or all the rest: but that cannot be the power our author speaks of here, it is not a power by grant and commission, but the natural paternal power he supposes a father to have over his children. For 1. He says, *As Adam was lord of his children, so his children under him had a power over their own children*: they were then lords over their own children after the same manner, and by the same title, that Adam was, i.e. by right of generation, by right of fatherhood. 2. It is plain he means the natural power of fathers, because he limits it to be only over their own children; a delegated power has no such limitation, as only over their own children, it might be over others, as well as their own children. 3. If it were a delegated power, it must appear in scripture; but there is no ground in scripture to affirm, that Adam's children had any other power over theirs, than what they naturally had as fathers.

§. 69. But that he means here paternal power and no other, is past doubt, from the inference he makes in these words immediately following, *I see not then how the children of Adam, or of any man else, can be free from subjection to their parents*: whereby it appears that the power on one side, and the subjection on the other, our author here speaks of, is that natural power and subjection between parents and children: for that which every man's children owed, could be no other; and that our author always affirms to be absolute and unlimited. This natural power of parents over their children, Adam had over his posterity, says our author; and this power of parents over their children, his children had over theirs in his lifetime, says our author also; so that Adam, by a natural right of father, had an absolute unlimited power over all his posterity, and at the same time his children had by the same right absolute unlimited power over theirs. Here then are two absolute unlimited powers existing together, which I would have anybody reconcile one to another, or to common sense. For the salvo he has put in of subordination, makes it more absurd: to have one absolute, unlimited, nay, unlimitable power, in subordination to another, is so manifest a contradiction, that nothing can be more. *Adam is absolute prince with the unlimited authority of fatherhood over all his posterity*; all his posterity are then absolutely his subjects; and, as our author says, his slaves, children, and grandchildren, are equally in this state of subjection and slavery; and yet, says our author, the children of Adam have paternal, i.e. absolute unlimited power over their own children: which in plain English is, they are slaves and absolute princes at the same time, and in the same government; and one part of the subjects have an absolute unlimited power over the other by the natural right of parentage.

§. 70. If anyone will suppose, in favor of our author, that he here meant, that parents, who are in subjection themselves to the absolute authority of their father, have yet some power over their children; I confess he is something nearer the truth: but he will not at all hereby help our author for he nowhere speaking of the paternal power, but as an absolute unlimited authority, cannot be supposed to understand anything else here, unless he himself had limited it, and showed how far it reached. And that he means here paternal authority in that large extent, is plain from the immediately following words; *This subjection of children being*, says he, *the fountain of all regal authority*, p. 12. The subjection then that in the former line, he says, every man is in to his parents, and consequently what Adam's grandchildren were in to their parents, was that which was the fountain of all regal authority, i.e. according to our author, absolute unlimited authority. And thus Adam's children had regal authority over their children, while they themselves were subjects to their father, and fellow-subjects with their children. But let him mean as he pleases, it is plain he allows *Adam's children to have paternal power* p. 12. As also all other fathers to have *paternal power over their children, Observations*, 156. From whence one of these two things will necessarily follow, that either Adam's children, even in his lifetime, had, and so all fathers have, as he phrases it, p. 12. By right of fatherhood, *royal authority* over their children, or else, that Adam, by right of fatherhood, had not royal authority. For it cannot be but that paternal power does, or does not, give royal authority to them that have it: if it does not, then Adam could not be sovereign by this title, nor anybody else, and then there is an end of all our author's politics at once; if it does give royal authority, then everyone that has paternal power, has royal authority, and then by our author's patriarchal government, there will be as many kings as there are fathers.

§. 71. And thus what a monarchy he has set up, let him and his disciples consider. Princes certainly will have great reason to thank him for these new politics, which set up as many absolute kings in every country as there are fathers of children. And yet who can blame our author for it, it lying unavoidably in the way of one discoursing upon our author's principles? For having placed an *absolute power in fathers by right of begetting*, he could not easily resolve how much of this power belonged to a son over the children he had begotten; and so it fell out to be a very hard matter to give all the power, as he does, to Adam, and yet allow a part in his lifetime to his children, when they were parents, and which he knew not well how to deny them. This makes him so doubtful in his expressions, and so uncertain where to place this absolute natural power, which he calls *fatherhood*. Sometimes Adam alone has it all, as p. 13., *Observations*, 244, 245. & Pref.

Sometimes parents have it, which word scarce signifies the father alone, p. 12, 19.

Sometimes children during their father's lifetime, as p. 12.

Sometimes fathers of families, as p. 78 & 79.

Sometimes fathers indefinitely, *Observations*, 155.

Sometimes *the heir to Adam*, *Observations*, 253.

Sometimes *the posterity of Adam*, *Observations*, 244, 246.

Sometimes prime fathers, all sons or grandchildren of Noah, *Observations*, 244.

Sometimes *the eldest parents*, p. 12.

Sometimes all kings, p. 19.

Sometimes all that have supreme power, *Observations*, 245.

Sometimes *heirs to those first progenitors, who were at first the natural parents of the whole people*, p. 19.

Sometimes an elective king, p. 23.

Sometimes those, whether a few or a multitude, that govern the commonwealth, p. 23.

Sometimes he that can catch it, an usurper, p. 23. *Observations*, 155.

§. 72. Thus this new nothing, that is to carry with it all power, authority, and government; this fatherhood, which is to design the person, and establish the throne of monarchs, whom the people are to obey, may, according to Sir Robert, come into any hands, anyhow, and so by his politics give to democracy royal authority, and make an usurper a lawful prince. And if it will do all these fine feats, much good do our author and all his followers with their omnipotent fatherhood, which can serve for nothing but to unsettle and destroy all the lawful governments in the world, and to establish in their room disorder, tyranny, and usurpation.

CHAPTER VII
Of Fatherhood and Property, Considered Together as Fountains of Sovereignty

§. 73. In the foregoing chapters we have seen what Adam's monarchy was, in our author's opinion, and upon what titles he founded it. The foundations which he lays the chief stress on, as those from which he thinks he may best derive monarchical power to future princes, are two, viz. fatherhood and property, and therefore the way he proposes *to remove the absurdities and inconveniencies of the doctrine of natural freedom is, to maintain the natural and private dominion of Adam, Observations,* 222. Conformable hereunto, he tells us, *the grounds and principles of government necessarily depend upon the original of property, Observations,* 108. *The subjection of children to their parents is the fountain of all regal authority,* p. 12. *And all power on earth is either derived or usurped from the fatherly power, there being no other original to be found of any power whatsoever, Observations,* 158. I will not stand here to examine how it can be said without a contradiction, *that the first grounds and principles of government necessarily depend upon the original of property,* and yet, *that there is no other original of any power whatsoever, but that of the father;* it being hard to understand how there can be no other original but fatherhood, and yet that *the grounds and principles of government depend upon the original of property;* property and fatherhood being as far different as lord of a manor and father of children. Nor do I see how they will either of them agree with what our author says, *Observations,* 244. of God's sentence against Eve, Gen. 3. 16. That it is the original grant of government: so that if that were the original, government had not its original, by our author's own confession, either from property or fatherhood; and this text which he brings as a proof of Adam's power over Eve, necessarily contradicts what he says of the fatherhood, that it is the sole fountain of all power. For if Adam had any such regal power over Eve, as our author contends for, it must be by some other title than that of begetting.

§. 74. But I leave him to reconcile these contradictions, as well as many others, which may plentifully be found in him by anyone, who will but read him with a little attention, and shall come now to consider, how these two originals of government, Adam's natural and private dominion, will consist, and serve to make out and establish the titles of succeeding monarchs, who, as our author obliges them, must all derive their power from these fountains. Let us then suppose Adam made, by God's donation, lord and sole proprietor of the whole earth, in as large and ample a manner as Sir Robert could wish; let us suppose him also, by right of fatherhood, absolute ruler over his children with an unlimited supremacy, I ask then, upon Adam's death what becomes of both his natural and private dominion? And I doubt not it will be answered, that they descended to his next heir, as our author tells us in several places. But this way, it is plain, cannot possibly convey both his natural and private dominion to the same person. For should we allow, that all the property, all the estate of the father, ought to descend to the eldest son, (which will need some proof to establish it) and so he has by that title all the private dominion of the father, yet the father's natural dominion, the paternal power cannot descend to him by inheritance. For it being a right that accrues to a man only by begetting, no man can have this natural dominion over anyone he does not beget; unless it can be supposed, that a man can have a right to anything, without doing that upon which that right is solely founded. For if a father by begetting, and no other title, has natural dominion over his children, he that does not beget them cannot have this natural dominion over them: and therefore be it true or false, that our author says, *Observations*, 156. That every man *that is born, by his very birth becomes subject to him that begets him*, this necessarily follows, viz. That a man by his birth cannot become a subject to his brother, who did not beget him: unless it can be supposed that a man by the very same title can come to be under the natural and absolute dominion of two different men at once, or it be sense to say, that a man by birth is under the natural dominion of his father, only because he begat him, and a man by birth also is under the natural dominion of his eldest brother, though he did not beget him.

§. 75. If then the private dominion of Adam, i.e. his property in the creatures, descended at his death all entirely to his eldest son, his heir; (for, if it did not, there is presently an end of all Sir Robert's monarchy) and his natural dominion, the dominion a father has over his children by begetting them, belonged immediately, upon Adam's decease, equally to all his sons who had children, by the same title their father had it, the sovereignty founded upon property, and the sovereignty founded upon fatherhood, come to be divided: since Cain, as heir, had that or property alone, Seth, and the other sons, that of fatherhood equally with him. This is the best that can be made of our author's doctrine, and of the two titles of sovereignty he sets up in Adam, one of them will either signify nothing, or if they both must stand, they can serve only to confound the rights of princes, and disorder government in his posterity. For by building upon two titles to dominion, which cannot descend together, and which he allows may be separated, (for he yields that *Adam's children had their distinct territories by right of private dominion, Observations,* 210, p. 40) he makes it perpetually a doubt upon his principles where the sovereignty is, or to whom we owe our obedience, since fatherhood and property are distinct titles, and began presently upon Adam's death to be in distinct persons. And which then was to give way to the other?

§. 76. Let us take the account of it, as he himself gives it us. He tells us out of Grotius, that *Adam's children by donation, assignation, or some kind of cession before he was dead, had their distinct territories by right of private dominion; Abel had his flocks and pastures for them; Cain had his fields for corn, and the land of Nod, where he built him a city, Observations,* 210. Here it is obvious to demand, which of these two after Adam's death was sovereign? Cain, says our author, p. 19. By what title? As heir; *for heirs to progenitors, who were natural parents of their people, are not only lords of their own children, but also of their brethren,* says our author, p. 19. What was Cain heir to? Not the entire possessions, not all that which Adam had private dominion in, for our author allows that Abel by a title derived from his father, had his distinct territory for pasture by right of private dominion. What then Abel had by private dominion, was exempt from Cain's dominion. For he could not have private dominion over that which was under the private dominion of another, and therefore his sovereignty over his brother is gone with this private dominion, and so there are presently two sovereigns, and his imaginary title of fatherhood is out of doors, and Cain is no prince over his brother: or else, if Cain retain his sovereignty over Abel, notwithstanding his private dominion, it will follow, that the first grounds and principles of government have nothing to do with property, whatever our author says to the contrary. It is true, Abel did not outlive his father Adam, but that makes nothing to the argument, which will hold good against Sir Robert in Abel's issue, or in Seth, or any of the posterity of Adam, not descended from Cain.

§. 77. The same inconvenience he runs into about the three sons of Noah, who, as he says, p. 13. *had the whole world divided among them by their father.* I ask then, in which of the three shall we find the establishment of regal power after Noah's death? If in all three, as our author there seems to say; then it will follow, that regal power is founded in property of land, and follows private dominion, and not in paternal power, or natural dominion, and so there is an end of paternal power as the fountain of regal authority, and the so much magnified fatherhood quite vanishes. If the regal power descended to Shem as eldest, and heir to his father, then *Noah's division of the world by lot, to his sons or his ten years sailing about the Mediterranean to appoint each son his part,* which our author tells of, p. 15. was labor lost, his division of the world to them, was to ill, or to no purpose. For his grant to Cham and Japhet was little worth, if Shem, notwithstanding this grant, as soon as Noah was dead, was to be lord over them. Or, if this grant of private dominion to them, over their assigned territories, were good, here were set up two distinct sorts of power, not subordinate one to the other, with all those inconveniencies which he musters up against the power of the people, *Observations,* 158. which I shall set down in his own words, only changing property for people. *All power on earth is either derived or usurped from the fatherly power, there being no other original to be found of any power whatsoever: for if there should be granted two sorts of power, without any subordination of one to the other, they would be in perpetual strife which should be supreme, for two supremes cannot agree: if the fatherly power be supreme, then the power grounded on private dominion must be subordinate, and depend on it; and if the power grounded on property be supreme, then the fatherly power must submit to it, and cannot be exercised without the licence of the proprietors, which must quite destroy the frame and course of nature.* This is his own arguing against two distinct independent powers, which I have set down in his own words, only putting power rising from property, for *power of the people*, and when he has answered what he himself has urged here against two distinct powers, we shall be better able to see how, with any tolerable sense, he can derive all regal authority from the natural and private dominion of Adam, from fatherhood and property together, which are distinct titles, that do not always meet in the same person; and it is plain, by his own confession, presently separated as soon both as Adam's and Noah's death made way for succession: though our author frequently in his writings jumbles them together, and omits not to make use of either, where he thinks it will sound best to his purpose. But the absurdities of this will more fully appear in the next chapter, where we shall examine the ways of conveyance of the sovereignty of Adam, to princes that were to reign after him.

CHAPTER VIII
Of the Conveyance of Adam's Sovereign Monarchical Power

§. 78. Sir Robert, having not been very happy in any proof he brings for the sovereignty of Adam, is not much more fortunate in conveying it to future princes, who, if his politics be true, must all derive their titles from that first monarch. The ways he has assigned, as they lie scattered up and down in his writings, I will set down in his own words. In his preface he tells us, that *Adam being monarch of the whole world, none of his posterity had any right to possess anything, but by his grant or permission, or by succession from him.* Here he makes two ways of conveyance of anything Adam stood possessed of; and those are grants or succession. Again he says, *All kings either are, or are to be reputed, the next heirs to those first progenitors, who were at first the natural parents of the whole people,* p. 19. *There cannot be any multitude of men whatsoever, but that in it, considered by itself there is one man among them, that in nature hath a right to be the king of all the rest, as being the next heir to Adam, Observations,* 253. Here in these places inheritance is the only way he allows of conveying monarchical power to princes. In other places he tells us, *Observations,* 155. *All power on earth*

is either derived or usurped from the fatherly power, Observations,
158. All kings that now are, or ever were, are or were either fathers of
their people, or heirs of such fathers, or usurpers of the right of such
fathers, Observations, 253. And here he makes inheritance or usurpation the only ways whereby kings come by this original power:
but yet he tells us, *This fatherly empire, as it was of itself hereditary,*
so it was alienable by patent and seizable by an usurper, Observa-
tions, 190. So then here inheritance, grant, or usurpation, will convey it. And last of all, which is most admirable, he tells us, p. 100. *It*
skills not which way kings come by their power, whether by election,
donation, succession, or by any other means; for it is still the man-
ner of the government by supreme power, that makes them properly
kings, and not the means of obtaining their crowns. Which I think
is a full answer to all his whole hypothesis and discourse about
Adam's royal authority, as the fountain from which all princes were
to derive theirs: and he might have spared the trouble of speaking so much as he does, up and down, of heirs and inheritance,
if to make one properly a king, needs no more but governing by
supreme power, and it matters not by what means he came by it.

§. 79. By this notable way, our author may make Oliver[22] as properly king, as anyone else he could think of: and had he had the
happiness to live under Massanello's government,[23] he could not
by this his own rule have forborne to have done homage to him,
with O king live forever, since the manner of his government by
supreme power, made him properly king, who was but the day
before properly a fisherman. And if Don Quixote[24] had taught
his squire to govern with supreme authority, our author no doubt
could have made a most loyal subject in Sancho Pancha's island;
and he must needs have deserved some preferment in such gov-

22. Oliver Cromwell (1599–1658) was the most important general on the Parliamentary side in the English Civil War and later established de facto one-man rule
under the Protectorate (1653–1658), after dissolving the Rump Parliament. He
was seen by English royalists as the archvillain of the civil war period.

23. Tommaso Aniello (1622–1647) was an Italian fisherman who led a revolt in
Naples in 1647 against Spanish rule. In Locke's time, he was synonymous with
mob rule.

24. The novel *Don Quixote* (1615), written by Spanish author Miguel de
Cervantes (1547–1616). Locke owned several editions of *Don Quixote,* in both
English and French.

ernments, since I think he is the first politician, who, pretending to settle government upon its true basis, and to establish the thrones of lawful princes, ever told the world that he *was properly a king, whose manner of government was by supreme power, by what means soever he obtained it*: which in plain English is to say, that regal and supreme power is properly and truly his, who can by any means seize upon it: and if this be to be properly a king, I wonder how he came to think of, or where he will find, an usurper.

§. 80. This is so strange a doctrine, that the surprise of it has made me pass by, without their due reflection, the contradictions he runs into, by making sometimes inheritance alone, sometimes only grant or inheritance, sometimes only inheritance or usurpation, sometimes all these three, and at last election, or any other means, added to them, whereby Adam's royal authority, that is, his right to supreme rule, could be conveyed down to future kings and governors, so as to give them a title to the obedience and subjection of the people. But these contradictions lie so open, that the very reading of our author's own words will discover them to any ordinary understanding: and though what I have quoted out of him (with abundance more of the same strain and coherence which might be found in him) might well excuse me from any farther trouble in this argument, yet having proposed to myself, to examine the main parts of his doctrine, I shall a little more particularly consider how inheritance, grant, usurpation, or election, can any way make out government in the world upon his principles; or derive to anyone a right of empire from this regal authority of Adam, had it been never so well proved, that he had been absolute monarch, and lord of the whole world.

CHAPTER IX
Of Monarchy, by Inheritance from Adam

§. 81. Though it be never so plain, that there ought to be government in the world, nay, should all men be of our author's mind, that divine appointment had ordained it to be monarchical; yet, since men cannot obey anything, that cannot command, and ideas of government in the fancy, though never so perfect, though never so right, cannot give laws, nor prescribe rules to the actions of men; it would be of no behoof for the settling of order, and establishing of government in its exercise and use among men, unless there were a way also taught how to know the person, to whom it belonged to have this power, and exercise this dominion over others. It is in vain then to talk of subjection and obedience without telling us whom we are to obey. For were I never so fully persuaded that there ought to be magistracy and rule in the world; yet I am nevertheless at liberty still, till it appears who is the person that has right to my obedience; since, if there be no marks to know him by, and distinguish him that has right to rule from other men, it may be myself, as well as any other. And therefore, though submission to government be everyone's duty, yet since that signifies nothing but submitting to the direction and laws of such men as have authority to command, it is not enough to make a man a subject, to convince him that there is a regal power in the world; but there must be ways of designing, and knowing the person to whom this regal power of right belongs: and a man can never be obliged in conscience to submit to any power, unless he can be satisfied who is the person who has a right to exercise that power over him. If this were not so, there would be no distinction between pirates and lawful princes, he that has force is without any more ado to be obeyed, and crowns and sceptres would become the inheritance only of violence and rapine. Men too might as often and as innocently change their governors, as they do their physicians, if the person cannot be known who has a right to direct me, and whose prescriptions I am bound to follow. To settle therefore men's consciences, under an obligation to obedience, it is necessary that they know not only that there is a power somewhere in the world, but the person who by right is vested with this power over them.

§. 82. How successful our author has been in his attempts, to set up a monarchical absolute power in Adam, the reader may judge by what has been already said: but were that absolute monarchy as clear as our author would desire it, as I presume it is the contrary, yet it could be of no use to the government of mankind now in the world, unless he also make out these two things.

First, that this power of Adam was not to end with him, but was upon his decease conveyed entire to some other person, and so on to posterity.

Secondly, that the princes and rulers now on earth are possessed of this power of Adam, by a right way of conveyance derived to them.

§. 83. If the first of these fail, the power of Adam, were it never so great, never so certain, will signify nothing to the present governments and societies in the world, but we must seek out some other original of power for the government of polities than this of Adam, or else there will be none at all in the world. If the latter fail, it will destroy the authority of the present governors, and absolve the people from subjection to them, since they, having no better a claim than others to that power, which is alone the fountain of all authority, can have no title to rule over them.

§. 84. Our author, having fancied an absolute sovereignty in Adam, mentions several ways of its conveyance to princes, that were to be his successors; but that which he chiefly insists on, is that of inheritance, which occurs so often in his several discourses, and I having in the foregoing chapter quoted several of these passages, I shall not need here again to repeat them. This sovereignty he erects, as has been said, upon a double foundation, viz. that of property, and that of fatherhood. One was the right he was supposed to have in all creatures, a right to possess the earth with the beasts, and other inferior ranks of things in it, for his private use, exclusive of all other men. The other was the right he was supposed to have, to rule and govern men, all the rest of mankind.

§. 85. In both these rights, there being supposed an exclusion of all other men, it must be upon some reason peculiar to Adam, that they must both be founded. That of his property our author supposes to arise from God's immediate donation, Gen. 1. 28. and that of fatherhood from the act of begetting: now in all inheritance, if the heir succeed not to the reason upon which his father's right was founded, he cannot succeed to the right which follows from it. For example, Adam had a right of property in the creatures upon the donation and grant of God almighty, who was lord and proprietor of them all: let this be so as our author tells us, yet upon his death his heir can have no title to them, no such right of property in them, unless the same reason, viz. God's donation, vested a right in the heir too. For if Adam could have had no property in, nor use of the creatures, without this positive donation from God, and this donation were only personally to Adam, his heir could have no right by it; but upon his death it must revert to God, the lord and owner again, for positive grants give no title farther than the express words convey it, and by which only it is held. And thus, as if our author himself contends, that donation, Gen. 1. 28. were made only to Adam personally, his heir could not succeed to his property in the creatures; and if it were a donation to any but Adam, let it be shown, that it was to his heir in our author's sense, i.e. to one of his children, exclusive of all the rest.

§. 86. But not to follow our author too far out of the way, the plain of the case is this. God having made man, and planted in him, as in all other animals, a strong desire of self-preservation, and furnished the world with things fit for food and raiment, and other necessaries of life, subservient to his design, that man should live and abide for some time upon the face of the earth, and not that so curious and wonderful a piece of workmanship, by his own negligence, or want of necessaries, should perish again, presently after a few moments continuance: God, I say, having made man and the world thus, spoke to him, (that is) directed him by his senses and reason, as he did the inferior animals by their sense and instinct, which he had placed in them to that purpose, to the use of those things, which were serviceable for his subsistence, and given him as means of his preservation. And therefore I doubt not, but before these words were pronounced, Gen. 1. 28, 29. (if they must be understood literally to have been spoken) and without any such verbal donation, man had a right to an use of the creatures, by the will and grant of God. For the desire, strong desire of preserving his life and being, having been planted in him as a principle of action by God himself, reason, which was the voice of God in him, could not but teach him and assure him, that pursuing that natural inclination he had to preserve his being, he followed the will of his Maker, and therefore had a right to make use of those creatures, which by his reason or senses he could discover would be serviceable thereunto. And thus man's property in the creatures was founded upon the right he had to make use of those things that were necessary or useful to his being.

§. 87. This being the reason and foundation of Adam's property, gave the same title, on the same ground, to all his children, not only after his death, but in his lifetime: so that here was no privilege of his heir above his other children, which could exclude them from an equal right to the use of the inferior creatures, for the comfortable preservation of their beings, which is all the property man has in them; and so Adam's sovereignty built on property, or, as our author calls it, private dominion, comes to nothing. Every man had a right to the creatures, by the same title Adam had, viz. by the right everyone had to take care of, and provide for their subsistence: and thus men had a right in common, Adam's children in common with him. But if anyone had began, and made himself a property in any particular thing, (which how he, or anyone else, could do, shall be shown in another place) that thing, that possession, if he disposed not otherwise of it by his positive grant, descended naturally to his children, and they had a right to succeed to it, and possess it.

§. 88. It might reasonably be asked here, how come children by this right of possessing, before any other, the properties of their parents upon their decease? For it being personally the parents, when they die, without actually transferring their right to another, why does it not return again to the common stock of mankind? It will perhaps be answered, that common consent has disposed of it to the children. Common practice, we see indeed, does so dispose of it but we cannot say, that it is the common consent of mankind; for that has never been asked, nor actually given: and if common tacit consent has established it, it would make but a positive, and not a natural right of children to inherit the goods of their parents: but where the practice is universal, it is reasonable to think the cause is natural. The ground then I think to be this. The first and strongest desire God planted in men, and wrought into the very principles of their nature, being that of self-preservation, that is the foundation of a right to the creatures for the particular support and use of each individual person himself. But, next to this, God planted in men a strong desire also of propagating their kind, and continuing themselves in their posterity, and this gives children a title to share in the property of their parents, and a right to inherit their possessions. Men are not proprietors of what they have, merely for themselves, their children have a title to part of it, and have their kind of right joined with their parents, in the possession which comes to be wholly theirs, when death, having put an end to their parents use of it, has taken them from their possessions, and this we call inheritance. Men being by a like obligation bound to preserve what they have begotten, as to preserve themselves, their issue come to have a right in the goods they are possessed of. That children have such a right, is plain from the laws of God, and that men are convinced that children have such a right, is evident from the law of the land, both which laws require parents to provide for their children.

§. 89. For children being by the course of nature, born weak, and unable to provide for themselves, they have by the appointment of God himself, who has thus ordered the course of nature, a right to be nourished and maintained by their parents, nay, a right not only to a bare subsistence, but to the conveniences and comforts of life, as far as the conditions of their parents can afford it. Hence it comes, that when their parents leave the world, and so the care due to their children ceases, the effects of it are to extend as far as possibly they can, and the provisions they have made in their lifetime, are understood to be intended, as nature requires they should, for their children, whom, after themselves, they are bound to provide for, though the dying parents, by express words, declare nothing about them, nature appoints the descent of their property to their children, who thus come to have a title, and natural right of inheritance to their father's goods, which the rest of mankind cannot pretend to.

§. 90. Were it not for this right of being nourished and maintained by their parents, which God and nature has given to children, and obliged parents to as a duty, it would be reasonable, that the father should inherit the estate of his son, and be preferred in the inheritance before his grandchild. For to the grandfather there is due a long score of care and expenses laid out upon the breeding and education of his son, which one would think in justice ought to be paid. But that having been done in obedience to the same law, whereby he received nourishment and education from his own parents, this score of education, received from a man's father, is paid by taking care, and providing for his own children; is paid, I say, as much as is required of payment by alteration of property, unless present necessity of the parents require a return of goods for their necessary support and subsistence. For we are not now speaking of that reverence, acknowledgment, respect and honor, that is always due from children to their parents, but of possessions and commodities of life valuable by money. But though it be incumbent on parents to bring up and provide for their children, yet this debt to their children does not quite cancel the score due to the parents, but only is made by nature preferable to it. For the debt a man owes his father, takes place, and gives the father a right to inherit the son's goods, where, for want of issue, the right of children does not exclude that title. And therefore a man having a right to be maintained by his children, where he needs it, and to enjoy also the comforts of life from them, when the necessary provision due to them and their children will afford it, if his son die without issue, the father has a right in nature to possess his goods, and inherit his estate, (whatever the municipal laws of some countries may absurdly direct otherwise), and so again his children and their issue from him, or, for want of such, his father and his issue. But where no such are to be found, i.e. no kindred, there we see the possessions of a private man revert to the community, and so in politic societies come into the hands of the public magistrate: but in the state of nature become again perfectly common, nobody having a right to inherit them: nor can anyone have a property in them, otherwise than in other things common by nature, of which I shall speak in its due place.

§. 91. I have been the larger, in showing upon what ground children have a right to succeed to the possession of their father's properties, not only because by it, it will appear, that if Adam had a property (a titular, insignificant, useless property; for it could be no better, for he was bound to nourish and maintain his children and posterity out of it) in the whole earth and its product, yet all his children coming to have, by the law of nature, and right of inheritance, a joint title, and right of property in it after his death,

it could convey no right of sovereignty to any one of his posterity over the rest: since everyone having a right of inheritance to
his portion, they might enjoy their inheritance, or any part of it
in common, or share it, or some parts of it, by division, as it best
liked them. But no one could pretend to the whole inheritance, or
any sovereignty supposed to accompany it, since a right of inheritance gave every one of the rest, as well as any one, a title to share
in the goods of his father. Not only upon this account, I say, have I
been so particular in examining the reason of children's inheriting
the property of their fathers, but also because it will give us farther light in the inheritance of rule and power, which in countries
where their particular municipal laws give the whole possession of
land entirely to the first-born, and descent of power has gone so
to men by this custom, some have been apt to be deceived into an
opinion, that there was a natural or divine right of primogeniture,
to both estate and power; and that the inheritance of both rule
over men, and property in things, sprang from the same original,
and were to descend by the same rules.

§. 92. Property, whose original is from the right a man has to use
any of the inferior creatures, for the subsistence and comfort of his
life, is for the benefit and sole advantage of the proprietor, so that
he may even destroy the thing, that he has property in by his use of
it, where need requires: but government being for the preservation
of every man's right and property, by preserving him from the
violence or injury of others, is for the good of the governed. For
the magistrate's sword being for a terror to evil doers, and by that
terror to enforce men to observe the positive laws of the society,
made conformable to the laws of nature, for the public good, i.e.
the good of every particular member of that society, as far as by
common rules it can be provided for; the sword is not given the
magistrate for his own good alone.

§. 93. Children therefore, as has been shown by the dependence
they have on their parents for subsistence, have a right of inheritance to their father's property, as that which belongs to them for
their proper good and behoof, and therefore are fitly termed goods,
wherein the first-born has not a sole or peculiar right by any law
of God and nature, the younger children having an equal title with

him, founded on that right they all have to maintenance, support, and comfort from their parents, and nothing else. But government being for the benefit of the governed, and not the sole advantage of the governors, (but only for theirs with the rest, as they make a part of that politic body, each of whose parts and members are taken care of, and directed in its peculiar functions for the good of the whole, by the laws of the society) cannot be inherited by the same title, that children have to the goods of their father. The right a son has to be maintained and provided with the necessaries and conveniences of life out of his father's stock, gives him a right to succeed to his father's property for his own good, but this can give him no right to succeed also to the rule, which his father had over other men. All that a child has right to claim from his father is nourishment and education, and the things nature furnishes for the support of life: but he has no right to demand rule or dominion from him: he can subsist and receive from him the portion of good things, and advantages of education naturally due to him, without empire and dominion. That (if his father has any) was vested in him, for the good and behoof of others, and therefore the son cannot claim or inherit it by a title, which is founded wholly on his own private good and advantage.

§. 94. We must know how the first ruler, from whom anyone claims, came by his authority, upon what ground anyone has empire, what his title is to it, before we can know who has a right to succeed him in it, and inherit it from him. If the agreement and consent of men first gave a sceptre into anyone's hand, or put a crown on his head, that also must direct its descent and conveyance. For the same authority, that made the first a lawful ruler, must make the second too, and so give right of succession: in this case inheritance, or primogeniture, can in itself have no right, no pretence to it, any farther than that consent, which established the form of the government, has so settled the succession. And thus we see, the succession of crowns, in several countries, places it on different heads, and he comes by right of succession to be a prince in one place, who would be a subject in another.

§. 95. If God, by his positive grant and revealed declaration, first gave rule and dominion to any man, he that will claim by that title,

must have the same positive grant of God for his succession: for
if that has not directed the course of its descent and conveyance
down to others, nobody can succeed to this title of the first ruler.
Children have no right of inheritance in this; and primogeniture
can lay no claim to it, unless God, the author of this constitution,
has so ordained it. Thus we see, the pretensions of Saul's family, who received his crown from the immediate appointment of
God, ended with his reign; and David, by the same title that Saul
reigned, viz. God's appointment, succeeded in his throne, to the
exclusion of Jonathan, and all pretensions of paternal inheritance.
And if Solomon had a right to succeed his father, it must be by
some other title, than that of primogeniture. A cadet, or sister's
son, must have the preference in succession, if he has the same title
the first lawful prince had: and in dominion that has its foundation
only in the positive appointment of God himself, Benjamin, the
youngest, must have the inheritance of the Crown, if God so direct
as well as one of that tribe had the first possession.

§. 96. If paternal right, the act of begetting, give a man rule and
dominion, inheritance or primogeniture can give no title, for he
that cannot succeed to his father's title, which was begetting, cannot succeed to that power over his brethren, which his father had
by paternal right over them. But of this I shall have occasion to
say more in another place. This is plain in the meantime, that any
government, whether supposed to be at first founded in paternal
right, consent of the people, or the positive appointment of God
himself, which can supersede either of the other, and so begin a
new government upon a new foundation, I say, any government
began upon either of these, can by right of succession come to those
only, who have the title of him they succeed to. Power founded on
contract can descend only to him, who has right by that contract:
power founded on begetting, he only can have that begets; and
power founded on the positive grant or donation of God, he only
can have by right of succession, to whom that grant directs it.

§. 97. From what I have said, I think this is clear, that a right to the
use of the creatures, being founded originally in the right a man
has to subsist and enjoy the conveniences of life, and the natural right children have to inherit the goods of their parents, being

founded in the right they have to the same subsistence and commodities of life, out of the stock of their parents, who are therefore
taught by natural love and tenderness to provide for them, as a
part of themselves: and all this being only for the good of the proprietor, or heir; it can be no reason for children's inheriting of rule
and dominion, which has another original and a different end. Nor
can primogeniture have any pretence to a right of solely inheriting
either property or power, as we shall, in its due place, see more
fully. It is enough to have shown here, that Adam's property, or
private dominion, could not convey any sovereignty or rule to his
heir, who not having a right to inherit all his father's possessions,
could not thereby come to have any sovereignty over his brethren:
and therefore, if any sovereignty on account of his property had
been vested in Adam, which in truth there was not; yet it would
have died with him.

§. 98. As Adam's sovereignty, if, by virtue of being proprietor of
the world, he had any authority over men, could not have been
inherited by any of his children over the rest, because they had
the same title to divide the inheritance, and every one had a right
to a portion of his father's possessions; so neither could Adam's
sovereignty by right of fatherhood, if any such he had, descend
to any one of his children. For it being, in our author's account, a
right acquired by begetting to rule over those he had begotten, it
was not a power possible to be inherited, because the right being
consequent to, and built on, an act perfectly personal, made that
power so too, and impossible to be inherited. For paternal power,
being a natural right rising only from the relation of father and
son, is as impossible to be inherited as the relation itself, and a
man may pretend as well to inherit the conjugal power the husband, whose heir he is, had over his wife, as he can to inherit the
paternal power of a father over his children. For the power of the
husband being founded on contract, and the power of the father
on begetting, he may as well inherit the power obtained by the
conjugal contract, which was only personal, as he may the power
obtained by begetting, which could reach no farther than the person of the begetter, unless begetting can be a title to power in him,
that does not beget.

§. 99. Which makes it a reasonable question to ask, whether Adam, dying before Eve, his heir, (suppose Cain or Seth) should have had by right of inheriting Adam's fatherhood, sovereign power over Eve his mother. For Adam's fatherhood being nothing but a right he had to govern his children, because he begot them, he that inherits Adam's fatherhood, inherits nothing, even in our author's sense, but the right Adam had to govern his children, because he begot them: so that the monarchy of the heir would not have taken in Eve, or if it did, it being nothing but the fatherhood of Adam descended by inheritance, the heir must have right to govern Eve, because Adam begot her; for fatherhood is nothing else.

§. 100. Perhaps it will be said with our author, that a man can alien his power over his child, and what may be transferred by compact, may be possessed by inheritance. I answer, a father cannot alien the power he has over his child, he may perhaps to some degrees forfeit it, but cannot transfer it: and if any other man acquire it, it is not by the father's grant, but by some act of his own. For example, a father, unnaturally careless of his child, sells or gives him to another man; and he again exposes him: a third man finding him, breeds up, cherishes, and provides for him as his own. I think in this case, nobody will doubt, but that the greatest part of filial duty and subjection was here owing, and to be paid to this foster-father: and if anything could be demanded from the child by either of the other, it could only be due to his natural father, who perhaps might have forfeited his right to much of that duty comprehended in the command, *Honour your parents*, but could transfer none of it to another. He that purchased, and neglected the child, got by his purchase and grant of the father, no title to duty or honor from the child, but only he acquired it, who by his own authority, performing the office and care of a father, to the forlorn and perishing infant, made himself, by paternal care, a title to proportional degrees of paternal power. This will be more easily admitted upon consideration of the nature of paternal power, for which I refer my reader to the second book.

§. 101. To return to the argument in hand: this is evident, that paternal power arising only from begetting, for in that our author places it alone, can neither be transferred nor inherited: and he that does not beget, can no more have paternal power, which arises from thence, than he can have a right to anything, who performs not the condition, to which only it is annexed. If one should ask, by what law has a father power over his children? It will be answered, no doubt, by the law of nature, which gives such a power over them, to him that begets them. If one should ask likewise, by what law does our author's heir come by a right to inherit? I think it would be answered, by the law of nature too. For I find not that our author brings one word of scripture to prove the right of such an heir he speaks of. Why then the law of nature gives fathers paternal power over their children, because they did beget them, and the same law of nature gives the same paternal power to the heir over his brethren, who did not beget them: whence it follows, that either the father has not his paternal power by begetting, or else that the heir has it not at all. For it is hard to understand how the law of nature, which is the law of reason, can give the paternal power to the father over his children, for the only reason of begetting, and to the first-born over his brethren without this only reason, i.e. for no reason at all: and if the eldest, by the law of nature, can inherit this paternal power, without the only reason that gives a title to it, so may the youngest as well as he, and a stranger as well as either; for where there is no reason for anyone, as there is not, but for him that begets, all have an equal title. I am sure our author offers no reason, and when anybody does, we shall see whether it will hold or no.

§. 102. In the meantime it is as good sense to say, that by the law of nature a man has right to inherit the property of another, because he is of kin to him, and is known to be of his blood, and therefore, by the same law of nature, an utter stranger to his blood has right to inherit his estate: as to say that, by the law of nature, he that begets them has paternal power over his children, and therefore, by the law of nature, the heir that begets them not, has this paternal power over them: or supposing the law of the land gave absolute power over their children, to such only who nursed them, and fed their children themselves, could anybody pretend, that this law gave anyone, who did no such thing, absolute power over those, who were not his children?

§. 103. When therefore it can be shown, that conjugal power can belong to him that is not a husband, it will also I believe be proved, that our author's paternal power, acquired by begetting, may be inherited by a son, and that a brother, as heir to his father's power, may have paternal power, over his brethren, and by the same rule conjugal power too, but till then, I think we may rest satisfied, that the paternal power of Adam, this sovereign authority of father-hood, were there any such, could not descend to, nor be inherited by, his next heir. Fatherly power, I easily grant our author, if it will do him any good, can never be lost, because it will be as long in the world as there are fathers: but none of them will have Adam's paternal power, or derive theirs from him, but everyone will have his own, by the same title Adam had his, viz. by begetting, but not by inheritance, or succession, no more than husbands have their conjugal power by inheritance from Adam. And thus we see, as Adam had no such property, no such paternal power, as gave him sovereign jurisdiction over mankind; so likewise his sovereignty built upon either of these titles, if he had any such, could not have descended to his heir, but must have ended with him. Adam there-fore, as has been proved, being neither monarch, nor his imagi-nary monarchy hereditable, the power which is now in the world, is not that which was Adam's, since all that Adam could have upon our author's grounds, either of property or fatherhood, necessarily died with him, and could not be conveyed to posterity by inheri-tance. In the next place we will consider, whether Adam had any such heir, to inherit his power, as our author talks of.

CHAPTER X
Of the Heir to Adam's Monarchical Power

§. 104. Our author tells us, *Observations*, 253. *That it is a truth undeniable, that there cannot be any multitude of men whatsoever, either great or small, though gathered together from the several cor-ners and remotest regions of the world, but that in the same mul-titude, considered by itself, there is one man among them, that in nature hath a right to be king of all the rest, as being the next heir to Adam, and all the other subject to him, every man by nature is a king or a subject.* And again, p. 20. *If Adam himself were still living, and now ready to die, it is certain that there is one man, and but one in the world, who is next heir.* Let this *multitude of men be,* if our author pleases, all the princes upon the earth, there will then be, by our author's rule, *one among them, that in nature has a right to be king of all the rest, as being the right heir to Adam;* an excellent way to establish the thrones of princes, and settle the obedience of their subjects, by setting up a hundred, or perhaps a thousand titles (if there be so many princes in the world) against any king now reigning, each as good, upon our author's grounds, as his who wears the crown. If this right of heir carry any weight with it, if it be the *ordinance of God,* as our author seems to tell us, *Observations,* 244. must not all be subject to it, from the highest to the lowest? Can those who wear the name of princes, without having the right of being heirs to Adam, demand obedience from their subjects by this title, and not be bound to pay it by the same law? Either governments in the world are not to be claimed, and held by this title of Adam's heir, and then the starting of it is to no purpose, the being or not being Adam's heir, signifies nothing as to the title of dominion; or if it really be, as our author says, the true title to government and sovereignty, the first thing to be done, is to find out this true heir of Adam, seat him in his throne, and then all the kings and princes of the world ought to come and resign up their crowns and sceptres to him, as things that belong no more to them, than to any of their subjects.

§. 105. For either this right in nature, of Adam's heir, to be king over all the race of men, (for altogether they make one multitude) is a right not necessary to the making of a lawful king, and so there may be lawful kings without it, and then kings' titles and power depend not on it, or else all the kings in the world but one are not lawful kings, and so have no right to obedience: either this title of heir to Adam is that whereby kings hold their crowns, and have a right to subjection from their subjects, and then one only can have it, and the rest being subjects can require no obedience from other men, who are but their fellow subjects, or else it is not the title whereby kings rule, and have a right to obedience from their subjects, and then kings are kings without it, and this dream of the natural sovereignty of Adam's heir is of no use to obedience and government. For if kings have a right to dominion, and the obedience of their subjects, who are not, nor can possibly be, heirs to Adam, what use is there of such a title, when we are obliged to obey without it? If kings, who are not heirs to Adam, have no right to sovereignty, we are all free, till our author, or anybody for him, will show us Adam's right heir. If there be but one heir of Adam, there can be but one lawful king in the world, and nobody in conscience can be obliged to obedience till it be resolved who that is; for it may be anyone, who is not known to be of a younger house, and all others have equal titles. If there be more than one heir of Adam, everyone is his heir, and so everyone has regal power. For if two sons can be heirs together, then all the sons are equally heirs, and so all are heirs, being all sons, or sons' sons of Adam. Between these two the right of heir cannot stand: for by it either but one only man, or all men are kings. Take which you please, it dissolves the bonds of government and obedience; since, if all men are heirs, they can owe obedience to nobody; if only one, nobody can be obliged to pay obedience to him, till he be known and his title made out.

CHAPTER XI
Who Heir?

§. 106. The great question which in all ages has disturbed mankind, and brought on them the greatest part of those mischiefs which have ruined cities, depopulated countries, and disordered the peace of the world, has been, not whether there be power in the world, nor whence it came, but who should have it. The settling of this point being of no smaller moment than the security of princes, and the peace and welfare of their estates and kingdoms, a reformer of politics, one would think, should lay this sure, and be very clear in it. For if this remain disputable, all the rest will be to very little purpose, and the skill used in dressing up power with all the splendor and temptation absoluteness can add to it, without showing who has a right to have it, will serve only to give a greater edge to man's natural ambition, which of itself is but too keen. What can this do but set men on the more eagerly to scramble, and so lay a sure and lasting foundation of endless contention and disorder, instead of that peace and tranquility, which is the business of government, and the end of human society?

§. 107. This designation of the person our author is more than ordinary obliged to take care of, because he, affirming that the assignment of civil power is by divine institution, has made the conveyance as well as the power itself sacred: so that no consideration, no act or art of man, can divert it from that person, to whom, by this divine right, it is assigned, no necessity or contrivance can substitute another person in his room. For if the assignment of civil power be by divine institution, and Adam's heir be he to whom it is thus assigned, as in the foregoing chapter our author tells us, it would be as much sacrilege for anyone to be king, who was not Adam's heir, as it would have been among the Jews, for anyone to have been priest, who had not been of Aaron's posterity: for not only the priesthood in general being by divine institution, but the assignment of it to the sole line and posterity of Aaron, made it impossible to be enjoyed or exercised by anyone, but those persons who were the offspring of Aaron: whose succession therefore was carefully observed, and by that the persons who had a right to the priesthood certainly known.

§. 108. Let us see then what care our author has taken, to make us know who is this heir, who by *divine institution has a right to be king over all men.* The first account of him we meet with is, p. 12. in these words: *This subjection of children, being the fountain of all regal authority, by the ordination of God himself; it follows, that civil power, not only in general, is by divine institution, but even the assignment of it, specifically to the eldest parents.* Matters of such consequence as this is, should be in plain words, as little liable, as might be, to doubt or equivocation; and I think, if language be capable of expressing anything distinctly and clearly, that of kindred, and the several degrees of nearness of blood, is one. It were therefore to be wished, that our author had used a little more intelligible expressions here, that we might have better known, who it is, to whom the assignment of civil power is made by divine institution, or at least would have told us what he meant by eldest parents. For I believe, if land had been assigned or granted to him, and the eldest parents of his family, he would have thought it had needed an interpreter, and it would scarce have been known to whom it next belonged.

§. 109. In propriety of speech, and certainly propriety of speech is necessary in a discourse of this nature, *eldest parents* signifies either the eldest men and women that have had children, or those who have longest had issue: and then our author's assertion will be, that those fathers and mothers, who have been longest in the world, or longest fruitful, have by divine institution a right to civil power. If there be any absurdity in this, our author must answer for it: and if his meaning be different from my explication, he is to be blamed, that he would not speak it plainly. This I am sure, parents cannot signify heirs male, nor eldest parents an infant child: who yet may sometimes be the true heir, if there can be but one. And we are hereby still as much at a loss, who civil power belongs to, notwithstanding this assignment by divine institution, as if there had been no such assignment at all, or our author had said nothing of it. This of eldest parents leaving us more in the dark, who by divine institution has a right to civil power, than those who never heard anything at all of heir, or descent, of which our author is so full. And though the chief matter of his writing be to teach obedience to those, who have a right to it, which he tells us is conveyed by descent, yet who those are, to whom this right by descent belongs, he leaves, like the philosopher's stone in politics, out of the reach of anyone to discover from his writings.

§. 110. This obscurity cannot be imputed to want of language in so great a master of style as Sir Robert is, when he is resolved with himself what he would say: and therefore, I fear, finding how hard it would be to settle rules of descent by institution, and how little it would be to his purpose, or conduce to the clearing and establishing the titles of princes, if such rules of descent were settled, he chose rather to content himself with doubtful and general terms, which might make no ill sound in men's ears, who were willing to be pleased with them, rather than offer any clear rules of descent of this fatherhood of Adam, by which men's consciences might be satisfied to whom it descended, and know the persons who had a right to regal power, and with it to their obedience.

§. 111. How else is it possible, that laying so much stress, as he does, upon descent, and Adam's heir, next heir, true heir, he should never tell us what heir means, nor the way to know who the next or true heir is? This, I do not remember, he does anywhere expressly handle, but, where it comes in his way, very warily and doubtfully touches: though it be so necessary, that without it all discourses of government and obedience upon his principles would be to no purpose, and fatherly power, never so well made out, will be of no use to anybody. Hence he tells us, *Observations*, 244. *That not only the constitution of power in general, but the limitation of it to one kind, (i.e.) monarchy, and the determination of it to the individual person and line of Adam, are all three ordinances of God, neither Eve nor her children could either limit Adam's power, or join others with him; and what was given unto Adam was given in his person to his posterity.* Here again our author informs us, that the divine ordinance hath limited the descent of Adam's monarchical power. To whom? To Adam's line and posterity, says our author. A notable limitation, a limitation to all mankind. For if our author can find anyone among mankind, that is not of the line and posterity of Adam, he may perhaps tell him, who this next heir of Adam is: but for us, I despair how this limitation of Adam's empire to his line and posterity will help us to find out one heir. This limitation indeed of our author will save those the labor, who would look for him among the race of brutes, if any such there were; but will very little contribute to the discovery of one next heir among men, though it make a short and easy determination of the question about the descent of Adam's regal power, by telling us, that the line and posterity of Adam is to have it, that is, in plain English, anyone may have it, since there is no person living that has not the title of being of the line and posterity of Adam, and while it keeps there, it keeps within our author's limitation by God's ordinance. Indeed, p. 19. he tells us, that such *heirs are not only lords of their own children, but of their brethren,* whereby, and by the words fol-lowing, which we shall consider anon, he seems to insinuate, that the eldest son is heir: but he nowhere, that I know, says it in direct words, but by the instances of Cain and Jacob, that there follow, we may allow this to be so far his opinion concerning heirs, that where there are diverse children, the eldest son has the right to be heir. That primogeniture cannot give any title to paternal power, we have already shown. That a father may have a natural right to some kind of power over his children, is easily granted, but that an elder brother has so over his brethren, remains to be proved. God or nature has not anywhere, that I know, placed such jurisdiction in the first born, nor can reason find any such natural superiority among brethren. The law of Moses gave a double portion of the goods and possessions to the eldest, but we find not anywhere that naturally, or by God's institution, superiority or dominion belonged to him, and the instances there brought by our author are but slender proofs of a right to civil power and dominion in the first born, and do rather show the contrary.

§. 112. His words are in the afore cited place: *And therefore we find God told Cain of his brother Abel: his desire shall be subject unto thee, and thou shall rule over him.* To which I answer,

1. These words of God to Cain, are by many interpreters, with great reason, understood in a quite different sense than what our author uses them in.

2. Whatever was meant by them, it could not be, that Cain, as elder, had a natural dominion over Abel; for the words are conditional: *If thou dost well* and so personal to Cain, and whatever was signified by them, did depend on his carriage, and not follow his birthright, and therefore could by no means be an establishment of dominion in the first born in general. For before this Abel had his distinct territories by right of private dominion, as our author himself confesses, *Observations*, 210, which he could not have had to the prejudice of the heir's title, if by divine institution, Cain as heir were to inherit all his father's dominion.

3. If this were intended by God as the charter of primogeniture, and the grant of dominion to elder brothers in general as such, by right of inheritance, we might expect it should have included all his brethren. For we may well suppose, Adam, from whom the world was to be peopled, had by this time, that these were grown up to be men, more sons than these two: whereas Abel himself is not so much as named; and the words in the original can scarce, with any good construction, be applied to him.

4. It is too much to build a doctrine of so mighty consequence upon so doubtful and obscure a place of scripture, which may be well, nay better, understood in a quite different sense, and so can

be but an ill proof, being as doubtful as the thing to be proved by it, especially when there is nothing else in scripture or reason to be found, that favors or supports it.

§. 113. It follows, p. 19. *Accordingly when Jacob bought his brother's birth-right, Isaac blessed him thus; be lord over thy brethren, and let the sons of thy mother bow before thee.* Another instance, I take it, brought by our author to evince dominion due to birthright, and an admirable one it is. For it must be no ordinary way of reasoning in a man, that is pleading for the natural power of kings, and against all compact, to bring for proof of it, an example, where his own account of it founds all the right upon compact, and settles empire in the younger brother, unless buying and selling be no compact; for he tells us, *when Jacob bought his brother's birth-right.* But passing by that, let us consider the history itself, with what use our author makes of it, and we shall find these following mistakes about it.

1. That our author reports this, as if Isaac had given Jacob this blessing, immediately upon his purchasing the birthright; for he says, *when Jacob bought Isaac blessed him*; which is plainly otherwise in the scripture. For it appears, there was a distance of time between, and if we will take the story in the order it lies, it must be no small distance; all Isaac's sojourning in Gerar, and transactions with Abimelech, Gen. 26. coming between, Rebecca being then beautiful, and consequently young, but Isaac, when he blessed Jacob, was old and decrepit; and Esau also complains of Jacob, Gen. 27. 36. that two times he had supplanted him, *He took away my birth-right*, says he, *and behold now he hath taken away my blessing*; words, that I think signify distance of time and difference of action.

2. Another mistake of our author's is, that he supposes Isaac gave Jacob the blessing, and bid him be lord over his brethren, because he had the birthright: for our author brings this example to prove, that he that has the birthright, has thereby a right to be lord over his brethren. But it is also manifest by the text, that Isaac had no consideration of Jacob's having bought the birthright, for when he blessed him, he considered him not as Jacob, but took him for Esau. Nor did Esau understand any such connection between birthright and the blessing; for he says, *He hath supplanted me*

these two times, he took away my birth-right, and behold now he
hath taken away my blessing: whereas had the blessing, which was
to be lord over his brethren, belonged to the birthright, Esau could
not have complained of this second, as a cheat, Jacob having got
nothing but what Esau had sold him, when he sold him his birthright; so that it is plain, dominion, if these words signify it, was not
understood to belong to the birthright.

§. 114. And that in those days of the patriarchs, dominion was not
understood to be the right of the heir, but only a greater portion
of goods, is plain from Gen. 21. 10. for Sarah, taking Isaac to be
heir, says, *Cast out this bondwoman and her son, for the son of this*
bondwoman shall not be heir with my son: whereby could be meant
nothing, but that he should not have a pretence to an equal share
of his father's estate after his death, but should have his portion
presently, and begone. Accordingly we read, Gen. 25. 5, 6. That
Abraham gave all he had unto Isaac, but unto the sons of the concu-
bines which Abraham had, Abraham gave gifts, and sent them away
from Isaac his son, while he yet lived. That is, Abraham having given
portions to all his other sons, and sent them away, that which he
had reserved, being the greatest part of his substance, Isaac as heir
possessed after his death, but by being heir, he had no right to be
lord over his brethren; for if he had, why should Sarah endeavor to
rob him of one of his subjects, or lessen the number of his slaves,
by desiring to have Ishmael sent away?

§. 115. Thus, as under the law, the privilege of birthright was nothing but a double portion, so we see that before Moses, in the patriarch's time, from whence our author pretends to take his model,
there was no knowledge, no thought, that birthright gave rule or
empire, paternal or kingly authority, to any one over his brethren.
If this be not plain enough in the story of Isaac and Ishmael, he
that will look into 1 Chron. 5. 12. may read these words, *Reuben*
was the first born, but forasmuch as he defiled his father's bed, his
birth-right, was given unto the sons of Joseph, the son of Israel, and
the genealogy is not to be reckoned after the birth-right; for Judah
prevailed above his brethren, and of him came the chief ruler; but the
birth-right was Joseph's. What this birthright was, Jacob blessing
Joseph, Gen. 48. 22. tells us in these words, *Moreover I have given*

thee one portion above thy brethren, which I took out of the hand of
the Amorite, with my sword and with my bow. Whereby it is not
only plain, that the birthright was nothing but a double portion,
but the text in Chronicles is express against our author's doctrine,
and shows that dominion was no part of the birthright. For it tells
us, that Joseph had the birthright, but Judah the dominion. One
would think our author were very fond of the very name of birthright, when he brings this instance of Jacob and Esau, to prove that
dominion belongs to the heir over his brethren.

§. 116. 1. Because it will be but an ill example to prove, that dominion by God's ordination belonged to the eldest son, because Jacob
the youngest here had it, let him come by it how he would. For if
it prove anything, it can only prove, against our author, that the
assignment of dominion to the eldest is not by divine institution,
which would then be unalterable. For if by the law of God, or
nature, absolute power and empire belongs to the eldest son and
his heirs, so that they are supreme monarchs, and all the rest of
their brethren slaves, our author gives us reason to doubt whether
the eldest son has a power to part with it, to the prejudice of his
posterity, since he tells us, *Observations*, 158. that *in grants and*
gifts that have their original from God or nature, no inferior power
of man can limit or make any law of prescription against them.

§. 117. 2. Because this place, Gen. 27. 29. brought by our author,
concerns not at all the dominion of one brother over the other, nor
the subjection of Esau to Jacob. For it is plain in the history, that
Esau was never subject to Jacob, but lived apart in mount Seir,
where he founded a distinct people and government, and was himself prince over them, as much as Jacob was in his own family. This
text, if considered, can never be understood of Esau himself, or the
personal dominion of Jacob over him: for the words brethren and
sons of thy mother, could not be used literally by Isaac, who knew
Jacob had only one brother; and these words are so far from being
true in a literal sense, or establishing any dominion in Jacob over
Esau, that in the story we find the quite contrary, for Gen. 32. Jacob
several times calls Esau lord, and himself his servant, and Gen.
33. *he bowed himself seven times to the ground to Esau.* Whether
Esau then were a subject and vassal (nay, as our author tells us,

all subjects are slaves) to Jacob, and Jacob his sovereign prince by birthright, I leave the reader to judge; and to believe if he can, that these words of Isaac, *Be lord over thy brethren, and let thy mothers sons bow down to thee*, confirmed Jacob in a sovereignty over Esau, upon the account of the birthright he had got from him.

§. 118. He that reads the story of Jacob and Esau, will find there was never any jurisdiction or authority, that either of them had over the other after their father's death: they lived with the friendship and equality of brethren, neither lord, neither slave to his brother, but independent each of other, were both heads of their distinct families, where they received no laws from one another, but lived separately, and were the roots out of which sprang two distinct people under two distinct governments. This blessing then of Isaac, whereon our author would build the dominion of the elder brother, signifies no more, but what Rebecca had been told from God, Gen. 25. 23. *Two nations are in thy womb, and two manner of people shall be separated from thy bowels, and the one people shall be stronger than the other people, and the elder shall serve the younger*; and so Jacob blessed Judah, Gen. 49. and gave him the scepter and dominion, from whence our author might have argued as well, that jurisdiction and dominion belongs to the third son over his brethren, as well as from this blessing of Isaac, that it belonged to Jacob: both these places contain only predictions of what should long after happen to their posterities, and not any declaration of the right of inheritance to dominion in either. And thus we have our author's two great and only arguments to prove, that heirs are lords over their brethren.

1. Because God tells Cain, Gen. 4. that however sin might set upon him, he ought or might be master of it: for the most learned interpreters understand the words of sin, and not of Abel, and give so strong reasons for it, that nothing can convincingly be inferred from so doubtful a text, to our author's purpose.

2. Because in this of Gen. 27. Isaac foretells that the Israelites, the posterity of Jacob, should have dominion over the Edomites, the posterity of Esau; therefore says our author, heirs are lords of their brethren: I leave anyone to judge of the conclusion.

§. 119. And now we see how our author has provided for the descending, and conveyance down of Adam's monarchical power, or paternal dominion to posterity, by the inheritance of his heir, succeeding to all his father's authority, and becoming upon his death as much lord as his father was, not only over his own children, but over his brethren, and all descended from his father, and so *in infinitum*. But yet who this heir is, he does not once tell us; and all the light we have from him in this so fundamental a point, is only, that in his instance of Jacob, by using the word *birthright*, as that which passed from Esau to Jacob, he leaves us to guess, that by heir, he means the eldest son; though I do not remember he anywhere mentions expressly the title of the first born, but all along keeps himself under the shelter of the indefinite term *heir*. But taking it to be his meaning, that the eldest son is heir, (for if the eldest be not, there will be no pretence why the sons should not be all heirs alike) and so by right of primogeniture has dominion over his brethren; this is but one step toward the settlement of succession, and the difficulties remain still as much as ever, till he can show us who is meant by right heir, in all those cases which may happen where the present possessor has no son. This he silently passes over, and perhaps wisely too: for what can be wiser after one has affirmed, that *the person having that power, as well as the power and form of government, is the ordinance of God, and by divine institution, vid. Observations,* 254. p. 12. than to be careful, not to start any question concerning the person, the resolution whereof will certainly lead him into a confession, that God and nature has determined nothing about him? And if our author cannot show who by right of nature, or a clear positive law of God, has the next right to inherit the dominion of this natural monarch he has been at such pains about, when he died without a son, he might have spared his pains in all the rest, it being more necessary for the settling men's consciences, and determining their subjection and allegiance, to show them who by original right, superior and antecedent to the will, or any act of men, has a title to this paternal jurisdiction, than it is to show that by nature there was such a jurisdiction: it being to no purpose for me to know there is such a paternal power, which I ought, and am disposed to obey, unless, where there are many pretenders, I also know the person that is rightly invested and endowed with it.

§. 120. For the main matter in question being concerning the duty of my obedience, and the obligation of conscience I am under to pay it to him that is of right my lord and ruler, I must know the person that this right of paternal power resides in, and so empowers him to claim obedience from me. For let it be true what he says, p. 12. That *civil power not only in general is by divine institution, but even the assignment of it specifically to the eldest parents*; and *Observations*, 254. *That not only the power, or right of government, but the form of the power of governing, and the person having that power, are all the ordinance of God*; yet unless he shows us in all cases, who is this person ordained by God, who is this eldest parent, all his abstract notions of monarchical power will signify just nothing, when they are to be reduced to practice, and men are conscientiously to pay their obedience. For paternal jurisdiction being not the thing to be obeyed, because it cannot command, but is only that which gives one man a right which another has not, and if it come by inheritance, another man cannot have, to command and be obeyed; it is ridiculous to say, I pay obedience to the paternal power, when I obey him, to whom paternal power gives no right to my obedience; for he can have no divine right to my obedience, who cannot show his divine right to the power of ruling over me, as well as that by divine right there is such a power in the world.

§. 121. And hence not being able to make out any princes' title to government, as heir to Adam, which therefore is of no use, and had been better let alone, he is fain to resolve all into present possession, and make civil obedience as due to an usurper, as to a lawful king; and thereby the usurper's title as good. His words are, *Observations*, 253. and they deserve to be remembered: *If an usurper dispossess the true heir, the subject's obedience to the fatherly power must go along, and wait upon God's providence.* But I shall leave his title of usurpers to be examined in its due place, and desire my sober reader to consider what thanks princes owe such politics as this, which can suppose paternal power, (i.e.) a right to government in the hands of a Cade, or a Cromwell,[25] and so all obedience being due to paternal power, the obedience of subjects

25. Jack Cade (1420–1450) was a commoner who led a popular revolt against the government of King Henry VI, in Kent in 1450. Like Tommaso Aniello, Cade became synonymous with mob rule. For Cromwell, see the note at I: 79.

will be due to them, by the same right, and upon as good grounds, as it is to lawful princes; and yet this, as dangerous a doctrine as it is, must necessarily follow from making all political power to be nothing else, but Adam's paternal power by right and divine institution, descending from him, without being able to show to whom it descended, or who is heir to it.

§. 122. To settle government in the world, and to lay obligations to obedience on any man's conscience, it is necessary (supposing with our author that all power be nothing but the being possessed of Adam's fatherhood) to satisfy him, who has a right to this power, this fatherhood, when the possessor dies without sons to succeed immediately to it, as it was to tell him, that upon the death of the father, the eldest son had a right to it: for it is still to be remembered, that the great question is, (and that which our author would be thought to contend for, if he did not sometimes forget it) what persons have a right to be obeyed, and not whether there be a power in the world, which is to be called paternal, without knowing in whom it resides: for so it be a power, i.e. right to govern, it matters not, whether it be termed paternal or regal, natural or acquired; whether you call it supreme fatherhood, or supreme brotherhood, will be all one, provided we know who has it.

§. 123. I go on then to ask, whether in the inheriting of this paternal power, this supreme fatherhood, the grandson by a daughter has a right before a nephew by a brother? Whether the grandson by the eldest son, being an infant, before the younger son, a man and able? Whether the daughter before the uncle? Or any other man, descended by a male line? Whether a grandson by a young daughter, before a granddaughter by an elder daughter? Whether the elder son by a concubine, before a younger son by a wife? From whence also will arise many questions of legitimation, and what in nature is the difference between a wife and a concubine? For as to the municipal or positive laws of men, they can signify nothing here. It may farther be asked, Whether the eldest son, being a fool, shall inherit this paternal power, before the younger, a wise man? And what degree of folly it must be that shall exclude him? And who shall be judge of it? Whether the son of a fool, excluded for his folly, before the son of his wise brother who reigned? Who has the paternal power while the widow queen is with child by the deceased king, and nobody knows whether it will be a son or a daughter? Which shall be heir of two male twins, who by the dissection of the mother were laid open to the world? Whether a sister by the half blood, before a brother's daughter by the whole blood?

§. 124. These, and many more such doubts, might be proposed about the titles of succession, and the right of inheritance; and that not as idle speculations, but such as in history we shall find have concerned the inheritance of crowns and kingdoms; and if ours want them, we need not go farther for famous examples of it, than the other kingdom in this very island, which having been fully related by the ingenious and learned author of *Patriarcha non Monarcha*,[26] I need say no more of. Till our author has resolved all the doubts that may arise about the next heir, and showed that they are plainly determined by the law of nature, or the revealed law of God, all his suppositions of a monarchical, absolute, supreme, paternal power in Adam, and the descent of that power to his heirs, would not be of the least use to establish the authority, or make out the title, of any one prince now on earth, but would rather unsettle and bring all into question: for let our author tell us as long as he please, and let all men believe it too, that Adam had a paternal, and thereby a monarchical power; that this (the only power in the world) descended to his heirs, and that there is no other power in the world but this: let this be all as clear demonstration, as it is manifest error, yet if it be not past doubt, to whom this paternal power descends, and whose now it is, nobody can be under any obligation of obedience, unless anyone will say, that I am bound to pay obedience to paternal power in a man who has no more paternal power than I myself; which is all one as to say, I obey a man, because he has a right to govern, and if I be asked, how I know he has a right to govern, I should answer, it cannot be known, that he has any at all. For that cannot be the reason of my obedience, which I know not to be so; much less can that be a reason of my obedience, which nobody at all can know to be so.

26. This is a reference to the Whig tract *Patriarcha non monarcha* (1681), written against Filmer by Locke's personal friend James Tyrrell (1642–1718).

§. 125. And therefore all this ado about Adam's fatherhood, the greatness of its power, and the necessity of its supposal, helps nothing to establish the power of those that govern, or to determine the obedience of subjects who are to obey, if they cannot tell whom they are to obey, or it cannot be known who are to govern, and who to obey. In the state the world is now, it is irrecoverably ignorant, who is Adam's heir. This fatherhood, this monarchical power of Adam, descending to his heirs, would be of no more use to the government of mankind, than it would be to the quieting of men's consciences, or securing their health, if our author had assured them, that Adam had a power to forgive sins, or cure diseases, which by divine institution descended to his heir, while this heir is impossible to be known. And should not he do as rationally, who upon this assurance of our author went and confessed his sins, and expected a good absolution; or took physic with expectation of health, from anyone who had taken on himself the name of priest or physician, or thrust himself into those employments, saying, I acquiesce in the absolving power descending from Adam, or I shall be cured by the medicinal power descending from Adam; as he who says, I submit to and obey the paternal power descending from Adam, when it is confessed all these powers descend only to his single heir, and that heir is unknown.

§. 126. It is true, the civil lawyers have pretended to determine some of these cases concerning the succession of princes; but by our author's principles, they have meddled in a matter that belongs not to them: for if all political power be derived only from Adam, and be to descend only to his successive heirs, by the ordinance of God and divine institution, this is a right antecedent and paramount to all government; and therefore the positive laws of men cannot determine that which is itself the foundation of all law and government, and is to receive its rule only from the law of God and nature. And that being silent in the case, I am apt to think there is no such right to be conveyed this way: I am sure it would be to no purpose if there were, and men would be more at a loss concerning government, and obedience to governors, than if there were no such right; since by positive laws and compact, which divine institution (if there be any) shuts out, all these endless inextricable doubts can be safely provided against; but it can never be understood, how a divine natural right, and that of such moment as is all order and peace in the world, should be conveyed down to posterity, without any plain natural or divine rule concerning it. And there would be an end of all civil government, if the assignment of civil power were by divine institution to the heir, and yet by that divine institution the person of the heir could not be known. This paternal regal power, being by divine right only his, it leaves no room for human prudence, or consent, to place it anywhere else: for if only one man has a divine right to the obedience of mankind, nobody can claim that obedience, but he that can show that right; nor can men's consciences by any other pretence be obliged to it. And thus this doctrine cuts up all government by the roots.

§. 127. Thus we see how our author, laying it for a sure foundation, that the very person that is to rule, is the ordinance of God, and by divine institution, tells us at large, only that this person is the heir, but who this heir is, he leaves us to guess; and so this divine institution, which assigns it to a person whom we have no rule to know, is just as good as an assignment to nobody at all. But, whatever our author does, divine institution makes no such ridiculous assignments: nor can God be supposed to make it a sacred law, that one certain person should have a right to something, and yet not give rules to mark out, and know that person by, or give an heir a divine right to power, and yet not point out who that heir is. It is rather to be thought, that an heir had no such right by divine institution, than that God should give such a right to the heir, but yet leave it doubtful and undeterminable who such heir is.

§. 128. If God had given the land of Canaan to Abraham, and in general terms to somebody after him, without naming his seed, whereby it might be known who that somebody was, it would have been as good and useful an assignment, to determine the right to the land of Canaan, as it would to the determining the right of crowns, to give empire to Adam and his successive heirs after him, without telling who his heir is: for the word *heir*, without a rule to know who it is, signifies no more than somebody, I know not whom. God making it a divine institution, that men should not marry those who were near of kin, thinks it not enough to say, None of you shall approach to any that is near of kin to him, to uncover their nakedness: but moreover, gives rules to know who are those near of kin, forbidden by divine institution, or else that law would have been of no use, it being to no purpose to lay restraint, or give privileges to men, in such general terms, as the particular person concerned cannot be known by. But God not having anywhere said, The next heir shall inherit all his father's estate or dominion, we are not to wonder, that he has nowhere appointed who that heir should be, for never having intended any such thing, never designed any heir in that sense, we cannot expect he should any where nominate, or appoint any person to it, as we might, had it been otherwise. And therefore in scripture, though the word *heir* occur, yet there is no such thing as heir in our author's sense, one that was by right of nature to inherit all that his father had, exclusive of his brethren. Hence Sarah supposes, that if Ishmael stayed in the house, to share in Abraham's estate after his death, this son of a bond woman might be heir with Isaac: and therefore, says she, *Cast out this bondwoman and her son, for the son of this bondwoman shall not be heir with my son*; but this cannot excuse our author, who telling us there is, in every number of men, one who is right and next heir to Adam, ought to have told us what the laws of descent are. He having been so sparing to instruct us by rules, how to know who is heir, let us see in the next place, what his history out of scripture, on which he pretends wholly to build his government, gives us in this necessary and fundamental point.

§. 129. Our author, to make good the title of his book, p. 13. begins his history of the descent of Adam's regal power, p. 13. in these words: *This lordship which Adam by command had over the whole world, and by right descending from him, the patriarchs did enjoy, was as large*, &c. How does he prove that the patriarchs by descent did enjoy it? For dominion of life and death, says he, we find Judah the father pronounced sentence of death against Thamar his daughter-in-law for playing the harlot, p. 13. How does this prove that Judah had absolute and sovereign authority? He pronounced sentence of death. The pronouncing of sentence of death is not a certain mark of sovereignty, but usually the office of inferior magistrates. The power of making laws of life and death is indeed a mark of sovereignty, but pronouncing the sentence according to those laws may be done by others, and therefore this will but ill prove that he had sovereign authority: as if one should say, Judge Jefferies pronounced sentence of death in the late times, therefore Judge Jefferies[27] had sovereign authority. But it will be said, Judah did it not by commission from another, and therefore did it in his own right. Who knows whether he had any right at all? Heat of passion might carry him to do that which he had no authority to do. Judah had dominion of life and death: how does that appear? He exercised it, he pronounced sentence of death against Thamar, our author thinks it is very good proof, that because he did it, therefore he had a right to do it; he lay with her also: by the same way of proof, he had a right to do that too. If the consequence be good from doing to a right of doing, Absalom too may be reckoned among our author's sovereigns, for he pronounced such a sentence of death against his brother Amnon, and much upon a like occasion, and had it executed too, if that be sufficient to prove a dominion of life and death.

But allowing this all to be clear demonstration of sovereign power, who was it that had this lordship by right descending to him from Adam, as large and ample as the most absolute dominion of any monarch? Judah, says our author, Judah, a younger son of Jacob, his father and elder brethren living; so that if our author's own proof be to be taken, a younger brother may, in the life of his father and elder brothers, by right of descent, enjoy Adam's monarchical power; and if one so qualified may be monarch by descent, why may not every man? If Judah, his father and elder brother living, were one of Adam's heirs, I know not who can be excluded from this inheritance; all men by inheritance may be monarchs as well as Judah.

§. 130. Touching war, we see that Abraham commanded an army of three hundred and eighteen soldiers of his own family, and Esau met his brother Jacob with four hundred men at arms; for matter of peace, Abraham made a league with Abimelech, &c. p. 13. Is it not possible for a man to have three hundred and eighteen men

27. George Jefferies (1645–1689), 1st Baron Jefferies, was a strong enforcer, from the bench, of the royal policy of Charles II and James II. The Whigs despised him as the judge who presided over the trial of Algernon Sidney in 1683 and over the Bloody Assizes in 1685, in which hundreds of Whigs were executed following the failed Monmouth rebellion.

in his family, without being heir to Adam? A planter in the West Indies has more, and might, if he pleased, (who doubts?) muster them up and lead them out against the Indians, to seek reparation upon any injury received from them, and all this without the absolute dominion of a monarch, descending to him from Adam. Would it not be an admirable argument to prove, that all power by God's institution descended from Adam by inheritance, and that the very person and power of this planter were the ordinance of God, because he had power in his family over servants, born in his house, and bought with his money? For this was just Abraham's case: those who were rich in the patriarch's days, as in the West Indies now, bought men and maid servants, and by their increase, as well as purchasing of new, came to have large and numerous families, which though they made use of in war or peace, can it be thought the power they had over them was an inheritance descended from Adam, when it was the purchase of their money? A man's riding in an expedition against an enemy, his horse bought in a fair would be as good a proof that the owner enjoyed the lordship which Adam by command had over the whole world, by right of descending to him, as Abraham's leading out the servants of his family is, that the patriarchs enjoyed this lordship by descent from Adam: since the title to the power, the master had in both cases, whether over slaves or horses, was only from his purchase; and the getting a dominion over anything by bargain and money, is a new way of proving one had it by descent and inheritance.

§. 131. *But making war and peace are marks of sovereignty.* Let it be so in politic societies. May not therefore a man in the West Indies, who has with him sons of his own, friends, or companions, soldiers under pay, or slaves bought with money, or perhaps a band made up all of these, make war and peace, if there should be occasion, and ratify the articles too with an oath, without being a sovereign, an absolute king over those who went with him? He that says he cannot, must then allow many masters of ships, many private planters, to be absolute monarchs, for as much as this they have done. War and peace cannot be made for politic societies, but by the supreme power of such societies; because war and peace, giving a different motion to the force of such a politic body, none can make war or peace, but that which has the direction of the force of the whole body, and that in politic societies is only the supreme power. In voluntary societies for the time, he that has such a power by consent, may make war and peace, and so may a single man for himself, the state of war not consisting in the number of partisans, but the enmity of the parties, where they have no superior to appeal to.

§. 132. The actual making of war or peace, is no proof of any other power, but only of disposing those to exercise or cease acts of enmity for whom he makes it, and this power in many cases anyone may have without any politic supremacy: and therefore the making of war or peace will not prove that everyone that does so is a politic ruler, much less a king; for then commonwealths must be kings too, for they do as certainly make war and peace as monarchical government.

§. 133. But granting this a mark of sovereignty in Abraham, is it a proof of the descent to him of Adam's sovereignty over the whole world? If it be, it will surely be as good a proof of the descent of Adam's lordship to others too. And then commonwealths, as well as Abraham, will be heirs of Adam, for they make war and peace, as well as he. If you say, that the lordship of Adam does not by right descend to commonwealths, though they make war and peace, the same say I of Abraham, and then there is an end of your argument; if you stand to your argument, and say those that do make war and peace, as commonwealths do without doubt, do inherit Adam's lordship, there is an end of your monarchy, unless you will say, that commonwealths by descent enjoying Adam's lordship are monarchies, and that indeed would be a new way of making all the governments in the world monarchical.

§. 134. To give our author the honor of this new invention, for I confess it is not I have first found it out by tracing his principles, and so charged it on him, it is fit my readers know that (as absurd as it may seem) he teaches it himself, p. 23. Where he ingenuously says, *In all kingdoms and commonwealths in the world, whether the prince be the supreme father of the people, or but the true heir to such a father, or come to the Crown by usurpation or election, or whether some few or a multitude govern the commonwealth; yet still the authority that is in any one, or in many, or in all these, is the*

only right, and natural authority of a supreme father; which right
of fatherhood, he often tells us, is *regal and royal authority;* as particularly, p. 12. The page immediately preceding this instance of
Abraham. This regal authority, he says, those that govern commonwealths have: and if it be true, that regal and royal authority
be in those that govern commonwealths, it is as true that commonwealths are governed by kings: for if regal authority be in
him that governs, he that governs must needs be a king, and so all
commonwealths are nothing but downright monarchies, and then
what need any more ado about the matter? The governments of
the world are as they should be, there is nothing but monarchy in
it. This, without doubt, was the surest way our author could have
found, to turn all other governments, but monarchical, out of the
world.

§. 135. But all this scarce proves Abraham to have been a king as
heir to Adam. If by inheritance he had been king, Lot, who was of
the same family, must needs have been his subject, by that title,
before the servants in his family: but we see they lived as friends
and equals, and when their herdsmen could not agree, there was
no pretence of jurisdiction or superiority between them, but they
parted by consent, Gen. 13. Hence he is called both by Abraham,
and by the text, Abraham's brother, the name of friendship and
equality, and not of jurisdiction and authority, though he were
really but his nephew. And if our author knows that Abraham was
Adam's heir, and a king, it was more, it seems, than Abraham himself knew, or his servant whom he sent a wooing for his son; for
when he sets out the advantages of the match, Gen. 24. 35. Thereby
to prevail with the young woman and her friends, he says, *I am
Abraham's servant, and the Lord hath blessed my master greatly, and
he is become great; and he hath given him flocks and herds, and silver and gold, and men-servants and maid-servants, and camels and
asses: and Sarah, my master's wife, bare a son to my master when
she was old, and unto him hath he given all he hath.* Can one think
that a discreet servant that was thus particular to set out his master's
greatness, would have omitted the crown Isaac was to have, if he had
known of any such? Can it be imagined he should have neglected
to have told them on such an occasion as this, that Abraham was
a king, a name well known at that time, for he had nine of them

his neighbors, if he or his master had thought any such thing, the likeliest matter of all the rest, to make his errand successful?

§. 136. But this discovery it seems was reserved for our author to make two or three thousand years after, and let him enjoy the credit of it, only he should have taken care that some of Adam's land should have descended to this his heir, as well as all Adam's lordship, for though this lordship which Abraham, (if we may believe our author) as well as the other patriarchs, *by right descending to him did enjoy, was as large and ample as the absolutest dominion of any monarch which hath been since the creation.* Yet his estate, his territories, his dominions were very narrow and scanty, for he had not the possession of a foot of land, till he bought a field and a cave of the sons of Heth to bury Sarah in.

§. 137. The instance of Esau joined with this of Abraham, to prove that *the lordship which Adam had over the whole world, by right descending from him, the patriarchs did enjoy,* is yet more pleasant than the former. Esau met his brother Jacob with four hundred men at arms; he therefore was a king by right of heir to Adam. Four hundred armed men then, however got together, are enough to prove him that leads them, to be a king and Adam's heir. There have been Tories in Ireland, (whatever there are in other countries) who would have thanked our author for so honorable an opinion of them, especially if there had been nobody near with a better title of five hundred armed men, to question their royal authority of four hundred. It is a shame for men to trifle so, to say no worse of it, in so serious an argument. Here Esau is brought as a proof that Adam's lordship, *Adam's absolute dominion, as large as that of any monarch, descended by right to the patriarchs,* and in this very chap. p. 19. Jacob is brought as an instance of one, that by birthright was lord over his brethren. So we have here two brothers absolute monarchs by the same title, and at the same time heirs to Adam, the eldest, heir to Adam, because he met his brother with four hundred men, and the youngest, heir to Adam by birthright. *Esau enjoyed the lordship which Adam had over the whole world by right descending to him in as large and ample manner, as the absolutest dominion of any monarch, and at the same time, Jacob lord over him, by the right heirs have to be lords over their brethren. Risum teneatis?*[28] I never, I confess, met with any man of parts so dexterous as Sir Robert at this way of arguing: but it was his misfortune to light upon an hypothesis, that could not be accommodated to the nature of things, and human affairs, his principles could not be made to agree with that constitution and order, which God had settled in the world, and therefore must needs often clash with common sense and experience.

§. 138. In the next section, he tells us, *This patriarchal power continued not only till the flood, but after it, as the name patriarch doth in part prove.* The word *patriarch* does more than in part prove, that patriarchal power continued in the world as long as there were patriarchs, for it is necessary that patriarchal power should be while there are patriarchs, as it is necessary there should be paternal or conjugal power while there are fathers or husbands: but this is but playing with names. That which he would fallaciously insinuate is the thing in question to be proved, viz. that the lordship which Adam had over the world, the supposed absolute universal dominion of Adam by right descending from him, the patriarchs did enjoy. If he affirms such an absolute monarchy continued to the flood, in the world, I would be glad to know what records he has it from; for I confess I cannot find a word of it in my Bible: if by patriarchal power he means anything else, it is nothing to the matter in hand. And how the name *patriarch* in some part proves, that those, who are called by that name, had absolute monarchical power, I confess, I do not see, and therefore I think needs no answer till the argument from it be made out a little clearer.

§. 139. *The three sons of Noah had the world,* says our author, *divided among them by their father, for of them was the whole world overspread,* p. 14. The world might be overspread by the offspring of Noah's sons, though he never divided the world among them; for the earth might be replenished without being divided, so that all our author's argument here proves no such division. However, I allow it to him, and then ask, the world being divided among them, which of the three was Adam's heir? If Adam's lordship, Adam's monarchy, by right descended only to the eldest, then the other two could be but his subjects, his slaves; if by right it descended to

28. Latin for "Can you help laughing?"

all three brothers, by the same right, it will descend to all mankind, and then it will be impossible what he says, p. 19. *That heirs are lords of their brethren,* should be true, but all brothers, and consequently all men, will be equal and independent, all heirs to Adam's monarchy, and consequently all monarchs too, one as much as another. But it will be said, Noah their father divided the world among them, so that our author will allow more to Noah, than he will to God Almighty, *Observations,* 211. He thought it hard, that God himself should give the world to Noah and his sons, to the prejudice of Noah's birthright: his words are, *Noah was left sole heir to the world, why should it be thought that God would disinherit him of his birth right, and make him, of all men in the world, the only tenant in common with his children?* And yet here he thinks it fit that Noah should disinherit Shem of his birthright, and divide the world between him and his brethren, so that this birthright, when our author pleases, must, and when he pleases must not, be sacred and inviolable.

§. 140. If Noah did divide the world between his sons, and his assignment of dominions to them were good, there is an end of divine institution; all our author's discourse of Adam's heir, with whatsoever he builds on it, is quite out of doors; the natural power of kings falls to the ground; and then *the form of the power governing, and the person having that power,* will not be (as he says they are, *Observations,* 254.) *the ordinance of God,* but they will be ordinances of man. For if the right of the heir be the ordinance of God, a divine right, no man, father or not father, can alter it: if it be not a divine right, it is only human, depending on the will of man: and so where human institution gives it not, the first-born has no right at all above his brethren; and men may put government into what hands, and under what form, they please.

§. 141. He goes on, *Most of the civilest nations of the earth labour to fetch their original from some of the sons, or nephews of Noah,* p. 14. How many do most of the civilest nations amount to? And who are they? I fear the Chinese, a very great and civil people, as well as several other people of the East, West, North and South, trouble not themselves much about this matter. All that believe the Bible, which I believe are our author's *most of the nations,* must necessarily derive themselves from Noah, but for the rest of the world, they think little of his sons or nephews. But if the heralds and antiquaries of all nations, for it is these men generally that labor to find out the originals of nations, or all the nations themselves, should labor to fetch their original from some of the sons or nephews of Noah, what would this be to prove, that the lordship which Adam had over the whole world, by right descended to the patriarchs? Whoever, nations, or races of men, labor to fetch their original from, may be concluded to be thought by them, men of renown, famous to posterity, for the greatness of their virtues and actions; but beyond these they look not, nor consider who they were heirs to, but look on them as such as raised themselves, by their own virtue, to a degree that would give a luster to those who in future ages could pretend to derive themselves from them. But if it were Ogygis, Hercules, Brama, Tamerlane, Pharamond;[29] nay, if Jupiter and Saturn were the names from whence diverse races of men, both ancient and modern, have labored to derive their original; will that prove, that those men enjoyed the lordship of Adam, by right descending to them? If not, this is but a flourish of our author's to mislead his reader, that in itself signifies nothing.

§. 142. To as much purpose is what he tells us, p. 15. Concerning this division of the world, *That some say it was by lot, and others that Noah sailed round the Mediterranean in ten years and divided the world into Asia, Africa and Europe*, portions for his three sons. America then, it seems, was left to be his that could catch it. Why our author takes such pains to prove the division of the world by Noah to his sons, and will not leave out an imagination, though no better than a dream, that he can find anywhere to favor it, is hard to guess, since such a division, if it prove anything, must necessarily take away the title of Adam's heir; unless three brothers can together be heirs of Adam; and therefore the following words, *Howsoever the manner of this division be uncertain, yet it is most certain the division itself was by families from Noah and his children, over which the parents were heads and princes*, p. 15. If allowed him to be true, and of any force to prove, that all the power in the world is nothing but the lordship of Adam's descending by right, they

---

29. The legendary and semimythical leaders or founders of the Thebans, Dorians, Brahmans of India, Mongols, and French Merovingians, respectively.

will only prove, that the fathers of the children are all heirs to this lordship of Adam: for if in those days Cham and Japhet, and other parents, besides the eldest son, were heads and princes over their families, and had a right to divide the earth by families, what hinders younger brothers, being fathers of families, from having the same right? If Cham and Japhet were princes by right descending to them, notwithstanding any title of heir in their eldest brother, younger brothers by the same right descending to them are princes now; and so all our author's natural power of kings will reach no farther than their own children, and no kingdom, by this natural right, can be bigger than a family. For either this lordship of Adam over the whole world, by right descends only to the eldest son, and then there can be but one heir, as our author says, p. 19. Or else, it by right descends to all the sons equally, and then every father of a family will have it, as well as the three sons of Noah: take which you will, it destroys the present governments and kingdoms, that are now in the world, since whoever has this natural power of a king, by right descending to him, must have it, either as our author tells us Cain had it, and be lord over his brethren, and so be alone king of the whole world; or else, as he tells us here, Shem, Cham and Japhet had it, three brothers, and so be only prince of his own family, and all families independent one of another; all the world must be only one empire by the right of the next heir, or else every family be a distinct government of itself, by the lordship of Adam's descending to parents of families. And to this only tends all the proofs he here gives us of the descent of Adam's lordship: for continuing his story of this descent, he says;

§. 143. *In the dispersion of Babel, we must certainly find the establishment of royal power, throughout the kingdoms of the world,* p. 14. If you must find it, pray do, and you will help us to a new piece of history: but you must show it us before we shall be bound to believe, that regal power was established in the world upon your principles. For, that regal power was established in the kingdoms of the world, I think nobody will dispute, but that there should be kingdoms in the world, whose several kings enjoyed their crowns, by right descending to them from Adam, that we think not only apocrypha, but also utterly impossible. If our author has no better foundation for his monarchy than a supposition of what was done at the dispersion of Babel, the monarchy he erects thereon, whose top is to reach to heaven to unite mankind, will serve only to divide and scatter them as that tower did; and instead of establishing civil government and order in the world, will produce nothing but confusion.

§. 144. For he tells us, the nations they were divided into, *were distinct families, which had fathers for rulers over them; whereby it appears, that even in the confusion, God was careful to preserve the fatherly authority, by distributing the diversity of languages according to the diversity of families*, p. 14. It would have been a hard matter for anyone but our author to have found out so plainly, in the text he here brings, that all the nations in that dispersion were governed by fathers, and that God was careful to preserve the fatherly authority. The words of the text are; *These are the sons of Shem after their families, after their tongues in their lands, after their nations*; and the same thing is said of Cham and Japhet, after an enumeration of their posterities: in all which there is not one word said of their governors, or forms of government; of fathers, or fatherly authority. But our author, who is very quick sighted to spy out fatherhood, where nobody else could see any the least glimpses of it, tells us positively *their rulers were fathers, and God was careful to preserve the fatherly authority*; and why? Because those of the same family spoke the same language, and so of necessity in the division kept together. Just as if one should argue thus; Hannibal in his army, consisting of diverse nations, kept those of the same language together, therefore fathers were captains of each band, and Hannibal was careful of the fatherly authority. Or in peopling of Carolina, the English, French, Scotch and Welch that are there, plant themselves together, and by them the country is divided in their lands after their tongues, after their families, after their nations; therefore care was taken of the fatherly authority. Or because, in many parts of America, every little tribe was a distinct people, with a different language, one should infer, that therefore God *was careful to preserve the fatherly authority*, or that therefore their rulers *enjoyed Adam's lordship by right descending to them*, though we know not who were their governors, nor what their form of government, but only that they were divided into little independent societies, speaking different languages.

§. 145. The scripture says not a word of their rulers or forms of government, but only gives an account, how mankind came to be divided into distinct languages and nations; and therefore it is not to argue from the authority of scripture, to tell us positively, fathers were their rulers, when the scripture says no such thing, but to set up fancies of one's own brain, when we confidently aver matter of fact, where records are utterly silent. Upon a like ground, i.e. none at all, he says, *That they were not confused multitudes without heads and governors, and at liberty to choose what governors or governments they pleased.*

§. 146. For I demand, when mankind were all yet of one language, all congregated in the plain of Shinar, were they then all under one monarch, *who enjoyed the lordship of Adam by right descending to him?* If they were not, there were then no thoughts, it is plain, of Adam's heir, no right to government known then upon that title, no care taken, by God or man, of Adam's fatherly authority. If when mankind were but one people, dwelt altogether, and were of one language, and were upon building a city together; and when it was plain, they could not but know the right heir, for Shem lived till Isaac's time, a long while after the division at Babel; if then, I say, they were not under the monarchical government of Adam's fatherhood, by right descending to the heir, it is plain there was no regard had to the fatherhood, no monarchy acknowledged due to Adam's heir, no empire of Shem's in Asia, and consequently no such division of the world by Noah, as our author has talked of. As far as we can conclude anything from scripture in this matter, it seems from this place, that if they had any government, it was rather a commonwealth than an absolute monarchy: for the scripture tells us, Gen. 11. They said: it was not a prince commanded the building of this city and tower, it was not by the command of one monarch, but by the consultation of many, a free people, *let us build us a city*; they built it for themselves as freemen, not as slaves for their lord and master: *that we be not scattered abroad*; having a city once built, and fixed habitations to settle our abodes and families. This was the consultation and design of a people, that were at liberty to part asunder, but desired to keep in one body, and could not have been either necessary or likely in men tied together under the government of one monarch, who if they had been, as our author tells us, all slaves under the absolute dominion of a monarch, needed not have taken such care to hinder themselves from wandering out of the reach of his dominion. I demand whether this be not plainer in scripture than anything of *Adam's heir or fatherly authority*?

§. 147. But if being, as God says, Gen. 11. 6. One people, they had one ruler, one king by natural right, absolute and supreme over them, *what care had God to preserve the paternal authority of the supreme fatherhood*, if on a sudden he suffers seventy-two (for so many our author talks of) *distinct nations* to be erected out of it, under distinct governors, and at once to withdraw themselves from the obedience of their sovereign? This is to entitle God's care how, and to what we please. Can it be sense to say, that God was careful to preserve the fatherly authority in those who had it not? For if these were subjects under a supreme prince, what authority had they? Was it an instance of God's care to preserve the fatherly authority, when he took away the true supreme fatherhood of the natural monarch? Can it be reason to say, that God, for the preservation of fatherly authority, lets several new governments with their governors start up, who could not all have fatherly authority? And is it not as much reason to say, that God is careful to destroy fatherly authority, when he suffers one, who is in possession of it, to have his government torn in pieces, and shared by several of his subjects? Would it not be an argument just like this, for monarchical government to say, when any monarchy was shattered to pieces, and divided among revolted subjects, that God was careful to preserve monarchical power, by rending a settled empire into a multitude of little governments? If anyone will say, that what happens in providence to be preserved, God is careful to preserve as a thing therefore to be esteemed by men as necessary or useful, it is a peculiar propriety of speech, which everyone will not think fit to imitate: but this I am sure is impossible to be either proper, or true speaking, that Shem, for example, (for he was then alive) should have fatherly authority, or sovereignty by right of fatherhood, over that, one people at Babel, and that the next moment, Shem yet living, seventy-two others should have fatherly authority, or sovereignty by right of fatherhood, over the same people, divided into so many distinct governments; either these seventy-two fathers actually were rulers, just before the confusion, and then they were not one people, but that God himself says they were; or else they were a commonwealth, and then where was monarchy? Or else these seventy-two fathers had fatherly authority, but knew it not. Strange! That fatherly authority should be the only original of government among men, and yet all mankind not know it; and stranger yet, that the confusion of tongues should reveal it to them all of a sudden, that in an instant these seventy-two should know that they had fatherly power, and all others know that they were to obey it in them, and everyone know that particular fatherly authority to which he was a subject. He that can think this arguing from scripture, may from thence make out what model of an Utopia will best suit with his fancy or interest; and this fatherhood, thus disposed of, will justify both a prince who claims an universal monarchy and his subjects, who being fathers of families, shall quit all subjection to him, and canton his empire into less governments for themselves: for it will always remain a doubt in which of these the fatherly authority resided, till our author resolves us, whether Shem, who was then alive, or these seventy-two new princes, beginning so many new empires in his dominions, and over his subjects, had right to govern, since our author tells us, that both one and the other had fatherly, which is supreme, authority, and are brought in by him as instances of those who *did enjoy the lordship of Adam by right descending to them, which was as large and ample as the absolutest dominion of any monarch.* This at least is unavoidable, that if God *was careful to preserve the fatherly authority, in the seventy-two new erected nations,* it necessarily follows, that he was as careful to destroy all pretences of Adam's heir; since he took care, and therefore did preserve the fatherly authority in so many, at least seventy-one, that could not possibly be Adam's heirs, when the right heir (if God had ever ordained any such inheritance) could not but be known, Shem then living, and they being all one people.

§. 148. Nimrod is his next instance of enjoying this patriarchal power, p. 16. But I know not for what reason our author seems a little unkind to him, and says, that he *against right enlarged his empire, by seizing violently on the rights of other lords of families.* These lords of families here were called fathers of families, in his account of the dispersion at Babel: but it matters not how they were called, so we know who they are; for this fatherly authority must be in them, either as heirs to Adam, and so there could not be seventy-two, nor above one at once; or else as natural parents over their children, and so every father will have paternal authority over his children by the same right, and in as large extent as those seventy-two had, and so be independent princes over their own offspring. Taking his *lords of families* in this latter sense, (as it is hard to give those words any other sense in this place) he gives us a very pretty account of the original of monarchy, in these following words, p. 16. *And in this sense he may be said to be the author and founder of monarchy, viz.* As against right seizing violently on the rights of fathers over their children; which paternal authority, if it be in them, by right of nature, (for else how could those seventy-two come by it?) nobody can take from them without their own consents; and then I desire our author and his friends to consider, how far this will concern other princes, and whether it will not, according to his conclusion of that paragraph, resolve all regal power of those, whose dominions extend beyond their families, either into tyranny and usurpation, or election and consent of fathers of families, which will differ very little from consent of the people.

§. 149. All his instances, in the next section, p. 17. Of the twelve dukes of Edom, the nine kings in a little corner of Asia in Abraham's days, the thirty-one kings in Canaan destroyed by Joshua, and the care he takes to prove that these were all sovereign princes, and that every town in those days had a king, are so many direct proofs against him, that it was not *the lordship of Adam by right descending to them,* that made kings: for if they had held their royalties by that title, either there must have been but one sovereign over them all, or else every father of a family had been as good a prince, and had as good a claim to royalty, as these: for if all the sons of Esau had each of them, the younger as well as the eldest, the right of fatherhood, and so were sovereign princes after their father's death, the same right had their sons after them, and so on to all posterity; which will limit all the natural power of fatherhood, only to be over the issue of their own bodies, and their descendants, which power of fatherhood dies with the head of each family, and makes way for the like power of fatherhood to take place in each of his sons over their respective posterities, whereby the power of fatherhood will be preserved indeed, and is intelligible, but will not be at all to our author's purpose. None of the instances he brings are proofs of any power they had, as heirs of Adam's paternal authority by the title of his fatherhood descending to them; no, nor of any power they had by virtue of their own. For Adam's fatherhood being over all mankind, it could descend but to one at once, and from him to his right heir only, and so there could by that title be but one king in the world at a time: and by right of fatherhood, not descending from Adam, it must be only as they themselves were fathers, and so could be over none but their own posterity. So that if those twelve dukes of Edom; if Abraham and the nine kings his neighbors; if Jacob and Esau, and the thirty-one kings in Canaan, the seventy-two kings mutilated by Adonibeseck, the thirty-two kings that came to Benhadad, the seventy kings of Greece making war at Troy, were, as our author contends, all of them sovereign princes; it is evident that kings derived their power from some other original than fatherhood, since some of these had power over more than their own posterity; and it is demonstration, they could not be all heirs to Adam: for I challenge any man to make any pretence to power by right of fatherhood, either intelligible or possible in anyone, otherwise than either as Adam's heir, or as progenitor over his own descendants, naturally sprung from him. And if our author could show that any one of these princes, of which he gives us here so large a catalogue, had his authority by either of these titles, I think I might yield him the cause: though it is manifest they are all impertinent, and directly contrary to what he brings them to prove, viz. *That the lordship which Adam had over the world by right descended to the patriarchs.*

§. 150. Having told us, p. 16. *That the patriarchal government continued in Abraham, Isaac, and Jacob, until the Egyptian bondage,* p. 17. He tells us, *By manifest footsteps we may trace this paternal government unto the Israelites coming into Egypt, where the exercise of supreme patriarchal government was intermitted, because they were in subjection to a stronger prince.* What these footsteps are of paternal government, in our author's sense, i.e. of absolute monarchical power descending from Adam, and exercised by right of fatherhood, we have seen, that is for two-thousand two-hundred ninety years no footsteps at all: since in all that time he cannot produce any one example of any person who claimed or exercised regal authority by right of fatherhood; or show anyone who being a king was Adam's heir. All that his proofs amount to, is only this, that there were fathers, patriarchs and kings, in that age of the world; but that the fathers and patriarchs had any absolute arbitrary power, or by what titles those kings had theirs, and of what extent it was, the scripture is wholly silent; it is manifest by right of fatherhood they neither did, nor could claim any title to dominion and empire.

§. 151. To say, *that the exercise of supreme patriarchal government was intermitted, because they were in subjection to a stronger prince,* proves nothing but what I before suspected, viz. That patriarchal jurisdiction or government is a fallacious expression, and does not in our author signify (what he would yet insinuate by it) paternal and regal power, such an absolute sovereignty as he supposes was in Adam.

§. 152. For how can he say that *patriarchal jurisdiction was intermitted in Egypt,* where there was a king, under whose regal government the Israelites were, if patriarchal were absolute monarchical jurisdiction? And if it were not, but something else, why does he make such ado about a power not in question, and nothing to the purpose? The exercise of patriarchal jurisdiction, if patriarchal be regal, was not intermitted while the Israelites were in Egypt. It is true, the exercise of regal power was not then in the hands of any of the promised seed of Abraham, nor before neither that I know, but what is that to the intermission of *regal authority, as descending from Adam,* unless our author will have it, that this chosen line of Abraham had the right of inheritance to Adam's lordship? And then to what purpose are his instances of the seventy-two rulers, in whom the fatherly authority was preserved in the confusion at Babel? Why does he bring the twelve princes sons of Ishmael, and the dukes of Edom, and join them with Abraham, Isaac and Jacob, as examples of the exercise of true patriarchal government, if the exercise of patriarchal jurisdiction were intermitted in the world, whenever the heirs of Jacob had not supreme power? I fear,

supreme patriarchal jurisdiction was not only intermitted, but
from the time of the Egyptian bondage quite lost in the world,
since it will be hard to find, from that time downwards, anyone
who exercised it as an inheritance descending to him from the
patriarchs Abraham, Isaac and Jacob. I imagined monarchical
government would have served his turn in the hands of Pharaoh,
or anybody. But one cannot easily discover in all places what his
discourse tends to, as particularly in this place it is not obvious
to guess what he drives at, when he says, *the exercise of supreme
patriarchal jurisdiction in Egypt*, or how this serves to make out
the descent of Adam's lordship to the patriarchs, or anybody else.

§. 153. For I thought he had been giving us out of scripture, proofs
and examples of monarchical government, founded on paternal authority, descending from Adam; and not an history of the
Jews: among whom yet we find no kings, till many years after they
were a people: and when kings were their rulers, there is not the
least mention or room for a pretence that they were heirs to Adam,
or kings by paternal authority. I expected, talking so much as he
does of scripture, that he would have produced thence a series of
monarchs, whose titles were clear to Adam's fatherhood, and who,
as heirs to him, owned and exercised paternal jurisdiction over
their subjects, and that this was the true patriarchal government;
whereas he neither proves, that the patriarchs were kings, nor that
either kings or patriarchs were heirs to Adam, or so much is pretended to it: and one may as well prove, that the patriarchs were
all absolute monarchs; that the power both of patriarchs and kings
was only paternal; and that this power descended to them from
Adam; I say all these propositions may be as well proved by a confused account of a multitude of little kings in the West Indies, out
of Ferdinando Soto,[30] or any of our late histories of the Northern
America, or by our author's seventy kings of Greece, out of Homer,
as by anything he brings out of scripture, in that multitude of kings
he has reckoned up.

---

30. Also known as Hernando de Soto (1496–1542), a Spanish explorer who
claimed the Mississippi River for Spain and chronicled his contacts with North
American indigenous peoples.

§. 154. And methinks he should have let Homer[31] and his wars of Troy alone, since his great zeal to truth or monarchy carried him to such a pitch of transport against philosophers and poets, that he tells us in his preface, that there are *too many in these days, who please themselves in running after the opinions of philosophers and poets, to find out such an original of government, as might promise them some title to liberty, to the great scandal of Christianity, and bringing in of atheism.* And yet these heathens, philosopher Aristotle,[32] and poet Homer, are not rejected by our zealous Christian politician, whenever they offer anything that seems to serve his turn, whether to the great scandal of Christianity, and bringing in of atheism, let him look. This I cannot but observe, in authors who (it is visible) write not for truth, how ready zeal for interest and party is to entitle Christianity to their design, and to charge atheism on those who will not without examining submit to their doctrines, and blindly swallow their nonsense.

But to return to his scripture history, our author farther tells us, p. 18. That *after the return of the Israelites out of bondage, God, out of a special care of them, chose Moses and Joshua successively to govern as princes in the place and stead of the supreme fathers.* If it be true, that they returned out of bondage, it must be into a state of freedom, and must imply that both before and after this bondage they were free, unless our author will say, that changing of masters is returning out of bondage; or that a slave returns out of bondage, when he is removed from one galley to another. If then they returned out of bondage, it is plain that in those days, whatever our author in his preface says to the contrary, there were difference between a son, a subject and a slave; and that neither the patriarchs before, nor their rulers after this Egyptian bondage, numbered their sons or subjects among their possessions, and disposed of them with as absolute a dominion, as they did their other goods.

§. 155. This is evident in Jacob, to whom Reuben offered his two sons as pledges, and Judah was at last surety for Benjamin's safe

---

31. Homer was a Greek poet who lived during the eighth century BCE and was the author of the classic story of the Greek and Trojan War recounted in the *Iliad*.

32. Aristotle (384–322 BCE) was one of the most important Greek philosophers of the classical period. As Locke's readers were well aware, Aristotle almost certainly never read Filmer's primary source, the Bible, and died centuries before the advent of Christianity.

return out of Egypt: which all had been vain, superfluous, and but a sort of mockery, if Jacob had had the same power over every one of his family as he had over his ox or his ass, as an owner over his substance; and the offers that Reuben or Judah made had been such a security for returning of Benjamin, as if a man should take two lambs out of his lord's flock, and offer one as security, that he will safely restore the other.

§. 156. When they were out of this bondage, what then? *God out of a special care of them, the Israelites.* It is well that once in his book, he will allow God to have any care of the people, for in other places he speaks of mankind, as if God had no care of any part of them, but only of their monarchs, and that the rest of the people, the societies of men, were made as so many herds of cattle, only for the service, use, and pleasure of their princes.

§. 157. *Chose Moses and Joshua successively to govern as princes*; a shrewd argument our author has found out to prove God's care of the fatherly authority, and Adam's heirs, that here, as an expression of his care of his own people, he chooses those for princes over them, that had not the least pretence to either. The persons chosen were, Moses of the tribe of Levi, and Joshua of the tribe of Ephraim, neither of which had any title of fatherhood. But says our author, they were in the place and stead of the supreme fathers. If God had anywhere as plainly declared his choice of such fathers to be rulers, as he did of Moses and Joshua, we might believe Moses and Joshua were in their place and stead, but that being the question in debate, till that be better proved, Moses being chosen by God to be ruler of his people, will no more prove that government belonged to Adam's heir, or to the fatherhood, than God's choosing Aaron of the tribe of Levi to be priest, will prove that the priesthood belonged to Adam's heir, or the prime fathers, since God would choose Aaron to be priest, and Moses ruler in Israel, though neither of those offices were settled on Adam's heir, or the fatherhood.

§. 158. Our author goes on, *and after them likewise for a time he raised up judges, to defend his people in time of peril*, p. 18. This proves fatherly authority to be the original of government, and that it descended from Adam to his heirs, just as well as what went before: only here our author seems to confess, that these judges, who were all the governors they then had, were only men of valor, whom they made their generals to defend them in time of peril; and cannot God raise up such men, unless fatherhood have a title to government?

§. 159. But says our author, when *God gave the Israelites kings, he re-established the ancient and prime right of lineal succession to paternal government*, p. 18.

§. 160. How did God *re-establish* it? By a law, a positive command? We find no such thing. Our author means then, that when God gave them a king, in giving them a king, he *re-established the right*, &c. To re-establish de facto the right of lineal succession to paternal government, is to put a man in possession of that government which his fathers did enjoy, and he by lineal succession had a right to. For, first, if it were another government than what his ancestors had, it was not succeeding to an ancient right, but beginning a new one. For if a prince should give a man, besides his ancient patrimony, which for some ages his family had been [dispossessed][33] of, an additional estate, never before in the possession of his ancestors, he could not be said to re-establish the right of lineal succession to any more than what had been formerly enjoyed by his ancestors. If therefore the power the kings of Israel had, were anything more than Isaac or Jacob had, it was not the re-establishing in them the right of succession to a power, but giving them a new power, however you please to call it, paternal or not: and whether Isaac and Jacob had the same power that the kings of Israel had, I desire anyone, by what has been above said, to consider; and I do not think they will find, that either Abraham, Isaac, or Jacob, had any regal power at all.

§. 161. Next, there can be no *re-establishment of the prime and ancient right of lineal succession* to anything, unless he, that is put in possession of it, has the right to succeed, and be the true and next heir to him he succeeds to. Can that be a re-establishment which begins in a new family? Or that the *re-establishment of an ancient right of lineal succession*, when a crown is given to one, who

33. This is a replacement for *disseized*, the now rarely used term Locke employed in the original.

has no right of succession to it, and who, if the lineal succession had gone on, had been out of all possibility of pretence to it? Saul, the first king that God gave the Israelites, was of the tribe of Benjamin. Was the ancient and prime right of lineal succession re-established in him? The next was David, the youngest son of Jesse, of the posterity of Judah, Jacob's third son. Was the ancient and prime right of lineal succession to paternal government re-established in him? Or in Solomon, his younger son and successor in the throne? Or in Jeroboam over the ten tribes? Or in Athaliah, a woman who reigned six years an utter stranger to the royal blood? *If the ancient and prime right of lineal succession to paternal government* were *re-established* in any of these or their posterity, *the ancient and prime right of lineal succession to paternal government* belongs to younger brothers as well as elder, and may be re-established in any man living; for whatever younger brothers, by *ancient and prime right of lineal succession*, may have as well as the elder, that every living man may have a right to, by lineal succession, and Sir Robert as well as any other. And so what a brave right of lineal succession, to his paternal or regal government, our author has re-established, for the securing the rights and inheritance of crowns, where everyone may have it, let the world consider.

§. 162. But says our author however, p. 19. *Whensoever God made choice of any special person to be king, he intended that the issue also should have benefit thereof, as being comprehended sufficiently in the person of the father, although the father was only named in the grant.* This yet will not help out succession; for if, as our author says, the benefit of the grant be intended to the issue of the grantee, this will not direct the succession; since, if God give anything to a man and his issue in general, the claim cannot be to any one of that issue in particular; everyone that is of his race will have an equal right. If it be said, our author meant heir, I believe our author was as willing as anybody to have used that word, if it would have served his turn; but Solomon, who succeeded David in the throne, being no more his heir than Jeroboam, who succeeded him in the government of the ten tribes, was his issue; our author had reason to avoid saying, that God intended it to the heirs, when that would not hold in a succession, which our author could not except against; and so he has left his succession as undetermined, as if he had said nothing about it. For if the regal power be given by God to a man and his issue, as the land of Canaan was to Abraham and his seed, must they not all have a title to it, all share in it? And one may as well say, that by God's grant to Abraham and his seed, the land of Canaan was to belong only to one of his seed exclusive of all others, as by God's grant of dominion to a man and his issue, this dominion was to belong in peculiar to one of his issue exclusive of all others.

§. 163. But how will our author prove that whensoever God made choice of any special person to be a king, he intended that *the* (I suppose he means *his) issue also should have benefit thereof*? Has he so soon forgot Moses and Joshua, whom in this very section, he says, *God out of a special care chose to govern as princes*, and the judges that God raised up? Had not these princes, having the authority of the supreme fatherhood, the same power that the kings had, and being specially chosen by God himself, should not their issue have the benefit of that choice, as well as David's or Solomon's? If these had the paternal authority put into their hands immediately by God, why had not their issue the benefit of this grant in a succession to this power? Or if they had it as Adam's heirs, why did not their heirs enjoy it after them by right descending to them? For they could not be heirs to one another. Was the power the same, and from the same original, in Moses, Joshua and the Judges, as it was in David and the Kings; and was it inheritable in one, and not in the other? If it was not paternal authority, then God's own people were governed by those that had not paternal authority, and those governors did well enough without it: if it were paternal authority, and God chose the persons that were to exercise it, our author's rule fails, that whensoever God makes choice of any person to be supreme ruler (for I suppose the name king has no spell in it, it is not the title, but the power makes the difference) *he intends that the issue also should have the benefit of it,* since from their coming out of Egypt to David's time, four hundred years, *the issue was never so sufficiently comprehended in the person of the father,* as that any son, after the death of his father, succeeded to the government among all those judges that judged Israel. If, to avoid this, it be said, God always chose the person of the successor, and so, transferring the fatherly authority to him, excluded his issue from succeeding to it, that is manifestly not so in the story of Jephtha, where he articled with the people, and they made him judge over them, as is plain, Judges 11.

§. 164. It is in vain then to say, that *whensoever God chooses any special person* to have the exercise of *paternal authority* (for if that be not to be king, I desire to know the difference between a king and one having the exercise of paternal authority), *he intends the issue also should have the benefit of it,* since we find the authority, the judges had, ended with them, and descended not to their issue; and if the judges had not paternal authority, I fear it will trouble our author, or any of the friends to his principles, to tell who had then the paternal authority, that is, the government and supreme power among the Israelites; and I suspect they must confess that the chosen people of God continued a people several hundreds of years, without any knowledge or thought of this paternal authority, or any appearance of monarchical government at all.

§. 165. To be satisfied of this, he need but read the story of the Levite, and the war thereupon with the Benjamites, in the three last chapters of Judges: and when he finds, that the Levite appeals to the people for justice; that it was the tribes and the congregation, that debated, resolved, and directed all that was done on that occasion, he must conclude, either that God was not careful to preserve the fatherly authority among his own chosen people; or else that the fatherly authority may be preserved, where there is no monarchical government; if the latter, then it will follow, that though fatherly authority be never so well proved, yet it will not infer a necessity of monarchical government; if the former, it will seem very strange and improbable, that God should ordain fatherly authority to be so sacred among the sons of men, that there could be no power or government without it, and yet that among his own people, even while he is providing a government for them, and therein prescribes rules to the several states and relations of men, this great and fundamental one, this most material and necessary of all the rest, should be concealed, and lie neglected for four hundred years after.

§. 166. Before I leave this, I must ask how our author knows that *whensoever God makes choice of any special person to be king he*

intends that the issue should have the benefit thereof? Does God by
the law of nature or revelation say so? By the same law also he must
say, which of his issue must enjoy the Crown in succession, and
so point out the heir, or else leave his issue to divide or scramble
for the government: both alike absurd, and such as will destroy
the benefit of such grant to the issue. When any such declaration
of God's intention is produced, it will be our duty to believe God
intends it so; but till that be done, our author must show us some
better warrant, before we shall be obliged to receive him as the
authentic revealer of God's intentions.

§. 167. The issue, says our author, *is comprehended sufficiently in
the person of the father, although the father only was named in the
grant*: and yet God, when he gave the land of Canaan to Abraham,
Gen. 13. 15. thought fit to put his seed into the grant too. So the
priesthood was given to Aaron and his seed; and the crown God
gave not only to David, but his seed also: and however our author
assures us that *God intends, that the issue should have the benefit
of it, when he chooses any person to be king*, yet we see that the
kingdom which he gave to Saul, without mentioning his seed after
him, never came to any of his issue; and why, when God chose a
person to be king, he should intend, that his issue should have the
benefit of it, more than when he chose one to be judge in Israel, I
would fain know a reason; or why does a grant of fatherly authority to a king more comprehend the issue, than when a like grant is
made to a judge? Is paternal authority by right to descend to the
issue of one, and not of the other? There will need some reason to
be shown of this difference, more than the name, when the thing
given is the same fatherly authority, and the manner of giving it,
God's choice of the person, the same too; for I suppose our author,
when he says, *God raised up judges*, will by no means allow, they
were chosen by the people.

§. 168. But since our author has so confidently assured us of the
care of God to preserve the fatherhood, and pretends to build all
he says upon the authority of the scripture, we may well expect that
the people, whose law, constitution and history is chiefly contained
in the scripture, should furnish him with the clearest instances of
God's care of preserving the fatherly authority, in that people who

it is agreed he had a most peculiar care of. Let us see then what state this paternal authority or government was in among the Jews, from their beginning to be a people. It was omitted, by our author's confession, from their coming into Egypt, till their return out of that bondage, above two hundred years. From thence till God gave the Israelites a king, about four hundred years more, our author gives but a very slender account of it, nor indeed all that time are there the least footsteps of paternal or regal government among them. But then says our author, *God re-established the ancient and prime right of lineal succession to paternal government.*

§. 169. What a *lineal succession to paternal government* was then established, we have already seen. I only now consider how long this lasted, and that was to their captivity, about five hundred years from thence to their destruction by the Romans, above six hundred and fifty years after, the *ancient and prime right of lineal succession to paternal government* was again lost, and they continued a people in the promised land without it. So that of one thousand, seven hundred and fifty years that they were God's peculiar people, they had hereditary kingly government among them not one third of the time, and of that time there is not the least footstep of one moment of *paternal government, nor the re-establishment of the ancient and prime right of lineal succession* to it, whether we suppose it to be derived, as from its fountain, from David, Saul, Abraham, or, which upon our author's principles, is the only true; from Adam.

THE SECOND TREATISE

CONTENTS OF BOOK II

Book II

An Essay Concerning the True Original, Extent, and End of Civil Government

CHAPTER I
The Introduction

§. 1. It having been shown in the foregoing discourse,

(*1*). That Adam had not, either by natural right of fatherhood, or by positive donation from God, any such authority over his children, or dominion over the world, as is pretended.

(*2*). That if he had, his heirs, yet, had no right to it.

(*3*). That if his heirs had, there being no law of nature nor positive law of God that determines which is the right heir in all cases that may arise, the right of succession, and consequently of bearing rule, could not have been certainly determined.

(*4*). That if even that had been determined, yet the knowledge of which is the eldest line of Adam's posterity, being so long since utterly lost, that in the races of mankind and families of the world, there remains not to one above another, the least pretence to be the eldest house, and to have the right of inheritance.

All these premises having, as I think, been clearly made out, it is impossible that the rulers now on earth should make any benefit, or derive any the least shadow of authority from that, which is held to be the fountain of all power, Adam's private dominion and paternal jurisdiction; so that he that will not give just occasion to think that all government in the world is the product only of force and violence, and that men live together by no other rules but that of beasts, where the strongest carries it, and so lay a foundation for perpetual disorder and mischief, tumult, sedition and rebellion, (things that the followers of that hypothesis so loudly cry out against) must of necessity find out another rise of government, another original of political power, and another way of designing and knowing the persons that have it, than what Sir Robert Filmer has taught us.

§. 2. To this purpose, I think it may not be amiss, to set down what I take to be political power; that the power of a magistrate over a subject may be distinguished from that of a father over his children, a master over his servant, a husband over his wife, and a lord over his slave. All which distinct powers happening sometimes together in the same man, if he be considered under these different relations, it may help us to distinguish these powers one from another, and show the difference between a ruler of a commonwealth, a father of a family, and a captain of a galley.

§. 3. Political power, then, I take to be a right of making laws with penalties of death, and consequently all less penalties, for the regulating and preserving of property, and of employing the force of the community, in the execution of such laws, and in the defense of the commonwealth from foreign injury; and all this only for the public good.

CHAPTER II
Of the State of Nature

§. 4. To understand political power right, and derive it from its original, we must consider, what state all men are naturally in, and that is, a state of perfect freedom to order their actions, and dispose of their possessions and persons, as they think fit, within the bounds of the law of nature, without asking leave, or depending upon the will of any other man.

A state also of equality, wherein all the power and jurisdiction is reciprocal, no one having more than another; there being nothing more evident, than that creatures of the same species and rank, promiscuously born to all the same advantages of nature, and the use of the same faculties, should also be equal one amongst another without subordination or subjection, unless the lord and master of them all should, by any manifest declaration of his will, set one above another, and confer on him, by an evident and clear appointment, an undoubted right to dominion and sovereignty.

§. 5. This equality of men by nature, the judicious Hooker[1] looks upon as so evident in itself, and beyond all question, that he makes it the foundation of that obligation to mutual love amongst men, on which he builds the duties they owe one another, and from whence he derives the great maxims of justice and charity. His words are,

The like natural inducement hath brought men to know that it is no less their duty, to love others than themselves; for seeing those things which are equal, must needs all have one measure; if I cannot but wish to receive good, even as much at every man's hands, as any man can wish unto his own soul, how should I look to have any part of my desire herein satisfied, unless myself be careful to satisfy the like desire, which is undoubtedly in other men, being of one and the same nature? To have anything offered them repugnant to this desire, must needs in all respects grieve them as much as me; so that if I do harm, I must look to suffer, there being no reason that others should show greater measure of love to me, than they have by me shewed unto them: my desire therefore to be loved of my equals in nature as much as possible may be, imposeth upon me a natural duty of bearing to themward fully the like affection; from which relation of equality between ourselves and them that are as ourselves, what several rules and canons natural reason has drawn, for direction of life, no man is ignorant, Hooker's *Eccl. Pol. lib.* 1.

§. 6. But though this be a state of liberty, yet it is not a state of license: though man in that state have an uncontrollable liberty to dispose of his person or possessions, yet he has not liberty to destroy himself, or so much as any creature in his possession, but where some nobler use than its bare preservation calls for it. The state of nature has a law of nature to govern it, which obliges everyone: and reason, which is that law, teaches all mankind, who will but consult it, that being all equal and independent, no one ought to harm another in his life, health, liberty, or possessions: for men being all the workmanship of one omnipotent, and infinitely wise

---

1. Richard Hooker (1554–1600) was the preeminent English scholastic of the sixteenth century. His *Laws of Ecclesiastical Polity* (*Eccl. Pol. lib.*) (1597) was widely viewed as the authoritative political commentary in the established church tradition throughout the seventeenth century. Locke referred to Hooker frequently in the *Second Treatise* as a putative ally against Filmer, e.g., II: 5, 15, 60, 61, 74, 90, 91, 94, 111, 134, 135, 136, and 239.

maker; all the servants of one sovereign master, sent into the world by his order, and about his business; they are his property, whose workmanship they are, made to last during his, not one another's pleasure: and being furnished with like faculties, sharing all in one community of nature, there cannot be supposed any such subordination amongst us, that may authorize us to destroy one another, as if we were made for one another's uses, as the inferior ranks of creatures are for ours. Everyone, as he is bound to preserve himself, and not to quit his station wilfully, so by the like reason, when his own preservation comes not in competition, ought he, as much as he can, to preserve the rest of mankind, and may not, unless it be to do justice on an offender, take away, or impair the life, or what tends to the preservation of the life, the liberty, health, limb, or goods of another.

§. 7. And that all men may be restrained from invading others' rights, and from doing hurt to one another, and the law of nature be observed, which wills the peace and preservation of all mankind, the execution of the law of nature is, in that state, put into every man's hands, whereby everyone has a right to punish the transgressors of that law to such a degree, as may hinder its violation: for the law of nature would, as all other laws that concern men in this world be in vain, if there were nobody that in the state of nature had a power to execute that law, and thereby preserve the innocent and restrain offenders. And if anyone in the state of nature may punish another for any evil he has done, everyone may do so: for in that state of perfect equality, where naturally there is no superiority or jurisdiction of one over another, what any may do in prosecution of that law, everyone must needs have a right to do.

§. 8. And thus, in the state of nature, one man comes by a power over another; but yet no absolute or arbitrary power, to use a criminal, when he has got him in his hands, according to the passionate heats, or boundless extravagancy of his own will; but only to retribute to him, so far as calm reason and conscience dictates, what is proportionate to his transgression, which is so much as may serve for reparation and restraint: for these two are the only reasons, why one man may lawfully do harm to another, which is that we call punishment. In transgressing the law of nature, the offender declares himself to live by another rule than that of reason and common equity, which is that measure God has set to the actions of men, for their mutual security; and so he becomes dangerous to mankind, the tie, which is to secure them from injury and violence, being slighted and broken by him. Which being a trespass against the whole species, and the peace and safety of it, provided for by the law of nature, every man upon this score, by the right he has to preserve mankind in general, may restrain, or where it is necessary, destroy things noxious to them, and so may bring such evil on anyone, who has transgressed that law, as may make him repent the doing of it, and thereby deter him, and by his example others, from doing the like mischief. And in the case, and upon this ground, every man has a right to punish the offender, and be executioner of the law of nature.

§. 9. I doubt not but this will seem a very strange doctrine to some men: but before they condemn it, I desire them to resolve me, by what right any prince or state can put to death, or punish an alien, for any crime he commits in their country. It is certain their laws, by virtue of any sanction they receive from the promulgated will of the legislative, reach not a stranger: they speak not to him, nor, if they did, is he bound to hearken to them. The legislative authority, by which they are in force over the subjects of that commonwealth, has no power over him. Those who have the supreme power of making laws in England, France or Holland, are to an Indian, but like the rest of the world, men without authority: and therefore, if by the law of nature every man has not a power to punish offences against it, as he soberly judges the case to require, I see not how the magistrates of any community can punish an alien of another country; since, in reference to him, they can have no more power than what every man naturally may have over another.

§. 10. Besides the crime which consists in violating the law, and varying from the right rule of reason, whereby a man so far becomes degenerate, and declares himself to quit the principles of human nature, and to be a noxious creature, there is commonly injury done to some person or other, and some other man receives damage by his transgression: in which case he who has received any damage, has, besides the right of punishment common to him with other men, a particular right to seek reparation from him that has done it: and any other person, who finds it just, may also join with him that is injured, and assist him in recovering from the offender so much as may make satisfaction for the harm he has suffered.

§. 11. From these two distinct rights, the one of punishing the crime for restraint, and preventing the like offence, which right of punishing is in everybody; the other of taking reparation, which belongs only to the injured party, comes it to pass that the magistrate, who by being magistrate has the common right of punishing put into his hands, can often, where the public good demands not the execution of the law, remit the punishment of criminal offences by his own authority, but yet cannot remit the satisfaction due to any private man for the damage he has received. That, he who has suffered the damage has a right to demand in his own name, and he alone can remit: the damnified person has this power of appropriating to himself the goods or service of the offender, by right of self-preservation, as every man has a power to punish the crime, to prevent its being committed again, by the right he has of preserving all mankind, and doing all reasonable things he can in order to that end: and thus it is, that every man, in the state of nature, has a power to kill a murderer, both to deter others from doing the like injury, which no reparation can compensate, by the example of the punishment that attends it from everybody, and also to secure men from the attempts of a criminal, who having renounced reason, the common rule and measure God has given to mankind, has, by the unjust violence and slaughter he has committed upon one, declared war against all mankind, and therefore may be destroyed as a lion or a tiger, one of those wild savage beasts, with whom men can have no society nor security: and upon this is grounded that great law of nature, *Whoso sheddeth man's blood, by man shall his blood be shed.* And Cain was so fully convinced, that everyone had a right to destroy such a criminal, that after the murder of his brother, he cries out, *Everyone that findeth me, shall slay me*; so plain was it writ in the hearts of all mankind.

§. 12. By the same reason, may a man in the state of nature punish the lesser breaches of that law. It will perhaps be demanded, with death? I answer, each transgression may be punished to that degree, and with so much severity, as will suffice to make it an ill bargain to the offender, give him cause to repent, and terrify others from doing the like. Every offence, that can be committed in the state of nature, may in the state of nature be also punished equally, and as far forth as it may, in a commonwealth: for though it would be besides my present purpose, to enter here into the particulars of the law of nature, or its measures of punishment; yet, it is certain there is such a law, and that too, as intelligible and plain to a rational creature, and a studier of that law, as the positive laws of commonwealths; nay, possibly plainer; as much as reason is easier to be understood, than the fancies and intricate contrivances of men, following contrary and hidden interests put into words; for so truly are a great part of the municipal laws of countries, which are only so far right, as they are founded on the law of nature, by which they are to be regulated and interpreted.

§. 13. To this strange doctrine, viz. That in the state of nature everyone has the executive power of the law of nature, I doubt not but it will be objected, that it is unreasonable for men to be judges in their own cases, that self-love will make men partial to themselves and their friends: and on the other side, that ill nature, passion and revenge will carry them too far in punishing others; and hence nothing but confusion and disorder will follow, and that therefore God has certainly appointed government to restrain the partiality and violence of men. I easily grant, that civil government is the proper remedy for the inconveniences of the state of nature, which must certainly be great, where men may be judges in their own case, since it is easy to be imagined, that he who was so unjust as to do his brother an injury, will scarce be so just as to condemn himself for it: but I shall desire those who make this objection, to remember, that absolute monarchs are but men; and if government is to be the remedy of those evils, which necessarily follow from men's being judges in their own cases, and the state of nature is therefore not to be endured, I desire to know what kind of government that is, and how much better it is than the state of nature, where one man, commanding a multitude, has the liberty to be judge in his own case, and may do to all his subjects whatever he pleases, without the least liberty to anyone to question or control those who execute his pleasure? And in whatsoever he does, whether led by reason, mistake or passion, must be submitted to? Much better it is in the state of nature, wherein men are not bound to submit to the unjust will of another: and if he that judges, judges amiss in his own, or any other case, he is answerable for it to the rest of mankind.

§. 14. It is often asked as a mighty objection, where are, or ever were there any men in such a state of nature? To which it may suffice as an answer at present, that since all princes and rulers of independent governments all through the world, are in a state of nature, it is plain the world never was, nor ever will be, without numbers of men in that state. I have named all governors of independent communities, whether they are, or are not, in league with others: for it is not every compact that puts an end to the state of nature between men, but only this one of agreeing together mutually to enter into one community, and make one body politic; other promises, and compacts, men may make one with another, and yet still be in the state of nature. The promises and bargains for truck, &c. between the two men in the desert island, mentioned by Garcilasso de la Vega[2] in his history of Peru; or between a Swiss and an Indian, in the woods of America, are binding to them, though they are perfectly in a state of nature, in reference to one another: for truth and keeping of faith belongs to men, as men, and not as members of society.

§. 15. To those that say, there were never any men in the state of nature, I will not only oppose the authority of the judicious Hooker, *Eccl. Pol. lib.* 1. sect. 10. where he says, *The laws which have been hitherto mentioned, i.e. the laws of nature, do bind men absolutely, even as they are men, although they have never any settled fellowship, never any solemn agreement amongst themselves what to do, or not to do: but forasmuch as we are not by ourselves sufficient to furnish ourselves with competent store of things, needful for such a life as our nature doth desire, a life fit for the dignity of man; therefore to supply those defects and imperfections which are in us, as living*

---

2. See note at Section 57 of the *First Treatise*.

single and solely by ourselves, we are naturally induced to seek communion and fellowship with others: this was the cause of men's uniting themselves at first in politic societies. But I moreover affirm, that all men are naturally in that state, and remain so, till by their own consents they make themselves members of some politic society; and I doubt not in the sequel of this discourse, to make it very clear.

CHAPTER III
Of the State of War

§. 16. The state of war is a state of enmity and destruction: and therefore declaring by word or action, not a passionate and hasty, but a sedate settled design upon another man's life, puts him in a state of war with him against whom he has declared such an intention, and so has exposed his life to the other's power to be taken away by him, or anyone that joins with him in his defense, and espouses his quarrel; it being reasonable and just, I should have a right to destroy that which threatens me with destruction: for, by the fundamental law of nature, man being to be preserved as much as possible, when all cannot be preserved, the safety of the innocent is to be preferred: and one may destroy a man who makes war upon him, or has discovered an enmity to his being, for the same reason that he may kill a wolf or a lion; because such men are not under the ties of the common law of reason, have no other rule, but that of force and violence, and so may be treated as beasts of prey, those dangerous and noxious creatures, that will be sure to destroy him whenever he falls into their power.

§. 17. And hence it is, that he who attempts to get another man into his absolute power, does thereby put himself into a state of war with him; it being to be understood as a declaration of a design upon his life: for I have reason to conclude, that he who would get me into his power without my consent, would use me as he pleased when he had got me there, and destroy me too when he had a fancy to it; for nobody can desire to have me in his absolute power, unless it be to compel me by force to that which is against the right of my freedom, i.e. make me a slave. To be free from such force is the only security of my preservation; and reason bids me look on him, as an enemy to my preservation, who would take away that freedom which is the fence to it; so that he who makes an attempt to enslave me, thereby puts himself into a state of war with me. He that, in the state of nature, would take away the freedom that belongs to anyone in that state, must necessarily be supposed to have a design to take away everything else, that freedom being the foundation of all the rest; as he that, in the state of society, would take away the freedom belonging to those of that society or commonwealth, must be supposed to design to take away from them everything else, and so be looked on as in a state of war.

§. 18. This makes it lawful for a man to kill a thief who has not in the least hurt him nor declared any design upon his life any farther than by the use of force, so to get him in his power, as to take away his money or what he pleases, from him; because using force, where he has no right, to get me into his power, let his pretence be what it will, I have no reason to suppose that he, who would take away my liberty would not, when he had me in his power, take away everything else. And therefore it is lawful for me to treat him as one who has put himself into a state of war with me, i.e. kill him if I can; for to that hazard does he justly expose himself, whoever introduces a state of war and is aggressor in it.

§. 19. And here we have the plain difference between the state of nature and the state of war, which however some men have confounded, are as far distant, as a state of peace, good will, mutual assistance and preservation, and a state of enmity, malice, violence and mutual destruction, are one from another. Men living together according to reason, without a common superior on earth, with authority to judge between them, is properly the state of nature. But force, or a declared design of force, upon the person of another, where there is no common superior on earth to appeal to for relief, is the state of war: and it is the want of such an appeal gives a man the right of war even against an aggressor, though he be in society and a fellow subject. Thus a thief, whom I cannot harm, but by appeal to the law, for having stolen all that I am worth, I may kill, when he sets on me to rob me but of my horse or coat; because the law, which was made for my preservation, where it cannot interpose to secure my life from present force, which, if lost, is capable of no reparation, permits me my own defense, and the right of war, a liberty to kill the aggressor, because the aggressor allows not time to appeal to our common judge, nor the decision of the law, for remedy in a case where the mischief may be irreparable. Want of a common judge with authority, puts all men in a state of nature: force without right, upon a man's person, makes a state of war, both where there is, and is not, a common judge.

§. 20. But when the actual force is over, the state of war ceases between those that are in society, and are equally on both sides subjected to the fair determination of the law; because then there lies open the remedy of appeal for the past injury, and to prevent future harm: but where no such appeal is, as in the state of nature, for want of positive laws, and judges with authority to appeal to, the state of war once begun, continues, with a right to the innocent party to destroy the other whenever he can, until the aggressor offers peace, and desires reconciliation on such terms as may repair any wrongs he has already done, and secure the innocent for the future; nay, where an appeal to the law, and constituted judges, lies open, but the remedy is denied by a manifest perverting of justice, and a barefaced wresting of the laws to protect or indemnify the violence or injuries of some men, or party of men, there it is hard to imagine anything but a state of war: for wherever violence is used, and injury done, though by hands appointed to administer justice, it is still violence and injury, however colored with the name, pretences, or forms of law, the end whereof being to protect and redress the innocent, by an unbiased application of it, to all who are under it; wherever that is not bona fide done, war is made upon the sufferers, who having no appeal on earth to right them, they are left to the only remedy in such cases, an appeal to heaven.

§. 21. To avoid this state of war (wherein there is no appeal but to heaven, and wherein every the least difference is apt to end, where there is no authority to decide between the contenders) is one great reason of men's putting themselves into society, and quitting the state of nature: for where there is an authority, a power on earth, from which relief can be had by appeal, there the continuance of the state of war is excluded, and the controversy is decided

by that power. Had there been any such court, any superior jurisdiction on earth, to determine the right between Jephtha and the
Ammonites,[3] they had never come to a state of war: but we see
he was forced to appeal to heaven. *The Lord the Judge* (says he)
*be judge this day between the children of Israel and the children of
Ammon*, Judg. 11. 27. and then prosecuting, and relying on his
appeal, he leads out his army to battle: and therefore in such controversies, where the question is put, who shall be judge? It cannot
be meant, who shall decide the controversy; everyone knows what
Jephtha here tells us, that *the Lord the Judge* shall judge. Where
there is no judge on earth, the appeal lies to God in heaven. That
question then cannot mean, who shall judge, whether another
has put himself in a state of war with me, and whether I may, as
Jephtha did, appeal to heaven in it? Of that I myself can only be
judge in my own conscience, as I will answer it, at the great day, to
the supreme judge of all men.

CHAPTER IV
Of Slavery

§. 22. The natural liberty of man is to be free from any superior
power on earth, and not to be under the will or legislative authority of man, but to have only the law of nature for his rule. The
liberty of man, in society, is to be under no other legislative power,
but that established, by consent, in the commonwealth; nor under
the dominion of any will, or restraint of any law, but what that
legislative shall enact, according to the trust put in it. Freedom
then is not what Sir Robert Filmer tells us, *Observations*, A. 55.
*A liberty for everyone to do what he lists, to live as he pleases, and
not to be tied by any laws*: but freedom of men under government
is, to have a standing rule to live by, common to everyone of that
society, and made by the legislative power erected in it; a liberty to
follow my own will in all things, where the rule prescribes not; and
not to be subject to the inconstant, uncertain, unknown, arbitrary

---

3. Notice Locke's reluctance to mention crucial aspects of the Bible's story of
Jephtha (especially the sacrifice of his daughter), in chapter 11 of the book of
Judges.

will of another man: as freedom of nature is, to be under no other restraint but the law of nature.

§. 23. This freedom from absolute, arbitrary power, is so necessary to, and closely joined with a man's preservation, that he cannot part with it, but by what forfeits his preservation and life together: for a man, not having the power of his own life, cannot, by compact, or his own consent, enslave himself to anyone, nor put himself under the absolute, arbitrary power of another, to take away his life, when he pleases. Nobody can give more power than he has himself; and he that cannot take away his own life, cannot give another power over it. Indeed, having by his fault forfeited his own life, by some act that deserves death; he, to whom he has forfeited it, may (when he has him in his power) delay to take it, and make use of him to his own service, and he does him no injury by it: for, whenever he finds the hardship of his slavery outweigh the value of his life, it is in his power, by resisting the will of his master, to draw on himself the death he desires.

§. 24. This is the perfect condition of slavery, which is nothing else, but the state of war continued, between a lawful conqueror and a captive: for, if once compact enter between them, and make an agreement for a limited power on the one side, and obedience on the other, the state of war and slavery ceases, as long as the compact endures: for, as has been said, no man can, by agreement, pass over to another that which he has not in himself, a power over his own life.

I confess, we find amongst the Jews, as well as other nations, that men did sell themselves; but, it is plain, this was only to drudgery, not to slavery: for, it is evident, the person sold was not under an absolute, arbitrary, despotical power: for the master could not have power to kill him, at any time, whom, at a certain time, he was obliged to let go free out of his service; and the master of such a servant was so far from having an arbitrary power over his life, that he could not, at pleasure, so much as maim him, but the loss of an eye, or tooth, set him free, Exod. 21.

CHAPTER V
Of Property

§. 25. Whether we consider natural reason, which tells us, that men, being once born, have a right to their preservation, and consequently to meat and drink, and such other things as nature affords for their subsistence: or revelation, which gives us an account of those grants God made of the world to Adam, and to Noah, and his sons, it is very clear, that God, as king David says, Psal. 115. 16. *has given the earth to the children of men*; given it to mankind in common. But this being supposed, it seems to some a very great difficulty, how anyone should ever come to have a property in anything: I will not content myself to answer, that if it be difficult to make out property, upon a supposition that God gave the world to Adam, and his posterity in common, it is impossible that any man, but one universal monarch, should have any property upon a supposition, that God gave the world to Adam, and his heirs in succession, exclusive of all the rest of his posterity. But I shall endeavor to show, how men might come to have a property in several parts of that which God gave to mankind in common, and that without any express compact of all the commoners.

§. 26. God, who has given the world to men in common, has also given them reason to make use of it to the best advantage of life, and convenience. The earth, and all that is therein, is given to men for the support and comfort of their being. And though all the fruits it naturally produces, and beasts it feeds, belong to mankind in common, as they are produced by the spontaneous hand of nature; and nobody has originally a private dominion, exclusive of the rest of mankind, in any of them, as they are thus in their natural state: yet being given for the use of men, there must of necessity be a means to appropriate them some way or other, before they can be of any use, or at all beneficial to any particular man. The fruit, or venison, which nourishes the wild Indian, who knows no enclosure, and is still a tenant in common, must be his, and so his, i.e. a part of him, that another can no longer have any right to it, before it can do him any good for the support of his life.

§. 27. Though the earth, and all inferior creatures, be common to all men, yet every man has a property in his own person: this nobody has any right to but himself. The labor of his body, and the work of his hands, we may say are properly his. Whatsoever then he removes out of the state that nature has provided, and left it in, he has mixed his labor with, and joined to it something that is his own, and thereby makes it his property. It being by him removed from the common state nature has placed it in, it has by this labor something annexed to it, that excludes the common right of other men: for this labor being the unquestionable property of the laborer, no man but he can have a right to what that is once joined to, at least where there is enough, and as good, left in common for others.

§. 28. He that is nourished by the acorns he picked up under an oak, or the apples he gathered from the trees in the wood, has certainly appropriated them to himself. Nobody can deny but the nourishment is his. I ask then, when did they begin to be his? When he digested? Or when he ate? Or when he boiled? Or when he brought them home? Or when he picked them up? And it is plain, if the first gathering made them not his, nothing else could. That labor put a distinction between them and common: that added something to them more than nature, the common mother of all, had done; and so they became his private right. And will anyone say, he had no right to those acorns or apples, he thus appropriated, because he had not the consent of all mankind to make them his? Was it a robbery thus to assume to himself what belonged to all in common? If such a consent as that was necessary, man had starved, notwithstanding the plenty God had given him. We see in commons, which remain so by compact, that it is the taking any part of what is common, and removing it out of the state nature leaves it in, which begins the property; without which the common is of no use. And the taking of this or that part, does not depend on the express consent of all the commoners. Thus the grass my horse has bit; the turfs my servant has cut; and the ore I have dug in any place, where I have a right to them in common with others, become my property, without the assignation or consent of anybody. The labor that was mine, removing them out of that common state they were in, has fixed my property in them.

§. 29. By making an explicit consent of every commoner, necessary to anyone's appropriating to himself any part of what is given
in common, children or servants could not cut the meat, which
their father or master had provided for them in common, without
assigning to everyone his peculiar part. Though the water running
in the fountain be everyone's, yet who can doubt, but that in the
pitcher is his only who drew it out? His labor has taken it out of the
hands of nature, where it was common, and belonged equally to all
her children, and has thereby appropriated it to himself.

§. 30. Thus this law of reason makes the deer that Indian's who has
killed it; it is allowed to be his goods, who has bestowed his labor
upon it, though before it was the common right of everyone. And
amongst those who are counted the civilized part of mankind,
who have made and multiplied positive laws to determine property, this original law of nature, for the beginning of property, in
what was before common, still takes place; and by virtue thereof,
what fish anyone catches in the ocean, that great and still remaining common of mankind; or what ambergris anyone takes up here,
is by the labor that removes it out of that common state nature left
it in, made his property, who takes that pains about it. And even
amongst us, the hare that anyone is hunting, is thought his who
pursues her during the chase: for being a beast that is still looked
upon as common, and no man's private possession; whoever has
employed so much labor about any of that kind, as to find and pur-
sue her, has thereby removed her from the state of nature, wherein
she was common, and has begun a property.

§. 31. It will perhaps be objected to this, that if gathering the acorns,
or other fruits of the earth, &c. makes a right to them, then anyone
may engross as much as he will. To which I answer, Not so. The
same law of nature, that does by this means give us property, does
also bound that property too. *God has given us all things richly*,
1 Tim. 6. 17. is the voice of reason confirmed by inspiration. But
how far has he given it us? To enjoy.

As much as anyone can make use of to any advantage of life
before it spoils, so much he may by his labor fix a property in:
whatever is beyond this, is more than his share, and belongs to
others. Nothing was made by God for man to spoil or destroy. And

thus, considering the plenty of natural provisions there was a long time in the world, and the few spenders; and to how small a part of that provision the industry of one man could extend itself, and engross it to the prejudice of others; especially keeping within the bounds, set by reason, of what might serve for his use; there could be then little room for quarrels or contentions about property so established.

§. 32. But the chief matter of property being now not the fruits of the earth, and the beasts that subsist on it, but the earth itself; as that which takes in and carries with it all the rest; I think it is plain, that property in that too is acquired as the former. As much land as a man tills, plants, improves, cultivates, and can use the product of, so much is his property. He by his labor does, as it were, enclose it from the common. Nor will it invalidate his right, to say everybody else has an equal title to it; and therefore he cannot appropriate, he cannot enclose, without the consent of all his fellow commoners, all mankind. God, when he gave the world in common to all mankind, commanded man also to labor, and the penury of his condition required it of him. God and his reason commanded him to subdue the earth, i.e. improve it for the benefit of life, and therein lay out something upon it that was his own, his labor. He that in obedience to this command of God, subdued, tilled and sowed any part of it, thereby annexed to it something that was his property, which another had no title to, nor could without injury take from him.

§. 33. Nor was this appropriation of any parcel of land, by improving it, any prejudice to any other man, since there was still enough, and as good left; and more than the yet unprovided could use. So that, in effect, there was never the less left for others because of his enclosure for himself: for he that leaves as much as another can make use of, does as good as take nothing at all. Nobody could think himself injured by the drinking of another man, though he took a good draught, who had a whole river of the same water left him to quench his thirst: and the case of land and water, where there is enough of both, is perfectly the same.

§. 34. God gave the world to men in common; but since he gave it them for their benefit, and the greatest conveniences of life they were capable to draw from it, it cannot be supposed he meant it should always remain common and uncultivated. He gave it to the use of the industrious and rational, (and labor was to be his title to it) not to the fancy or covetousness of the quarrelsome and contentious. He that had as good left for his improvement, as was already taken up, needed not complain, ought not to meddle with what was already improved by another's labor: if he did, it is plain he desired the benefit of another's pains, which he had no right to, and not the ground which God had given him in common with others to labor on, and whereof there was as good left, as that already possessed, and more than he knew what to do with, or his industry could reach to.

§. 35. It is true, in land that is common in England, or any other country, where there is plenty of people under government, who have money and commerce, no one can enclose or appropriate any part, without the consent of all his fellow commoners; because this is left common by compact, i.e. by the law of the land, which is not to be violated. And though it be common, in respect of some men, it is not so to all mankind; but is the joint property of this country, or this parish. Besides, the remainder, after such enclosure, would not be as good to the rest of the commoners, as the whole was when they could all make use of the whole; whereas in the beginning and first peopling of the great common of the world, it was quite otherwise. The law man was under, was, rather, for appropriating. God commanded, and his wants forced him to labor. That was his property which could not be taken from him wherever he had fixed it. And hence subduing or cultivating the earth, and having dominion, we see are joined together. The one gave title to the other. So that God, by commanding to subdue, gave authority so far to appropriate: and the condition of human life, which requires labor and materials to work on, necessarily introduces private possessions.

§. 36. The measure of property nature has well set by the extent of men's labor and the conveniences of life: no man's labor could subdue, or appropriate all; nor could his enjoyment consume more than a small part; so that it was impossible for any man, this way, to entrench upon the right of another, or acquire to himself a property, to the prejudice of his neighbor, who would still have room for as good, and as large a possession (after the other had taken out his) as before it was appropriated. This measure did confine every man's possession to a very moderate proportion, and such as he might appropriate to himself, without injury to anybody, in the first ages of the world, when men were more in danger to be lost, by wandering from their company, in the then-vast wilderness of the earth, than to be straitened for want of room to plant in. And the same measure may be allowed still without prejudice to anybody, as full as the world seems: for supposing a man, or family, in the state they were at first peopling of the world by the children of Adam, or Noah; let him plant in some inland, vacant places of America, we shall find that the possessions he could make himself, upon the measures we have given, would not be very large, nor, even to this day, prejudice the rest of mankind, or give them reason to complain, or think themselves injured by this man's encroachment, though the race of men have now spread themselves to all the corners of the world, and do infinitely exceed the small number was at the beginning. Nay, the extent of ground is of so little value, without labor, that I have heard it affirmed, that in Spain itself a man may be permitted to plough, sow and reap, without being disturbed, upon land he has no other title to, but only his making use of it. But, on the contrary, the inhabitants think themselves beholden to him, who, by his industry on neglected, and consequently waste land, has increased the stock of corn, which they wanted. But be this as it will, which I lay no stress on; this I dare boldly affirm, that the same rule of propriety, (viz.) that every man should have as much as he could make use of, would hold still in the world, without straitening anybody; since there is land enough in the world to suffice double the inhabitants, had not the invention of money, and the tacit agreement of men to put a value on it, introduced (by consent) larger possessions, and a right to them; which, how it has done, I shall by and by show more at large.

§. 37. This is certain, that in the beginning, before the desire of having more than man needed had altered the intrinsic value of things, which depends only on their usefulness to the life of man; or had agreed, that a little piece of yellow metal, which would keep without wasting or decay, should be worth a great piece of flesh, or a whole heap of corn; though men had a right to appropriate, by their labor, each one to himself, as much of the things of nature, as he could use: yet this could not be much, nor to the prejudice of others, where the same plenty was still left to those who would use the same industry. To which let me add, that he who appropriates land to himself by his labor, does not lessen, but increases the common stock of mankind: for the provisions serving to the support of human life, produced by one acre of enclosed and cultivated land, are (to speak much within compass) ten times more than those which are yielded by an acre of land of an equal richness lying waste in common. And therefore he that encloses land, and has a greater plenty of the conveniences of life from ten acres, than he could have from a hundred left to nature, may truly be said to give ninety acres to mankind: for his labor now supplies him with provisions out of ten acres, which were but the product of a hundred lying in common. I have here rated the improved land very low, in making its product but as ten to one, when it is much nearer a hundred to one: for I ask whether in the wild woods and uncultivated waste of America, left to nature, without any improvement, tillage or husbandry, a thousand acres yield the needy and wretched inhabitants as many conveniences of life, as ten acres of equally fertile land do in Devonshire, where they are well cultivated?

Before the appropriation of land, he who gathered as much of the wild fruit, killed, caught, or tamed as many of the beasts, as he could; he that so employed his pains about any of the spontaneous products of nature, as any way to alter them from the state which nature put them in, by placing any of his labor on them, did thereby acquire a propriety in them: but if they perished, in his possession, without their due use; if the fruits rotted, or the venison putrified, before he could spend it, he offended against the common law of nature, and was liable to be punished; he invaded his neighbor's share, for he had no right, farther than his use called for any of them, and they might serve to afford him conveniences of life.

§. 38. The same measures governed the possession of land too: whatsoever he tilled and reaped, laid up and made use of, before it spoiled, that was his peculiar right; whatsoever he enclosed, and could feed and make use of, the cattle and product was also his. But if either the grass of his enclosure rotted on the ground or the fruit of his planting perished without gathering and laying up, this part of the earth, notwithstanding his enclosure, was still to be looked on as waste, and might be the possession of any other. Thus, at the beginning, Cain might take as much ground as he could till, and make it his own land and yet leave enough to Abel's sheep to feed on; a few acres would serve for both their possessions. But as families increased, and industry enlarged their stocks, their possessions enlarged with the need of them; but yet it was commonly without any fixed property in the ground they made use of, till they incorporated, settled themselves together, and built cities; and then, by consent, they came in time, to set out the bounds of their distinct territories, and agree on limits between them and their neighbors; and by laws within themselves, settled the properties of those of the same society: for we see, that in that part of the world which was first inhabited, and therefore like to be best peopled, even as low down as Abraham's time, they wandered with their flocks, and their herds, which was their substance, freely up and down; and this Abraham did, in a country where he was a stranger. Whence it is plain, that at least a great part of the land lay in common; that the inhabitants valued it not, nor claimed property in any more than they made use of. But when there was not room enough in the same place, for their herds to feed together, they by consent, as Abraham and Lot did, Gen. 13. 5. separated and enlarged their pasture, where it best liked them. And for the same reason Esau went from his father, and his brother, and planted in Mount Seir, Gen. 36. 6.

§. 39. And thus, without supposing any private dominion, and property in Adam, over all the world, exclusive of all other men, which can no way be proved, nor anyone's property be made out from it; but supposing the world given, as it was, to the children of men in common, we see how labor could make men distinct titles to several parcels of it, for their private uses; wherein there could be no doubt of right, no room for quarrel.

§. 40. Nor is it so strange, as perhaps before consideration it may appear, that the property of labor should be able to overbalance the community of land: for it is labor indeed that puts the difference of value on everything; and let anyone consider what the difference is between an acre of land planted with tobacco or sugar, sown with wheat or barley, and an acre of the same land lying in common, without any husbandry upon it, and he will find, that the improvement of labor makes the far greater part of the value. I think it will be but a very modest computation to say, that of the products of the earth useful to the life of man nine tenths are the effects of labor: nay, if we will rightly estimate things as they come to our use, and cast up the several expenses about them, what in them is purely owing to nature, and what to labor, we shall find, that in most of them ninety-nine hundredths are wholly to be put on the account of labor.

§. 41. There cannot be a clearer demonstration of anything, than several nations of the Americans are of this, who are rich in land, and poor in all the comforts of life; whom nature having furnished as liberally as any other people, with the materials of plenty, i.e. a fruitful soil, apt to produce in abundance, what might serve for food, raiment, and delight; yet for want of improving it by labor, have not one hundredth part of the conveniences we enjoy: and a king of a large and fruitful territory there, feeds, lodges, and is clad worse than a day-laborer in England.

§. 42. To make this a little clearer, let us but trace some of the ordinary provisions of life, through their several progresses, before they come to our use, and see how much they receive of their value from human industry. Bread, wine and cloth, are things of daily use, and great plenty; yet notwithstanding, acorns, water and leaves, or skins, must be our bread, drink and clothing, did not labor furnish us with these more useful commodities: for whatever bread is more worth than acorns, wine than water, and cloth or silk, than leaves, skins or moss, that is wholly owing to labor and industry; the one of these being the food and raiment which unassisted nature furnishes us with; the other, provisions which our industry and pains prepare for us, which how much they exceed the other in value, when anyone has computed, he will then see how much labor makes the far greatest part of the value of things we enjoy in this world: and the ground which produces the materials, is scarce to be reckoned in, as any, or at most, but a very small part of it; so little, that even amongst us, land that is left wholly to nature, that has no improvement of pasturage, tillage, or planting, is called, as indeed it is, waste; and we shall find the benefit of it amount to little more than nothing. This shows how much numbers of men are to be preferred to largeness of dominions; and that the increase of lands,[4] and the right employing of them, is the great art of government: and that prince, who shall be so wise and godlike, as by established laws of liberty to secure protection and encouragement to the honest industry of mankind, against the oppression of power and narrowness of party, will quickly be too hard for his neighbors: but this by the by. To return to the argument in hand.

§. 43. An acre of land, that bears here twenty bushels of wheat, and another in America, which, with the same husbandry, would do the like, are, without doubt, of the same natural intrinsic value: but yet the benefit mankind receives from the one in a year, is worth 5£ and from the other possibly not worth a penny, if all the profit an Indian received from it were to be valued, and sold here; at least, I may truly say, not one thousandth. It is labor then which puts the greatest part of value upon land, without which it would scarcely be worth anything: it is to that we owe the greatest part of all its useful products; for all that the straw, bran, bread, of that acre of wheat, is more worth than the product of an acre of as good land, which lies waste, is all the effect of labor: for it is not barely the ploughman's pains, the reaper's and thresher's toil, and the baker's sweat, is to be counted into the bread we eat; the labor of those who broke the oxen, who dug and wrought the iron and stones, who felled and framed the timber employed about the plough, mill, oven, or any other utensils, which are a vast number, requisite to this corn, from its being seed to be sown to its being made bread, must all be charged on the account of labor, and received as an effect of that: nature and the earth furnished only the almost worthless materials, as in themselves. It would be a strange catalogue of things, that industry provided and made

4. There is some debate over whether the correct reading is "increase of lands" as it appears in the sixth edition or "increase in hands" as it appears is some earlier editions. The former would imply territorial expansionism whereas "hands" would suggest increased population due to increased agricultural productivity.

use of, about every loaf of bread, before it came to our use, if we could trace them; iron, wood, leather, bark, timber, stone, bricks, coals, lime, cloth, dyeing drugs, pitch, tar, masts, ropes, and all the materials made use of in the ship, that brought any of the commodities made use of by any of the workmen, to any part of the work; all which it would be almost impossible, at least too long, to reckon up.

§. 44. From all which it is evident, that though the things of nature are given in common, yet man, by being master of himself, and proprietor of his own person, and the actions or labor of it, had still in himself the great foundation of property; and that, which made up the great part of what he applied to the support or comfort of his being, when invention and arts had improved the conveniences of life, was perfectly his own, and did not belong in common to others.

§. 45. Thus labor, in the beginning, gave a right of property, wherever anyone was pleased to employ it upon what was common, which remained a long while the far greater part, and is yet more than mankind makes use of. Men, at first, for the most part, contented themselves with what unassisted nature offered to their necessities: and though afterwards, in some parts of the world, (where the increase of people and stock, with the use of money, had made land scarce, and so of some value) the several communities settled the bounds of their distinct territories, and by laws within themselves regulated the properties of the private men of their society, and so, by compact and agreement, settled the property which labor and industry began; and the leagues that have been made between several states and kingdoms, either expressly or tacitly disowning all claim and right to the land in the other's possession, have, by common consent, given up their pretences to their natural common right, which originally they had to those countries, and so have, by positive agreement, settled a property amongst themselves, in distinct parts and parcels of the earth; yet there are still great tracts of ground to be found, which (the inhabitants thereof not having joined with the rest of mankind, in the consent of the use of their common money) lie waste, and are more than the people who dwell on it do, or can make use of, and so still lie in common; though this can scarce happen amongst that part of mankind that have consented to the use of money.

§. 46. The greatest part of things really useful to the life of man, and such as the necessity of subsisting made the first commoners of the world look after, as it does the Americans now, are generally things of short duration; such as, if they are not consumed by use, will decay and perish of themselves: gold, silver and diamonds, are things that fancy or agreement has put the value on, more than real use, and the necessary support of life. Now of those good things which nature has provided in common, everyone had a right (as has been said) to as much as he could use, and property in all that he could affect with his labor; all that his industry could extend to, to alter from the state nature had put it in, was his. He that gathered a hundred bushels of acorns or apples, had thereby a property in them, they were his goods as soon as gathered. He was only to look, that he used them before they spoiled, else he took more than his share, and robbed others. And indeed it was a foolish thing, as well as dishonest, to hoard up more than he could make use of. If he gave away a part to anybody else, so that it perished not uselessly in his possession, these he also made use of. And if he also bartered away plums, that would have rotted in a week, for nuts that would last good for his eating a whole year, he did no injury; he wasted not the common stock; destroyed no part of the portion of goods that belonged to others, so long as nothing perished uselessly in his hands. Again, if he would give his nuts for a piece of metal, pleased with its color; or exchange his sheep for shells, or wool for a sparkling pebble or a diamond, and keep those by him all his life he invaded not the right of others, he might heap up as much of these durable things as he pleased; the exceeding of the bounds of his just property not lying in the largeness of his possession, but the perishing of anything uselessly in it.

§. 47. And thus came in the use of money, some lasting thing that men might keep without spoiling, and that by mutual consent men would take in exchange for the truly useful, but perishable supports of life.

§. 48. And as different degrees of industry were apt to give men possessions in different proportions, so this invention of money

gave them the opportunity to continue and enlarge them: for supposing an island, separate from all possible commerce with the
rest of the world, wherein there were but a hundred families, but
there were sheep, horses and cows, with other useful animals,
wholesome fruits, and land enough for corn for a hundred thousand times as many, but nothing in the island, either because of its
commonness, or perishableness, fit to supply the place of money;
what reason could anyone have there to enlarge his possessions
beyond the use of his family, and a plentiful supply to its consump-
tion, either in what their own industry produced, or they could
barter for like perishable, useful commodities, with others? Where
there is not something, both lasting and scarce, and so valuable
to be hoarded up, there men will not be apt to enlarge their possessions of land, were it never so rich, never so free for them to
take: for I ask, what would a man value ten thousand, or a hundred
thousand acres of excellent land, ready cultivated, and well stocked
too with cattle, in the middle of the inland parts of America, where
he had no hopes of commerce with other parts of the world, to
draw money to him by the sale of the product? It would not be
worth the enclosing, and we should see him give up again to the
wild common of nature, whatever was more than would supply the
conveniences of life to be had there for him and his family.

§. 49. Thus in the beginning all the world was America, and more
so than that is now; for no such thing as money was anywhere
known. Find out something that has the use and value of money
amongst his neighbors, you shall see the same man will begin presently to enlarge his possessions.

§. 50. But since gold and silver, being little useful to the life of man
in proportion to food, raiment, and carriage, has its value only
from the consent of men, whereof labor yet makes, in great part,
the measure, it is plain, that men have agreed to disproportionate
and unequal possession of the earth, they having, by a tacit and
voluntary consent, found out, a way how a man may fairly possess
more land than he himself can use the product of, by receiving in
exchange for the overplus gold and silver, which may be hoarded
up without injury to anyone; these metals not spoiling or decay-
ing in the hands of the possessor. This distribution of things in an

inequality of private possessions, men have made practicable out of the bounds of society, and without compact, only by putting a value on gold and silver, and tacitly agreeing in the use of money: for in governments, the laws regulate the right of property, and the possession of land is determined by positive constitutions.

§. 51. And thus, I think, it is very easy to conceive, without any difficulty, how labor could at first begin a title of property in the common things of nature, and how the spending it upon our uses bounded it. So that there could then be no reason of quarrelling about title, nor any doubt about the largeness of possession it gave. Right and convenience went together; for as a man had a right to all he could employ his labor upon, so he had no temptation to labor for more than he could make use of. This left no room for controversy about the title, nor for encroachment on the right of others; what portion a man carved to himself, was easily seen; and it was useless, as well as dishonest, to carve himself too much, or take more than he needed.

CHAPTER VI
Of Paternal Power

§. 52. It may perhaps be censured as an impertinent criticism, in a discourse of this nature, to find fault with words and names, that have obtained in the world: and yet possibly it may not be amiss to offer new ones, when the old are apt to lead men into mistakes, as this of paternal power probably has done, which seems so to place the power of parents over their children wholly in the father, as if the mother had no share in it; whereas, if we consult reason or revelation, we shall find, she has an equal title. This may give one reason to ask, whether this might not be more properly called parental power? For whatever obligation nature and the right of generation lays on children, it must certainly bind them equal to both the concurrent causes of it. And accordingly we see the positive law of God everywhere joins them together, without distinction, when it commands the obedience of children, *Honour thy father and thy mother*, Exod. 20. 12. *Whosoever curseth his father or his mother*, Lev. 20. 9. *Ye shall fear every man his mother and his father*, Lev. 19. 3. *Children, obey your parents*, &c. Eph. 6. 1. is the style of the Old and New Testament.

§. 53. Had but this one thing been well considered, without looking any deeper into the matter, it might perhaps have kept men from running into those gross mistakes, they have made, about this power of parents; which, however it might, without any great harshness, bear the name of absolute dominion, and regal authority, when under the title of paternal power it seemed appropriated to the father, would yet have sounded but oddly, and in the very name shown the absurdity, if this supposed absolute power over children had been called parental; and thereby have discovered, that it belonged to the mother too: for it will but very ill serve the turn of those men, who contend so much for the absolute power and authority of the fatherhood, as they call it, that the mother should have any share in it; and it would have but ill supported the monarchy they contend for, when by the very name it appeared, that that fundamental authority, from whence they would derive their government of a single person only, was not placed in one, but two persons jointly. But to let this of names pass.

§. 54. Though I have said above, Chap. II. That all men by nature are equal, I cannot be supposed to understand all sorts of equality: age or virtue may give men a just precedence: excellence of parts and merit may place others above the common level: birth may subject some, and alliance or benefits others, to pay an observance to those to whom nature, gratitude, or other respects, may have made it due: and yet all this consists with the equality, which all men are in, in respect of jurisdiction or dominion one over another; which was the equality I there spoke of, as proper to the business in hand, being that equal right, that every man has, to his natural freedom, without being subjected to the will or authority of any other man.

§. 55. Children, I confess, are not born in this full state of equality, though they are born to it. Their parents have a sort of rule and jurisdiction over them, when they come into the world, and for some time after, but it is but a temporary one. The bonds of this subjection are like the swaddling clothes they are wrapped up in, and supported by, in the weakness of their infancy. Age and reason as they grow up, loosen them, till at length they drop quite off, and leave a man at his own free disposal.

§. 56. Adam was created a perfect man, his body and mind in full possession of their strength and reason, and so was capable, from the first instant of his being to provide for his own support and preservation, and govern his actions according to the dictates of the law of reason which God had implanted in him. From him the world is peopled with his descendants, who are all born infants, weak and helpless, without knowledge or understanding: but to supply the defects of this imperfect state, till the improvement of growth and age has removed them, Adam and Eve, and after them all parents were, by the law of nature, under an obligation to pre-serve, nourish, and educate the children they had begotten; not as their own workmanship, but the workmanship of their own maker, the Almighty, to whom they were to be accountable for them.

§. 57. The law, that was to govern Adam, was the same that was to govern all his posterity, the law of reason. But his offspring having another way of entrance into the world, different from him, by a natural birth, that produced them ignorant and without the use of reason, they were not presently under that law; for nobody can be under a law, which is not promulgated to him; and this law being promulgated or made known by reason only, he that is not come to the use of his reason, cannot be said to be under this law; and Adam's children, being not presently as soon as born under this law of reason, were not presently free: for law, in its true notion, is not so much the limitation as the direction of a free and intelligent agent to his proper interest, and prescribes no farther than is for the general good of those under that law: could they be happier without it, the law, as a useless thing, would of itself vanish; and that ill deserves the name of confinement which hedges us in only from bogs and precipices. So that, however it may be mistaken, the end of law is not to abolish or restrain, but to preserve and enlarge freedom: for in all the states of created beings capable of laws, where there is no law, there is no freedom: for liberty is, to be free from restraint and violence from others; which cannot be, where there is no law: but freedom is not, as we are told, a liberty for every man to do what he lists: (for who could be free, when every other man's humor might domineer over him?) but a liberty to dispose, and order as he lists, his person, actions, possessions, and his whole property, within the allowance of those laws under which he is, and therein not to be subject to the arbitrary will of another, but freely follow his own.

§. 58. The power, then, that parents have over their children arises from that duty which is incumbent on them, to take care of their offspring, during the imperfect state of childhood. To inform the mind, and govern the actions of their yet ignorant nonage, till reason shall take its place, and ease them of that trouble, is what the children want, and the parents are bound to: for God having given man an understanding to direct his actions, has allowed him a freedom of will, and liberty of acting, as properly belonging thereunto, within the bounds of that law he is under. But while he is in an estate, wherein he has not understanding of his own to direct his will, he is not to have any will of his own to follow: he that understands for him, must will for him too; he must prescribe to his will, and regulate his actions; but when he comes to the estate that made his father a freeman, the son is a freeman too.

§. 59. This holds in all the laws a man is under, whether natural or civil. Is a man under the law of nature? What made him free of that law? What gave him a free disposing of his property, according to his own will, within the compass of that law? I answer; state of maturity wherein he might be supposed capable to know that law, that so he might keep his actions within the bounds of it. When he has acquired that state, he is presumed to know how far that law is to be his guide, and how far he may make use of his freedom, and so comes to have it; till then, somebody else must guide him, who is presumed to know how far the law allows a liberty. If such a state of reason, such an age of discretion made him free, the same shall make his son free too. Is a man under the law of England? What made him free of that law? That is, to have the liberty to dispose of his actions and possessions according to his own will, within the permission of that law? A capacity of knowing that law; which is supposed by that law, at the age of one and twenty years, and in some cases sooner. If this made the father free, it shall make the son free too. Till then we see the law allows the son to have no will, but he is to be guided by the will of his father or guardian, who is to understand for him. And if the father die, and fail to substitute a deputy in this trust; if he has not provided a tutor, to govern his son, during his minority, during his want of understanding, the law takes care to do it; some other must govern him, and be a will to him, till he has attained to a state of freedom, and his understanding be fit to take the government of his will. But after that, the father and son are equally free as much as tutor and pupil after nonage; equally subjects of the same law together, without any dominion left in the father over the life, liberty, or estate of his son, whether they be only in the state and under the law of nature, or under the positive laws of an established government.

§. 60. But if, through defects that may happen out of the ordinary course of nature, anyone comes not to such a degree of reason, wherein he might be supposed capable of knowing the law, and so living within the rules of it, he is never capable of being a free man, he is never let loose to the disposure of his own will (because he knows no bounds to it, has not understanding, its proper guide) but is continued under the tuition and government of others, all the time his own understanding is incapable of that charge. And so lunatics and idiots are never set free from the government of their parents; *children, who are not as yet come unto those years whereat they may have; and innocents which are excluded by a natural defect from ever having; thirdly, madmen, which for the present cannot possibly have the use of right reason to guide themselves, have for their guide, the reason that guides other men which are tutors over them, to seek and procure their good for them,* says Hooker, *Eccl. Pol. lib.* 1. sect. 7. All which seems no more than that duty, which God and nature has laid on man as well as other creatures, to preserve their offspring, till they can be able to shift for themselves, and will scarce amount to an instance or proof of parents' regal authority.

§. 61. Thus we are born free, as we are born rational; not that we have actually the exercise of either: age, that brings one, brings with it the other too. And thus we see how natural freedom and subjection to parents may consist together, and are both founded on the same principle. A child is free by his father's title, by his father's understanding, which is to govern him till he has it of his own. The freedom of a man at years of discretion, and the subjection of a child to his parents, while yet short of that age, are so consistent, and so distinguishable, that the most blinded contenders for monarchy, by right of fatherhood, cannot miss this difference; the most obstinate cannot but allow their consistency: for were their doctrine all true, were the right heir of Adam now known, and by that title settled a monarch in his throne, invested with all the absolute unlimited power Sir Robert Filmer talks of; if he should die as soon as his heir were born, must not the child, notwithstanding he were never so free, never so much sovereign, be in subjection to his mother and nurse, to tutors and governors, till age and education brought him reason and ability to govern himself and others? The necessities of his life, the health of his body, and the information of his mind, would require him to be directed by the will of others, and not his own; and yet will anyone think, that this restraint and subjection were inconsistent with, or spoiled him of that liberty or sovereignty he had a right to, or gave away his empire to those who had the government of his nonage? This government over him only prepared him the better and sooner for it. If anybody should ask me, when my son is of age to be free? I shall answer, just when his monarch is of age to govern. *But at what time*, says the judicious Hooker, *Eccl. Pol. lib.* 1. sect. 6. *a man may be said to have attained so far forth the use of reason, as suffices to make him capable of those laws whereby he is then bound to guide his actions: this is a great deal more easy for sense to discern, than for anyone by skill and learning to determine.*

§. 62. Commonwealths themselves take notice of, and allow, that there is a time when men are to begin to act like freemen, and therefore till that time require not oaths of fealty, or allegiance, or other public owning of, or submission to the government of their countries.

§. 63. The freedom then of man, and liberty of acting according to his own will, is grounded on his having reason, which is able to instruct him in that law he is to govern himself by, and make him know how far he is left to the freedom of his own will. To turn him loose to an unrestrained liberty, before he has reason to guide him, is not the allowing him the privilege of his nature to be free; but to thrust him out amongst brutes, and abandon him to a state as wretched, and as much beneath that of a man, as theirs. This is that which puts the authority into the parents' hands to govern the minority of their children. God has made it their business to employ this care on their offspring, and has placed in them suitable inclinations of tenderness and concern to temper this power, to apply it, as his wisdom designed it, to the children's good, as long as they should need to be under it.

§. 64. But what reason can hence advance this care of the parents due to their offspring into an absolute arbitrary dominion of the father, whose power reaches no farther, than by such a discipline, as he finds most effectual, to give such strength and health to their bodies, such vigor and rectitude to their minds, as may best fit his children to be most useful to themselves and others; and, if it be necessary to his condition, to make them work, when they are able, for their own subsistence. But in this power the mother too has her share with the father.

§. 65. Nay, this power so little belongs to the father by any peculiar right of nature, but only as he is guardian of his children, that when he quits his care of them, he loses his power over them, which goes along with their nourishment and education, to which it is inseparably annexed; and it belongs as much to the foster father of an exposed child, as to the natural father of another. So little power does the bare act of begetting give a man over his issue; if all his care ends there, and this be all the title he has to the name and authority of a father. And what will become of this paternal power in that part of the world, where one woman has more than one husband at a time? Or in those parts of America, where, when the husband and wife part, which happens frequently, the children are all left to the mother, follow her, and are wholly under her care and provision? If the father die while the children are young, do they not naturally everywhere owe the same obedience to their mother, during their minority, as to their father were he alive? And will anyone say, that the mother has a legislative power over her children? That she can make standing rules, which shall be of perpetual obligation, by which they ought to regulate all the concerns of their property, and bound their liberty all the course of their

lives? Or can she enforce the observation of them with capital punishments? For this is the proper power of the magistrate, of which
the father has not so much as the shadow. His command over his
children is but temporary, and reaches not their life or property:
it is but a help to the weakness and imperfection of their nonage,
a discipline necessary to their education: and though a father may
dispose of his own possessions as he pleases, when his children
are out of danger of perishing for want, yet his power extends not
to the lives or goods, which either their own industry, or another's
bounty has made theirs; nor to their liberty neither, when they are
once arrived to the enfranchisement of the years of discretion. The
father's empire then ceases, and he can from thence forwards no
more dispose of the liberty of his son, than that of any other man:
and it must be far from an absolute or perpetual jurisdiction, from
which a man may withdraw himself, having license from divine
authority to *leave father and mother, and cleave to his wife.*

§. 66. But though there be a time when a child comes to be as
free from subjection to the will and command of his father, as the
father himself is free from subjection to the will of anybody else,
and they are each under no other restraint, but that which is common to them both, whether it be the law of nature, or municipal
law of their country; yet this freedom exempts not a son from that
honor which he ought, by the law of God and nature, to pay his
parents. God having made the parents instruments in his great
design of continuing the race of mankind, and the occasions of
life to their children; as he has laid on them an obligation to nourish, preserve, and bring up their offspring; so he has laid on the
children a perpetual obligation of honoring their parents, which
containing in it an inward esteem and reverence to be shown by
all outward expressions, ties up the child from anything that may
ever injure or affront, disturb or endanger, the happiness or life of
those from whom he received his; and engages him in all actions of
defense, relief, assistance and comfort of those, by whose means he
entered into being, and has been made capable of any enjoyments
of life: from this obligation no state, no freedom can absolve children. But this is very far from giving parents a power of command
over their children, or an authority to make laws and dispose as
they please of their lives or liberties. It is one thing to owe honor,

respect, gratitude and assistance; another to require an absolute obedience and submission. The honor due to parents, a monarch in his throne owes his mother; and yet this lessens not his authority, nor subjects him to her government.

§. 67. The subjection of a minor places in the father a temporary government, which terminates with the minority of the child: and the honor due from a child places in the parents a perpetual right to respect, reverence, support and compliance too, more or less, as the father's care, cost, and kindness in his education, has been more or less. This ends not with minority, but holds in all parts and conditions of a man's life. The want of distinguishing these two powers, viz. that which the father has in the right of tuition, during minority, and the right of honor all his life, may perhaps have caused a great part of the mistakes about this matter: for to speak properly of them, the first of these is rather the privilege of children, and duty of parents, than any prerogative of paternal power. The nourishment and education of their children is a charge so incumbent on parents for their children's good, that nothing can absolve them from taking care of it: and though the power of commanding and chastising them go along with it, yet God has woven into the principles of human nature such a tenderness for their offspring, that there is little fear that parents should use their power with too much rigor; the excess is seldom on the severe side, the strong bias of nature drawing the other way. And therefore God almighty when he would express his gentle dealing with the Israelites, he tells them, that though he chastened them, *he chastened them as a man chastens his son*, Deut. 8. 5. i.e. with tenderness and affection, and kept them under no severer discipline than what was absolutely best for them, and had been less kindness to have slackened. This is that power to which children are commanded obedience, that the pains and care of their parents may not be increased, or ill rewarded.

§. 68. On the other side, honor and support, all that which gratitude requires to return for the benefits received by and from them, is the indispensable duty of the child, and the proper privilege of the parents. This is intended for the parents' advantage, as the other is for the child's; though education, the parents' duty, seems to have

most power, because the ignorance and infirmities of childhood
stand in need of restraint and correction; which is a visible exercise of rule, and a kind of dominion. And that duty which is comprehended in the word *honor*, requires less obedience, though the
obligation be stronger on grown, than younger children: for who
can think the command, Children obey your parents, requires in
a man, that has children of his own, the same submission to his
father, as it does in his yet young children to him; and that by this
precept he were bound to obey all his father's commands, if, out of
a conceit of authority, he should have the indiscretion to treat him
still as a boy?

§. 69. The first part then of paternal power, or rather duty, which
is education, belongs so to the father, that it terminates at a certain
season; when the business of education is over, it ceases of itself,
and is also alienable before: for a man may put the tuition of his
son in other hands; and he that has made his son an apprentice to
another, has discharged him, during that time, of a great part of
his obedience both to himself and to his mother. But all the duty of
honor, the other part, remains never the less entire to them; nothing can cancel that: it is so inseparable from them both, that the
father's authority cannot dispossess the mother of this right, nor
can any man discharge his son from honoring her that bore him.
But both these are very far from a power to make laws, and enforc-
ing them with penalties that may reach estate, liberty, limbs and
life. The power of commanding ends with nonage; and though,
after that, honor and respect, support and defense, and whatsoever gratitude can oblige a man to, for the highest benefits he is
naturally capable of, be always due from a son to his parents; yet
all this puts no scepter into the father's hand, no sovereign power
of commanding. He has no dominion over his son's property, or
actions; nor any right, that his will should prescribe to his son's in
all things; however it may become his son in many things, not very
inconvenient to him and his family, to pay a deference to it.

§. 70. A man may owe honor and respect to an ancient, or wise
man; defense to his child or friend; relief and support to the dis-
tressed; and gratitude to a benefactor, to such a degree, that all
he has, all he can do, cannot sufficiently pay it: but all these give

no authority, no right to anyone, of making laws over him from whom they are owing. And it is plain, all this is due not only to the bare title of father; not only because, as has been said, it is owing to the mother too; but because these obligations to parents, and the degrees of what is required of children, may be varied by the different care and kindness, trouble and expense, which is often employed upon one child more than another.

§. 71. This shows the reason how it comes to pass, that parents in societies, where they themselves are subjects, retain a power over their children, and have as much right to their subjection, as those who are in the state of nature. Which could not possibly be, if all political power were only paternal, and that in truth they were one and the same thing: for then, all paternal power being in the prince, the subject could naturally have none of it. But these two powers, political and paternal, are so perfectly distinct and separate; are built upon so different foundations, and given to so different ends, that every subject that is a father, has as much a paternal power over his children, as the prince has over his: and every prince, that has parents, owes them as much filial duty and obedience, as the meanest of his subjects do to theirs; and can therefore contain not any part or degree of that kind of dominion, which a prince or magistrate has over his subject.

§. 72. Though the obligation on the parents to bring up their children, and the obligation on children to honor their parents, contain all the power on the one hand, and submission on the other, which are proper to this relation, yet there is another power ordinarily in the father, whereby he has a tie on the obedience of his children; which though it be common to him with other men, yet the occasions of showing it, almost constantly happening to fathers in their private families, and the instances of it elsewhere being rare, and less taken notice of, it passes in the world for a part of paternal jurisdiction. And this is the power men generally have to bestow their estates on those who please them best. The possession of the father being the expectation and inheritance of the children, ordinarily in certain proportions, according to the law and custom of each country; yet it is commonly in the father's power to bestow it with a more sparing or liberal hand, according as the behavior of this or that child has comported with his will and humor.

§. 73. This is no small tie on the obedience of children: and there being always annexed to the enjoyment of land, a submission to the government of the country, of which that land is a part; it has been commonly supposed, that a father could oblige his posterity to that government, of which he himself was a subject, and that his compact held them; whereas, it being only a necessary condition annexed to the land, and the inheritance of an estate which is under that government, reaches only those who will take it on that condition, and so is no natural tie or engagement, but a voluntary submission: for every man's children being by nature as free as himself, or any of his ancestors ever were, may, while they are in that freedom, choose what society they will join themselves to, what commonwealth they will put themselves under. But if they will enjoy the inheritance of their ancestors, they must take it on the same terms their ancestors had it, and submit to all the conditions annexed to such a possession. By this power indeed fathers oblige their children to obedience to themselves, even when they are past minority, and most commonly too subject them to this or that political power: but neither of these by any peculiar right of fatherhood, but by the reward they have in their hands to enforce and recompense such a compliance; and is no more power than what a French man has over an English man, who by the hopes of an estate he will leave him, will certainly have a strong tie on his obedience: and if, when it is left him, he will enjoy it, he must certainly take it upon the conditions annexed to the possession of land in that country where it lies, whether it be France or England.

§. 74. To conclude then, though the father's power of commanding extends no farther than the minority of his children, and to a degree only fit for the discipline and government of that age; and though that honor and respect, and all that which the Latins called piety, which they indispensably owe to their parents all their lifetimes, and in all estates, with all that support and defense is due to them, gives the father no power of governing, i.e. making laws and enacting penalties on his children; though by all this he has no dominion over the property or actions of his son: yet it is obvious to conceive how easy it was, in the first ages of the world, and in places still, where the thinness of people gives families leave to separate into unpossessed quarters, and they have room to remove or plant themselves in yet vacant habitations, for the father of the family to become the prince of it;° he had been a ruler from the beginning of the infancy of his children: and since without some government it would be hard for them to live together, it was likeliest it should, by the express or tacit consent of the children when they were grown up, be in the father, where it seemed without any change barely to continue; when indeed nothing more was required to it, than the permitting the father to exercise alone, in his family, that executive power of the law of nature, which every free man naturally has, and by that permission resigning up to him a monarchical power, while they remained in it. But that this was not by any paternal right, but only by the consent of his children, is evident from hence, that nobody doubts, but if a stranger, whom chance or business had brought to his family, had there killed any of his children, or committed any other fact, he might condemn and put him to death, or otherwise have punished him, as well as any of his children; which it was impossible he should do by virtue of any paternal authority over one who was not his child, but by virtue of that executive power of the law of nature, which, as a man, he had a right to: and he alone could punish him in his family, where the respect of his children had laid by the exercise of such a power, to give way to the dignity° and authority they were willing should remain in him, above the rest of his family.

(°*It is no improbable opinion therefore, which the arch-philosopher was of, that the chief person in every household was always, as it were, a king: so when numbers of households joined themselves in civil societies together, kings were the first kind of governors amongst them, which is also, as it seemeth, the reason why the name of fathers continued still in them, who, of fathers, were made rulers; as also the ancient custom of governors to do as Melchizedec, and being kings, to exercise the office of priests, which fathers did at the first, grew perhaps by the same occasion. Howbeit, this is not the only kind of regiment that has been received in the world. The inconveniences of one kind have caused sundry others to be devised; so that in a word, all public regiment, of what kind soever, seemeth evidently to have risen from the deliberate advice, consultation and composition*

between men, judging it convenient and behoveful; there being no
impossibility in nature considered by itself, but that man might have
lived without any public regiment, Hooker's *Eccl. Pol. lib.* 1. sect.
10.)

§. 75. Thus it was easy, and almost natural for children by a tacit,
and scarce avoidable consent to make way for the father's authority
and government. They had been accustomed in their childhood to
follow his direction, and to refer their little differences to him, and
when they were men, who fitter to rule them? Their little properties, and less covetousness, seldom afforded greater controversies;
and when any should arise, where could they have a fitter umpire
than he, by whose care they had everyone been sustained and
brought up, and who had a tenderness for them all? It is no wonder that they made no distinction between minority and full age;
nor looked after one and twenty, or any other age that might make
them the free disposers of themselves and fortunes, when they
could have no desire to be out of their pupilage: the government
they had been under, during it, continued still to be more their
protection than restraint; and they could nowhere find a greater
security to their peace, liberties, and fortunes, than in the rule of
a father.

§. 76. Thus the natural fathers of families, by an insensible change,
became the politic monarchs of them too: and as they chanced to
live long, and leave able and worthy heirs, for several successions,
or otherwise; so they laid the foundations of hereditary, or elective kingdoms, under several constitutions and manners, according as chance, contrivance, or occasions happened to mould them.
But if princes have their titles in the father's right, and it be a sufficient proof of the natural right of fathers to political authority,
because they commonly were those in whose hands we find, de
facto, the exercise of government: I say, if this argument be good,
it will as strongly prove, that all princes, nay princes only, ought to
be priests, since it is as certain, that in the beginning, the father of
the family was priest, as that he was ruler in his own household.

CHAPTER VII
Of Political or Civil Society

§. 77. God having made man such a creature, that in his own judgment, it was not good for him to be alone, put him under strong
obligations of necessity, convenience, and inclination to drive him
into society, as well as fitted him with understanding and language
to continue and enjoy it. The first society was between man and
wife, which gave beginning to that between parents and children; to which, in time, that between master and servant came to
be added: and though all these might, and commonly did meet
together, and make up but one family, wherein the master or mistress of it had some sort of rule proper to a family; each of these,
or all together, came short of political society, as we shall see, if we
consider the different ends, ties, and bounds of each of these.

§. 78. Conjugal society is made by a voluntary compact between
man and woman; and though it consists chiefly in such a communion and right in one another's bodies as is necessary to its chief
end, procreation; yet it draws with it mutual support and assistance, and a communion of interests too, as necessary not only to
unite their care and affection, but also necessary to their common
offspring, who have a right to be nourished, and maintained by
them, till they are able to provide for themselves.

§. 79. For the end of conjunction, between male and female, being
not barely procreation, but the continuation of the species; this
conjunction between male and female ought to last, even after
procreation, so long as is necessary to the nourishment and support of the young ones, who are to be sustained even after procreation, till they are able to shift and provide for themselves. This
rule, which the infinite wise maker has set to the works of his
hands, we find the inferior creatures steadily obey. In those vivipa-
rous animals which feed on grass, the conjunction between male
and female lasts no longer than the very act of copulation; because
the teat of the dam being sufficient to nourish the young, till it
be able to feed on grass, the male only begets, but concerns not
himself for the female or young, to whose sustenance he can contribute nothing. But in beasts of prey the conjunction lasts longer:

because the dam not being able well to subsist herself, and nourish her numerous offspring by her own prey alone, a more laborious, as well as more dangerous way of living, than by feeding on grass, the assistance of the male is necessary to the maintenance of their common family, which cannot subsist till they are able to prey for themselves, but by the joint care of male and female. The same is to be observed in all birds, (except some domestic ones, where plenty of food excuses the cock from feeding, and taking care of the young brood) whose young needing food in the nest, the cock and hen continue mates, till the young are able to use their wing, and provide for themselves.

§. 80. And herein I think lies the chief, if not the only reason, why the male and female in mankind are tied to a longer conjunction than other creatures, viz. because the female is capable of conceiving, and de facto is commonly with child again, and brings forth too a new birth, long before the former is out of a dependency for support on his parents help, and able to shift for himself, and has all the assistance is due to him from his parents: whereby the father, who is bound to take care for those he has begot, is under an obligation to continue in conjugal society with the same woman longer than other creatures, whose young being able to subsist of themselves, before the time of procreation returns again, the conjugal bond dissolves of itself, and they are at liberty, till Hymen at his usual anniversary season summons them again to choose new mates. Wherein one cannot but admire the wisdom of the great Creator, who having given to man foresight, and an ability to lay up for the future, as well as to supply the present necessity, has made it necessary, that society of man and wife should be more lasting, than of male and female amongst other creatures; that so their industry might be encouraged, and their interest better united, to make provision and lay up goods for their common issue, which uncertain mixture, or easy and frequent solutions of conjugal society would mightily disturb.

§. 81. But though these are ties upon mankind, which make the conjugal bonds more firm and lasting in man, than the other species of animals; yet it would give one reason to enquire, why this compact, where procreation and education are secured, and inheritance taken care for, may not be made determinable, either by consent, or at a certain time, or upon certain conditions, as well as any other voluntary compacts, there being no necessity in the nature of the thing, nor to the ends of it, that it should always be for life; I mean, to such as are under no restraint of any positive law, which ordains all such contracts to be perpetual.

§. 82. But the husband and wife, though they have but one common concern, yet having different understandings, will unavoidably sometimes have different wills too; it therefore being necessary that the last determination, i.e. the rule, should be placed somewhere; it naturally falls to the man's share, as the abler and the stronger. But this reaching but to the things of their common interest and property, leaves the wife in the full and free possession of what by contract is her peculiar right, and gives the husband no more power over her life than she has over his; the power of the husband being so far from that of an absolute monarch that the wife has in many cases a liberty to separate from him, where natural right, or their contract allows it; whether that contract be made by themselves in the state of nature, or by the customs or laws of the country they live in; and the children upon such separation fall to the father or mother's lot, as such contract does determine.

§. 83. For all the ends of marriage being to be obtained under politic government, as well as in the state of nature, the civil magistrate does not abridge the right or power of either naturally necessary to those ends, viz. procreation and mutual support and assistance while they are together; but only decides any controversy that may arise between man and wife about them. If it were otherwise, and that absolute sovereignty and power of life and death naturally belonged to the husband, and were necessary to the society between man and wife, there could be no matrimony in any of those countries where the husband is allowed no such absolute authority. But the ends of matrimony requiring no such power in the husband, the condition of conjugal society put it not in him, it being not at all necessary to that state. Conjugal society could subsist and attain its ends without it; nay, community of goods, and the power over them, mutual assistance and maintenance, and other things belonging to conjugal society, might be varied and regulated by that contract which unites man and wife in that society, as far as may consist with procreation and the bringing up of children till they could shift for themselves; nothing being necessary to any society, that is not necessary to the ends for which it is made.

§. 84. The society between parents and children, and the distinct rights and powers belonging respectively to them, I have treated of so largely, in the foregoing chapter that I shall not here need to say anything of it. And I think it is plain, that it is far different from a political society.

§. 85. Master and servant are names as old as history, but given to those of far different condition; for a freeman makes himself a servant to another, by selling him, for a certain time, the service he undertakes to do, in exchange for wages he is to receive: and though this commonly puts him into the family of his master, and under the ordinary discipline thereof; yet it gives the master but a temporary power over him, and no greater than what is contained in the contract between them. But there is another sort of servants, which by a peculiar name we call slaves, who being captives taken in a just war, are by the right of nature subjected to the absolute dominion and arbitrary power of their masters. These men having, as I say, forfeited their lives, and with it their liberties, and lost their estates; and being in the state of slavery, not capable of any property, cannot in that state be considered as any part of civil society; the chief end whereof is the preservation of property.

§. 86. Let us therefore consider a master of a family with all these subordinate relations of wife, children, servants, and slaves, united under the domestic rule of a family; which, what resemblance soever it may have in its order, offices, and number too, with a little commonwealth, yet is very far from it, both in its constitution, power and end: or if it must be thought a monarchy, and the paterfamilias the absolute monarch in it, absolute monarchy will have but a very shattered and short power, when it is plain, by what has been said before, that the master of the family has a very distinct and differently limited power, both as to time and extent, over those several persons that are in it; for excepting the slave (and the family is as much a family, and his power as paterfamilias as great, whether there be any slaves in his family or no) he has no legislative power of life and death over any of them, and none too but what a mistress of a family may have as well as he. And he certainly can have no absolute power over the whole family, who has but a very limited one over every individual in it. But how a family, or any other society of men, differ from that which is properly political society, we shall best see, by considering wherein political society itself consists.

§. 87. Man being born, as has been proved, with a title to perfect freedom, and an uncontrolled enjoyment of all the rights and privileges of the law of nature, equally with any other man, or number of men in the world, has by nature a power, not only to preserve his property, that is, his life, liberty and estate, against the injuries and attempts of other men; but to judge of, and punish the breaches of that law in others, as he is persuaded the offence deserves, even with death itself, in crimes where the heinousness of the fact, in his opinion, requires it. But because no political society can be, nor subsist, without having in itself the power to preserve the property, and in order thereunto, punish the offences of all those of that society; there, and there only is political society, where every one of the members has quitted this natural power, resigned it up into the hands of the community in all cases that exclude him not from appealing for protection to the law established by it. And thus all private judgment of every particular member being excluded, the community comes to be umpire, by settled standing rules, indifferent, and the same to all parties; and by men having authority from the community, for the execution of those rules, decides all the differences that may happen between any members of that society concerning any matter of right; and punishes those offences which any member has committed against the society, with such penalties as the law has established: whereby it is easy to discern, who are, and who are not, in political society together. Those who are united into one body, and have a common established law and judicature to appeal to, with authority to decide controversies between them, and punish offenders, are in civil society one with another: but those who have no such common appeal, I mean on earth, are still in the state of nature, each being, where there is no other, judge for himself, and executioner; which is, as I have before showed it, the perfect state of nature.

§. 88. And thus the commonwealth comes by a power to set down what punishment shall belong to the several transgressions which they think worthy of it, committed amongst the members of that society, (which is the power of making laws) as well as it has the power to punish any injury done unto any of its members, by any-one that is not of it, (which is the power of war and peace;) and all this for the preservation of the property of all the members of that society, as far as is possible. But though every man who has entered into civil society, and is become a member of any commonwealth, has thereby quitted his power to punish offences, against the law of nature, in prosecution of his own private judgment, yet with the judgment of offences, which he has given up to the legislative in all cases, where he can appeal to the magistrate, he has given a right to the commonwealth to employ his force, for the execution of the judgments of the commonwealth, whenever he shall be called to it; which indeed are his own judgments, they being made by himself, or his representative. And herein we have the original of the legislative and executive power of civil society, which is to judge by standing laws, how far offences are to be punished, when committed within the commonwealth; and also to determine, by occasional judgments founded on the present circumstances of the fact, how far injuries from without are to be vindicated; and in both these to employ all the force of all the members, when there shall be need.

§. 89. Wherever therefore any number of men are so united into one society, as to quit everyone his executive power of the law of nature, and to resign it to the public, there and there only is a politi-cal, or civil society. And this is done, wherever any number of men, in the state of nature, enter into society to make one people, one body politic, under one supreme government; or else when anyone joins himself to, and incorporates with any government already made: for hereby he authorizes the society, or which is all one, the legislative thereof, to make laws for him, as the public good of the society shall require; to the execution whereof, his own assistance (as to his own decrees) is due. And this puts men out of a state of nature into that of a commonwealth, by setting up a judge on earth, with authority to determine all the controversies, and redress the injuries that may happen to any member of the commonwealth; which judge is the legislative, or magistrates appointed by it. And wherever there are any number of men, however associated, that have no such decisive power to appeal to, there they are still in the state of nature.

§. 90. Hence it is evident, that absolute monarchy, which by some men is counted the only government in the world, is indeed inconsistent with civil society, and so can be no form of civil government at all: for the end of civil society, being to avoid, and remedy those inconveniences of the state of nature, which necessarily follow from every man's being judge in his own case, by setting up a known authority, to which everyone of that society may appeal upon any injury received, or controversy that may arise, and which everyone of the society ought to obey;° wherever any persons are, who have not such an authority to appeal to, for the decision of any difference between them, there those persons are still in the state of nature; and so is every absolute prince, in respect of those who are under his dominion.

(°*The public power of all society is above every soul contained in the same society; and the principal use of that power is, to give laws unto all that are under it, which laws in such cases we must obey, unless there be reason showed which may necessarily inforce, that the law of reason, or of God, doth enjoin the contrary,* Hooker's *Eccl. Pol. lib.* 1. sect. 16.)

§. 91. For he being supposed to have all, both legislative and executive power in himself alone, there is no judge to be found, no appeal lies open to anyone, who may fairly, and indifferently, and with authority decide, and from whose decision relief and redress may be expected of any injury or inconvenience, that may be suffered from the prince, or by his order: so that such a man, however entitled, Czar, or Grand Seignior, or how you please, is as much in the state of nature, with all under his dominion, as he is with the rest of mankind: for wherever any two men are, who have no standing rule, and common judge to appeal to on earth, for the determination of controversies of right between them, there they are still in the state of nature, and under all the inconveniences of it,° with only this woeful difference to the subject, or rather slave of an absolute prince: that whereas, in the ordinary state of nature, he has a liberty to judge of his right, and according to the best of his power, to maintain it; now, whenever his property is invaded by the will and order of his monarch, he has not only no appeal, as those in society ought to have, but as if he were degraded from the common state of rational creatures, is denied a liberty to judge of, or to defend his right; and so is exposed to all the misery and inconveniences, that a man can fear from one, who being in the unrestrained state of nature, is yet corrupted with flattery, and armed with power.

(°*To take away all such mutual grievances, injuries and wrongs, i.e. such as attend men in the state of nature, there was no way but only by growing into composition and agreement amongst themselves, by ordaining some kind of government public, and by yielding themselves subject thereunto, that unto whom they granted authority to rule and govern, by them the peace, tranquillity and happy estate of the rest might be procured. Men always knew that where force and injury was offered, they might be defenders of themselves; they knew that however men may seek their own commodity, yet if this were done with injury unto others, it was not to be suffered, but by all men, and all good means to be withstood. Finally, they knew that no man might in reason take upon him to determine his own right, and according to his own determination proceed in maintenance thereof, in as much as every man is towards himself, and them whom he greatly affects, partial; and therefore that strifes and troubles would be endless, except they gave their common consent, all to be ordered by some, whom they should agree upon, without which consent there would be no reason that one man should take upon him to be lord or judge over another, Hooker's Eccl. Pol. lib. 1. sect. 10.*)*

§. 92. For he that thinks absolute power purifies men's blood, and corrects the baseness of human nature, need read but the history of this, or any other age, to be convinced of the contrary. He that would have been insolent and injurious in the woods of America, would not probably be much better in a throne; where perhaps learning and religion shall be found out to justify all that he shall do to his subjects, and the sword presently silence all those that dare question it: for what the protection of absolute monarchy is, what kind of fathers of their countries it makes princes to be and to what a degree of happiness and security it carries civil society, where this sort of government is grown to perfection, he that will look into the late relation of Ceylon,[5] may easily see.

§. 93. In absolute monarchies indeed, as well as other governments of the world, the subjects have an appeal to the law, and judges to decide any controversies, and restrain any violence that may happen between the subjects themselves, one amongst another. This everyone thinks necessary, and believes he deserves to be thought a declared enemy to society and mankind, who should go about to take it away. But whether this be from a true love of mankind and society, and such a charity as we owe all one to another, there is reason to doubt: for this is no more than what every man, who loves his own power, profit, or greatness, may and naturally must do, keep those animals from hurting, or destroying one another, who labor and drudge only for his pleasure and advantage; and so are taken care of, not out of any love the master has for them, but love of himself, and the profit they bring him: for if it be asked, what security, what fence is there, in such a state, against the violence and oppression of this absolute ruler? The very question can scarce be borne. They are ready to tell you, that it deserves death only to ask after safety. Between subject and subject, they will grant, there must be measures, laws and judges, for their mutual peace and security: but as for the ruler, he ought to be absolute, and is above all such circumstances; because he has power to do more hurt and wrong, it is right when he does it. To ask how you may be guarded from harm, or injury, on that side where the strongest hand is to do it, is presently the voice of faction and rebellion: as if when men quitting the state of nature entered into society, they agreed that all of them but one, should be under the restraint of laws, but that he should still retain all the liberty of the state of nature, increased with power, and made licentious by impunity. This is to think, that men are so foolish, that they take care to avoid what mischiefs may be done them by pole-cats, or foxes; but are content, nay, think it safety, to be devoured by lions.

5. A 1680 historical account of the Island of Ceylon (modern Sri Lanka) by English explorer Robert Knox (1641–1720).

§. 94. But whatever flatterers may talk to amuse people's understandings, it hinders not men from feeling; and when they per-
ceive, that any man, in what station soever, is out of the bounds of
the civil society which they are of, and that they have no appeal on
earth against any harm, they may receive from him, they are apt
to think themselves in the state of nature, in respect of him whom
they find to be so; and to take care, as soon as they can, to have that
safety and security in civil society, for which it was first instituted,
and for which only they entered into it. And therefore, though
perhaps at first, (as shall be showed more at large hereafter in the
following part of this discourse) some one good and excellent man
having got a preeminency amongst the rest, had this deference paid
to his goodness and virtue, as to a kind of natural authority, that
the chief rule, with arbitration of their differences, by a tacit consent devolved into his hands, without any other caution, but the
assurance they had of his uprightness and wisdom; yet when time,
giving authority, and (as some men would persuade us) sacredness
to customs, which the negligent, and unforeseeing innocence of
the first ages began, had brought in successors of another stamp,
the people finding their properties not secure under the government, as then it was, (whereas government has no other end but
the preservation of property) could never be safe nor at rest, nor
think themselves in civil society, till the legislature was placed in
collective bodies of men, call them senate, parliament, or what
you please.° By which means every single person became subject,
equally with other the meanest men, to those laws, which he himself, as part of the legislative, had established; nor could anyone, by
his own authority; avoid the force of the law, when once made; nor
by any pretence of superiority plead exemption, thereby to license
his own, or the miscarriages of any of his dependents.°° No man
in civil society can be exempted from the laws of it: for if any man
may do what he thinks fit, and there be no appeal on earth, for
redress or security against any harm he shall do; I ask, whether he
be not perfectly still in the state of nature, and so can be no part
or member of that civil society; unless anyone will say, the state of
nature and civil society are one and the same thing, which I have
never yet found anyone so great a patron of anarchy as to affirm.

(°*At the first, when some certain kind of regiment was once
appointed, it may be that nothing was then farther thought upon for*

the manner of governing, but all permitted unto their wisdom and discretion, which were to rule, till by experience they found this for all parts very inconvenient, so as the thing which they had devised for a remedy, did indeed but increase the sore, which it should have cured. They saw, that to live by one man's will, became the cause of all men's misery. This constrained them to come unto laws, wherein all men might see their duty beforehand, and know the penalties of transgressing them. Hooker's *Eccl. Pol. lib.* 1. sect. 10.)

(°°*Civil law being the act of the whole body politic, doth therefore overrule each several part of the same body.* Hooker, ibid.)

CHAPTER VIII
Of the Beginning of Political Societies

§. 95. Men being, as has been said, by nature, all free, equal, and independent, no one can be put out of this estate, and subjected to the political power of another, without his own consent. The only way whereby anyone divests himself of his natural liberty, and puts on the bonds of civil society, is by agreeing with other men to join and unite into a community for their comfortable, safe, and peaceable living one another, in a secure enjoyment of their properties, and a greater security against any, that are not of it. This any number of men may do, because it injures not the freedom of the rest; they are left as they were in the liberty of the state of nature. When any number of men have so consented to make one community or government, they are thereby presently incorporated, and make one body politic, wherein the majority have a right to act and conclude the rest.

§. 96. For when any number of men have, by the consent of every individual, made a community, they have thereby made that community one body, with a power to act as one body, which is only by the will and determination of the majority: for that which acts any community, being only the consent of the individuals of it, and it being necessary to that which is one body to move one way; it is necessary the body should move that way whither the greater force carries it, which is the consent of the majority: or else it is impossible it should act or continue one body, one community, which the consent of every individual that united into it, agreed that it should; and so everyone is bound by that consent to be concluded by the majority. And therefore we see, that in assemblies, empowered to act by positive laws, where no number is set by that positive law which empowers them, the act of the majority passes for the act of the whole, and of course determines, as having, by the law of nature and reason, the power of the whole.

§. 97. And thus every man, by consenting with others to make one body politic under one government, puts himself under an obligation, to everyone of that society, to submit to the determination of the majority, and to be concluded by it; or else this original compact, whereby he with others incorporates into one society, would signify nothing, and be no compact, if he be left free, and under no other ties than he was in before in the state of nature. For what appearance would there be of any compact? What new engagement if he were no farther tied by any decrees of the society, than he himself thought fit, and did actually consent to? This would be still as great a liberty, as he himself had before his compact, or anyone else in the state of nature has, who may submit himself, and consent to any acts of it if he thinks fit.

§. 98. For if the consent of the majority shall not, in reason, be received as the act of the whole, and conclude every individual; nothing but the consent of every individual can make anything to be the act of the whole: but such a consent is next impossible ever to be had, if we consider the infirmities of health, and avocations of business, which in a number, though much less than that of a commonwealth, will necessarily keep many away from the public assembly. To which if we add the variety of opinions, and contrariety of interests, which unavoidably happen in all collections of men, the coming into society upon such terms would be only like Cato's coming into the theatre,[6] only to go out again. Such a constitution as this would make the mighty *Leviathan* of a shorter duration, than the feeblest creatures, and not let it outlast the day it was born in: which cannot be supposed, till we can think, that

6. The Roman hero Cato the Younger was said to have conspicuously stridden out of a theatre in protest at what he took to be indecent and immoral behavior on stage.

rational creatures should desire and constitute societies only to be dissolved: for where the majority cannot conclude the rest, there they cannot act as one body, and consequently will be immediately dissolved again.

§. 99. Whosoever therefore out of a state of nature unite into a community, must be understood to give up all the power, necessary to the ends for which they unite into society, to the majority of the community, unless they expressly agreed in any number greater than the majority. And this is done by barely agreeing to unite into one political society, which is all the compact that is, or needs be, between the individuals, that enter into, or make up a commonwealth. And thus that, which begins and actually constitutes any political society, is nothing but the consent of any number of freemen capable of a majority to unite and incorporate into such a society. And this is that, and that only, which did, or could give beginning to any lawful government in the world.

§. 100. To this I find two objections made.

First, that there are no instances to be found in story, of a company of men independent, and equal one amongst another, that met together, and in this way began and set up a government.

Secondly, it is impossible of right that men should do so, because all men being born under government, they are to submit to that, and are not at liberty to begin a new one.

§. 101. To the first there is this to answer. That it is not at all to be wondered, that history gives us but a very little account of men that lived together in the state of nature. The inconveniences of that condition, and the love and want of society, no sooner brought any number of them together, but they presently united and incorporated, if they designed to continue together. And if we may not suppose men ever to have been in the state of nature, because we hear not much of them in such a state, we may as well suppose the armies of Salmanasser or Xerxes[7] were never children, because we hear little of them, till they were men, and embodied in armies. Government is everywhere antecedent to records, and letters

---

7. Salmanasser (or Shalmanesar) was a ninth-century BCE Assyrian king who conquered ancient Israel, and Xerxes was a Persian emperor of the fifth century (519–465 BCE) famous for his defeat by the Greeks at Salamis, in 480 BCE.

seldom come in amongst a people till a long continuation of civil society has, by other more necessary arts, provided for their safety, ease, and plenty: and then they begin to look after the history of their founders, and search into their original, when they have out-lived the memory of it: for it is with commonwealths as with par-ticular persons, they are commonly ignorant of their own births and infancies: and if they know anything of their original, they are beholding, for it, to the accidental records that others have kept of it. And those that we have, of the beginning of any polities in the world, excepting that of the Jews, where God himself immediately interposed, and which favors not at all paternal dominion, are all either plain instances of such a beginning as I have mentioned, or at least have manifest footsteps of it.

§. 102. He must show a strange inclination to deny evident mat-ter of fact, when it agrees not with his hypothesis, who will not allow that the beginning of Rome and Venice were by the unit-ing together of several men free and independent one of another, amongst whom there was no natural superiority or subjection. And if Josephus Acosta's[8] word may be taken, he tells us, that in many parts of America there was no government at all.

There are great and apparent conjectures, says he, *that these men,* speaking of those of Peru, *for a long time had neither kings nor commonwealths, but lived in troops, as they do this day in Florida, the Cheriquanas, those of Brazil, and many other nations, which have no certain kings, but as occasion is offered, in peace or war, they choose their captains as they please, lib. 1. c. 25.*

If it be said, that every man there was born subject to his father, or the head of his family; that the subjection due from a child to a father took not away his freedom of uniting into what political society he thought fit, has been already proved. But be that as it will, these men, it is evident, were actually free; and what-ever superiority some politicians now would place in any of them, they themselves claimed it not, but by consent were all equal, till by the same consent they set rulers over themselves. So that their politic societies all began from a voluntary union, and the mutual

8. José de Acosta (1539–1600) was a Spanish Jesuit missionary whose *Natural and Moral History of the Indies* (1604) was a widely read account of the New World in Locke's time.

agreement of men freely acting in the choice of their governors, and forms of government.

§. 103. And I hope those who went away from Sparta with Palantus,[9] mentioned by Justin, 1. iii. c. 4. will be allowed to have been free-men independent one of another, and to have set up a government over themselves, by their own consent. Thus I have given several examples, out of history, of people free and in the state of nature that being met together incorporated and began a commonwealth. And if the want of such instances be an argument to prove that government were not, nor could not be so begun, I suppose the contenders for paternal empire were better let it alone, than urge it against natural liberty. For if they can give so many instances, out of history, of governments begun upon paternal right, I think (though at best an argument from what has been, to what should of right be, has no great force) one might, without any great danger, yield them the cause. But if I might advise them in the case, they would do well not to search too much into the original of governments, as they have begun de facto, lest they should find, at the foundation of most of them, something very little favorable to the design they promote, and such a power as they contend for.

§. 104. But to conclude, reason being plain on our side, that men are naturally free, and the examples of history showing, that the governments of the world, that were begun in peace, had their beginning laid on that foundation, and were made by the consent of the people; there can be little room for doubt, either where the right is, or what has been the opinion, or practice of mankind, about the first erecting of governments.

§. 105. I will not deny that if we look back as far as history will direct us, toward the original of commonwealths, we shall generally find them under the government and administration of one man. And I am also apt to believe, that where a family was numerous enough to subsist by itself, and continued entire together, without

9. A Spartan who was chosen by his peers to be leader of the Dorian colony at Tarentum in Italy in the eighth century BCE. This is a reference to an account in the work *Ex Trogi Pompei, historiis* authored by Latin historian Marcus Junianius Justinus of the Roman Empire who lived in the second or third century CE.

mixing with others, as it often happens, where there is much land, and few people, the government commonly began in the father. For the father having, by the law of nature, the same power with every man else to punish, as he thought fit, any offences against that law, might thereby punish his transgressing children, even when they were men, and out of their pupilage; and they were very likely to submit to his punishment, and all join with him against the offender, in their turns, giving him thereby power to execute his sentence against any transgression, and so in effect make him the law-maker, and governor over all that remained in conjunction with his family. He was fittest to be trusted; paternal affection secured their property and interest under his care; and the custom of obeying him, in their childhood, made it easier to submit to him, rather than to any other. If therefore they must have one to rule them, as government is hardly to be avoided amongst men that live together; who so likely to be the man as he that was their common father; unless negligence, cruelty, or any other defect of mind or body made him unfit for it? But when either the father died, and left his next heir, for want of age, wisdom, courage, or any other qualities, less fit for rule; or where several families met, and consented to continue together; there, it is not to be doubted, but they used their natural freedom, to set up him, whom they judged the ablest, and most likely, to rule well over them. Conformable hereunto we find the people of America, who (living out of the reach of the conquering swords, and spreading domination of the two great empires of Peru and Mexico) enjoyed their own natural freedom, though, ceteris paribus, they commonly prefer the heir of their deceased king; yet if they find him any way weak, or incapable, they pass him by, and set up the stoutest and bravest man for their ruler.

§. 106. Thus, though looking back as far as records give us any account of peopling the world, and the history of nations, we commonly find the government to be in one hand; yet it destroys not that which I affirm, viz. that the beginning of politic society depends upon the consent of the individuals, to join into, and make one society; who, when they are thus incorporated, might set up what form of government they thought fit. But this having given occasion to men to mistake, and think, that by nature government was monarchical, and belonged to the father, it may not be amiss here to consider, why people in the beginning generally pitched upon this form, which though perhaps the father's preeminency might, in the first institution of some commonwealths, give a rise to, and place in the beginning, the power in one hand; yet it is plain that the reason, that continued the form of government in a single person, was not any regard, or respect to paternal authority; since all petty monarchies, that is, almost all monarchies, near their original, have been commonly, at least upon occasion, elective.

§. 107. First then, in the beginning of things, the father's government of the childhood of those sprung from him, having accustomed them to the rule of one man, and taught them that where it was exercised with care and skill, with affection and love to those under it, it was sufficient to procure and preserve to men all the political happiness they sought for in society. It was no wonder that they should pitch upon, and naturally run into that form of government, which from their infancy they had been all accustomed to; and which, by experience, they had found both easy and safe. To which, if we add, that monarchy being simple, and most obvious to men, whom neither experience had instructed in forms of government, nor the ambition or insolence of empire had taught to beware of the encroachments of prerogative, or the inconveniences of absolute power, which monarchy in succession was apt to lay claim to, and bring upon them, it was not at all strange, that they should not much trouble themselves to think of methods of restraining any exorbitances of those to whom they had given the authority over them, and of balancing the power of government, by placing several parts of it in different hands. They had neither felt the oppression of tyrannical dominion, nor did the fashion of the age, nor their possessions, or way of living, (which afforded little matter for covetousness or ambition) give them any reason to apprehend or provide against it; and therefore it is no wonder they put themselves into such a frame of government, as was not only, as I said, most obvious and simple, but also best suited to their present state and condition; which stood more in need of defense against foreign invasions and injuries, than of multiplicity of laws. The equality of a simple poor way of living, confining their desires within the narrow bounds of each man's small property, made few controversies, and so no need of many laws to decide them, or variety of officers to superintend the process, or look after the execution of justice, where there were but few trespasses, and few offenders. Since then those, who like one another so well as to join into society, cannot but be supposed to have some acquaintance and friendship together, and some trust one in another; they could not but have greater apprehensions of others, than of one another: and therefore their first care and thought cannot but be supposed to be, how to secure themselves against foreign force. It was natural for them to put themselves under a frame of government which might best serve to that end, and choose the wisest and bravest man to conduct them in their wars, and lead them out against their enemies, and in this chiefly be their ruler.

§. 108. Thus we see, that the kings of the Indians in America, which is still a pattern of the first ages in Asia and Europe, while the inhabitants were too few for the country, and want of people and money gave men no temptation to enlarge their possessions of land, or contest for wider extent of ground, are little more than generals of their armies; and though they command absolutely in war, yet at home and in time of peace they exercise very little dominion, and have but a very moderate sovereignty, the resolutions of peace and war being ordinarily either in the people, or in a council. Though the war itself, which admits not of plurality of governors, naturally devolves the command into the king's sole authority.

§. 109. And thus in Israel itself, the chief business of their judges, and first kings, seems to have been to be captains in war, and leaders of their armies; which (besides what is signified by going out and in before the people, which was, to march forth to war, and home again in the heads of their forces) appears plainly in the story of Jephtha. The Ammonites making war upon Israel, the Gileadites in fear send to Jephtha, a bastard of their family whom they had cast off, and article with him, if he will assist them against the Ammonites, to make him their ruler; which they do in these words, *And the people made him head and captain over them*, Judg. 11.11. which was, as it seems, all one as to be judge. *And he judged Israel*, Judg. 12. 7. that is, was their captain-general six years. So when Jotham upbraids the Shechemites with the obligation they had to Gideon, who had been their judge and ruler, he tells them, *He fought for you, and adventured his life far, and delivered you out of the hands of Midian,* Judg. 9. 17. Nothing mentioned of him but what he did as a general: and indeed that is all is found in his history, or in any of the rest of the judges. And Abimelech particularly is called king, though at most he was but their general. And when, being weary of the ill conduct of Samuel's sons, the children of Israel desired a king, *like all the nations to judge them, and to go out before them, and to fight their battles,* I. Sam 8. 20. God granting their desire, says to Samuel, *I will send thee a man, and thou shalt anoint him to be captain over my people Israel, that he may save my people out of the hands of the Philistines,* 9. 16. As if the only business of a king had been to lead out their armies, and fight in their defense; and accordingly at his inauguration pouring a vial of oil upon him, declares to Saul, *that the Lord had anointed him to be captain over his inheritance,* 10. 1. And therefore those, who after Saul's being solemnly chosen and saluted king by the tribes at Mispah, were unwilling to have him their king, make no other objection but this, *How shall this man save us?* 5. 27. as if they should have said, this man is unfit to be our king, not having skill and conduct enough in war, to be able to defend us. And when God resolved to transfer the government to David, it is in these words, *But now thy kingdom shall not continue: the Lord has sought him a man after his own heart, and the Lord has commanded him to be captain over his people,* 13. 14. As if the whole kingly authority were nothing else but to be their general: and therefore the tribes who had stuck to Saul's family, and opposed David's reign, when they came to Hebron with terms of submission to him, they tell him, amongst other arguments they had to submit to him as to their king, that he was in effect their king in Saul's time, and therefore they had no reason but to receive him as their king now. Also (say they) *in time past, when Saul was king over us, thou wast he that leddest out and broughtest in Israel, and the Lord said unto thee, Thou shalt feed my people Israel, and thou shalt be a captain over Israel.*

§. 110. Thus, whether a family by degrees grew up into a commonwealth, and the fatherly authority being continued on to the elder son, everyone in his turn growing up under it, tacitly submitted to it, and the easiness and equality of it not offending anyone, everyone acquiesced, till time seemed to have confirmed it, and settled a right of succession by prescription: or whether several families, or the descendants of several families, whom chance, neighborhood, or business brought together, uniting into society, the need of a general, whose conduct might defend them against their enemies in war, and the great confidence the innocence and sincerity of that poor but virtuous age, (such as are almost all those which begin governments, that ever come to last in the world) gave men one of another, made the first beginners of commonwealths generally put the rule into one man's hand, without any other express limitation or restraint, but what the nature of the thing, and the end of government required: whichever of these it was that at first put the rule into the hands of a single person, certain it is nobody was entrusted with it but for the public good and safety, and to those ends, in the infancies of commonwealths, those who had it commonly used it. And unless they had done so, young societies could not have subsisted; without such nursing fathers tender and careful of the public weal, all governments would have sunk under the weakness and infirmities of their infancy, and the prince and the people had soon perished together.

§. 111. But though the golden age (before vain ambition, and *amor sceleratus habendi*, evil concupiscence, had corrupted men's minds into a mistake of true power and honor) had more virtue, and consequently better governors, as well as less vicious subjects, and there was then no stretching prerogative on the one side, to oppress the people; nor consequently on the other, any dispute about privilege, to lessen or restrain the power of the magistrate, and so no contest between rulers and people about governors or government: yet, when ambition and luxury in future ages° would retain and increase the power, without doing the business for which it was given; and aided by flattery, taught princes to have distinct and separate interests from their people, men found it necessary to examine more carefully the original and rights of government; and to find out ways to restrain the exorbitances, and prevent the abuses of that power, which they having entrusted in another's hands only for their own good, they found was made use of to hurt them.

(°*At first, when some certain kind of regiment was once approved, it may be nothing was then farther thought upon for the manner of governing, but all permitted unto their wisdom and discretion which were to rule, till by experience they found this for all parts very inconvenient, so as the thing which they had devised for a remedy, did indeed but increase the sore which it should have cured. They saw, that to live by one man's will, became the cause of all men's misery. This constrained them to come unto laws wherein all men might see their duty before hand, and know the penalties of transgressing them.* Hooker's *Eccl. Pol. lib.* 1. sect. 10.)

§. 112. Thus we may see how probable it is, that people that were naturally free, and by their own consent either submitted to the government of their father, or united together out of different families to make a government, should generally put the rule into one man's hands, and choose to be under the conduct of a single person, without so much as by express conditions limiting or regulating his power, which they thought safe enough in his honesty and prudence; though they never dreamed of monarchy being *jure divino*, which we never heard of amongst mankind, till it was revealed to us by the divinity of this last age; nor ever allowed paternal power to have a right to dominion, or to be the foundation of all government. And thus much may suffice to show, that as far as we have any light from history, we have reason to conclude, that all peaceful beginnings of government have been laid in the consent of the people. I say peaceful, because I shall have occasion in another place to speak of conquest, which some esteem a way of beginning of governments.

The other objection I find urged against the beginning of polities, in the way I have mentioned, is this, viz.

§. 113. That all men being born under government, some or other, it is impossible any of them should ever be free, and at liberty to unite together, and begin a new one, or ever be able to erect a lawful government.

If this argument be good; I ask, how came so many lawful monarchies into the world? For if anybody, upon this supposition,

can show me any one man in any age of the world free to begin a
lawful monarchy, I will be bound to show him ten other freemen
at liberty, at the same time to unite and begin a new government
under a regal, or any other form; it being demonstration, that if
anyone, born under the dominion of another, may be so free as
to have a right to command others in a new and distinct empire,
everyone that is born under the dominion of another may be so
free too, and may become a ruler, or subject, of a distinct separate
government. And so by this their own principle, either all men,
however born, are free, or else there is but one lawful prince, one
lawful government in the world. And then they have nothing to
do, but barely to show us which that is. Which when they have
done, I doubt not but all mankind will easily agree to pay obedience to him.

§. 114. Though it be a sufficient answer to their objection, to show
that it involves them in the same difficulties that it does those they
use it against; yet I shall endeavor to discover the weakness of this
argument a little farther. All men, say they, are born under government, and therefore they cannot be at liberty to begin a new one.
Everyone is born a subject to his father, or his prince, and is therefore under the perpetual tie of subjection and allegiance.

It is plain mankind never owned nor considered any such natural subjection that they were born in, to one or to the other that
tied them, without their own consents, to a subjection to them and
their heirs.

§. 115. For there are no examples so frequent in history, both
sacred and profane, as those of men withdrawing themselves, and
their obedience, from the jurisdiction they were born under, and
the family or community they were bred up in, and setting up new
governments in other places; from whence sprang all that number of petty commonwealths in the beginning of ages, and which
always multiplied, as long as there was room enough, till the stronger, or more fortunate, swallowed the weaker; and those great
ones again breaking to pieces, dissolved into lesser dominions.
All which are so many testimonies against paternal sovereignty,
and plainly prove, that it was not the natural right of the father
descending to his heirs, that made governments in the beginning,

since it was impossible, upon that ground, there should have been so many little kingdoms; all must have been but only one universal monarchy, if men had not been at liberty to separate themselves from their families, and the government, be it what it will, that was set up in it, and go and make distinct commonwealths and other governments, as they thought fit.

§. 116. This has been the practice of the world from its first beginning to this day; nor is it now any more hindrance to the freedom of mankind, that they are born under constituted and ancient polities, that have established laws, and set forms of government, than if they were born in the woods, amongst the unconfined inhabitants, that ran loose in them: for those, who would persuade us, that by being born under any government, we are naturally subjects to it, and have no more any title or pretence to the freedom of the state of nature, have no other reason (bating[10] that of paternal power, which we have already answered) to produce for it, but only, because our fathers or progenitors passed away their natural liberty, and thereby bound up themselves and their posterity to a perpetual subjection to the government, which they themselves submitted to. It is true, that whatever engagements or promises anyone has made for himself, he is under the obligation of them, but cannot, by any compact whatsoever, bind his children or posterity: for his son, when a man, being altogether as free as the father, any act of the father can no more give away the liberty of the son, than it can of anybody else: he may indeed annex such conditions to the land, he enjoyed as a subject of any commonwealth, as may oblige his son to be of that community, if he will enjoy those possessions which were his father's; because that estate being his father's property, he may dispose, or settle it, as he pleases.

§. 117. And this has generally given the occasion to mistake in this matter; because commonwealths not permitting any part of their dominions to be dismembered, nor to be enjoyed by any but those of their community, the son cannot ordinarily enjoy the possessions of his father, but under the same terms his father did, by becoming a member of the society; whereby he puts himself presently under the government he finds there established, as much as any other subject of that commonwealth. And thus the consent of

10. See I: 12 Note 9.

freemen, born under government, which only makes them members of it, being given separately in their turns, as each comes to be of age, and not in a multitude together; people take no notice of it, and thinking it not done at all, or not necessary, conclude they are naturally subjects as they are men.

§. 118. But, it is plain, governments themselves understand it otherwise; they claim no power over the son, because of that they had over the father; nor look on children as being their subjects, by their fathers being so. If a subject of England has a child, by an English woman in France, whose subject is he? Not the king of England's; for he must have leave to be admitted to the privileges of it: nor the king of France's; for how then has his father a liberty to bring him away, and breed him as he pleases? And who ever was judged as a traitor or deserter, if he left, or warred against a country, for being barely born in it of parents that were aliens there? It is plain then, by the practice of governments themselves, as well as by the law of right reason, that a child is born a subject of no country or government. He is under his father's tuition and authority, till he comes to age of discretion; and then he is a freeman, at liberty what government he will put himself under, what body politic he will unite himself to: for if an Englishman's son, born in France, be at liberty, and may do so, it is evident there is no tie upon him by his father's being a subject of this kingdom; nor is he bound up by any compact of his ancestors. And why then has not his son, by the same reason, the same liberty, though he be born anywhere else? Since the power that a father has naturally over his children, is the same, wherever they be born, and the ties of natural obligations, are not bounded by the positive limits of kingdoms and commonwealths.

§. 119. Every man being, as has been shown, naturally free, and nothing being able to put him into subjection to any earthly power, but only his own consent; it is to be considered, what shall be understood to be a sufficient declaration of a man's consent, to make him subject to the laws of any government. There is a common distinction of an express and a tacit consent, which will concern our present case. Nobody doubts but an express consent, of any man entering into any society, makes him a perfect member of that society, a subject of that government. The difficulty is, what ought to be looked upon as a tacit consent, and how far it binds, i.e. how far anyone shall be looked on to have consented, and thereby submitted to any government, where he has made no expressions of it at all. And to this I say, that every man, that has any possessions, or enjoyment, of any part of the dominions of any government, does thereby give his tacit consent, and is as far forth obliged to obedience to the laws of that government, during such enjoyment, as anyone under it; whether this his possession be of land, to him and his heirs forever, or a lodging only for a week; or whether it be barely travelling freely on the highway; and in effect, it reaches as far as the very being of anyone within the territories of that government.

§. 120. To understand this the better, it is fit to consider, that every man, when he at first incorporates himself into any commonwealth, he, by his uniting himself thereunto, annexed also, and submits to the community, those possessions, which he has, or shall acquire, that do not already belong to any other government: for it would be a direct contradiction, for anyone to enter into society with others for the securing and regulating of property; and yet to suppose his land, whose property is to be regulated by the laws of the society, should be exempt from the jurisdiction of that government, to which he himself, the proprietor of the land, is a subject. By the same act therefore, whereby anyone unites his person, which was before free, to any commonwealth, by the same he unites his possessions, which were before free, to it also; and they become, both of them, person and possession, subject to the government and dominion of that commonwealth, as long as it has a being. Whoever therefore, from thenceforth, by inheritance, purchase, permission, or otherwise, enjoys any part of the land, so annexed to, and under the government of that commonwealth, must take it with the condition it is under; that is, of submitting to the government of the commonwealth, under whose jurisdiction it is, as far forth as any subject of it.

§. 121. But since the government has a direct jurisdiction only over the land, and reaches the possessor of it, (before he has actually incorporated himself in the society) only as he dwells upon, and enjoys that; the obligation anyone is under, by virtue of such enjoyment, to submit to the government, begins and ends with the enjoyment; so that whenever the owner, who has given nothing but such a tacit consent to the government, will, by donation, sale, or otherwise, quit the said possession, he is at liberty to go and incorporate himself into any other commonwealth; or to agree with others to begin a new one, *in vacuis locis*, in any part of the world, they can find free and unpossessed: whereas he, that has once, by actual agreement, and any express declaration, given his consent to be of any commonwealth, is perpetually and indispensably obliged to be, and remain unalterably a subject to it, and can never be again in the liberty of the state of nature; unless, by any calamity, the government he was under comes to be dissolved; or else by some public act cuts him off from being any longer a member of it.

§. 122. But submitting to the laws of any country, living quietly, and enjoying privileges and protection under them, makes not a man a member of that society: this is only a local protection and homage due to and from all those, who, not being in a state of war, come within the territories belonging to any government, to all parts whereof the force of its laws extends. But this no more makes a man a member of that society, a perpetual subject of that commonwealth, than it would make a man a subject to another, in whose family he found it convenient to abide for some time; though, while he continued in it, he were obliged to comply with the laws, and submit to the government he found there. And thus we see, that foreigners, by living all their lives under another government, and enjoying the privileges and protection of it, though they are bound, even in conscience, to submit to its administration, as far forth as any denizen; yet do not thereby come to be subjects or members of that commonwealth. Nothing can make any man so, but his actually entering into it by positive engagement, and express promise and compact. This is that, which I think, concerning the beginning of political societies, and that consent which makes anyone a member of any commonwealth.

CHAPTER IX
Of the Ends of Political Society and Government

§. 123. If man in the state of nature be so free, as has been said; if he be absolute lord of his own person and possessions, equal to the greatest, and subject to nobody, why will he part with his freedom? Why will he give up this empire, and subject himself to the dominion and control of any other power? To which it is obvious to answer, that though in the state of nature he has such a right, yet the enjoyment of it is very uncertain, and constantly exposed to the invasion of others: for all being kings as much as he, every man his equal, and the greater part no strict observers of equity and justice, the enjoyment of the property he has in this state is very unsafe, very unsecure. This makes him willing to quit a condition, which, however free, is full of fears and continual dangers: and it is not without reason, that he seeks out, and is willing to join in society with others, who are already united, or have a mind to unite, for the mutual preservation of their lives, liberties and estates, which I call by the general name, property.

§. 124. The great and chief end, therefore, of men's uniting into commonwealths, and putting themselves under government, is the preservation of their property. To which in the state of nature there are many things wanting.

First, there wants an established, settled, known law, received and allowed by common consent to be the standard of right and wrong, and the common measure to decide all controversies between them: for though the law of nature be plain and intelligible to all rational creatures; yet men being biased by their interest, as well as ignorant for want of study of it, are not apt to allow of it as a law binding to them in the application of it to their particular cases.

§. 125. Secondly, in the state of nature there wants a known and indifferent judge, with authority to determine all differences according to the established law: for everyone in that state being both judge and executioner of the law of nature, men being partial to themselves, passion and revenge is very apt to carry them too far, and with too much heat, in their own cases; as well as negligence, and unconcernedness, to make them too remiss in other men's.

§. 126. Thirdly, in the state of nature there often wants power to back and support the sentence when right, and to give it due execution. They who by any injustice offended, will seldom fail, where they are able, by force to make good their injustice; such resistance many times makes the punishment dangerous, and frequently destructive, to those who attempt it.

§. 127. Thus mankind, notwithstanding all the privileges of the state of nature, being but in an ill condition, while they remain in it, are quickly driven into society. Hence it comes to pass, that we seldom find any number of men live any time together in this state. The inconveniences that they are therein exposed to, by the irregular and uncertain exercise of the power every man has of punishing the transgressions of others, make them take sanctuary under the established laws of government, and therein seek the preservation of their property. It is this makes them so willingly give up everyone his single power of punishing, to be exercised by such alone, as shall be appointed to it amongst them; and by such rules as the community, or those authorized by them to that purpose, shall agree on. And in this we have the original right and rise of both the legislative and executive power, as well as of the governments and societies themselves.

§. 128. For in the state of nature, to omit the liberty he has of innocent delights, a man has two powers.

The first is to do whatsoever he thinks fit for the preservation of himself, and others within the permission of the law of nature: by which law, common to them all, he and all the rest of mankind are one community, make up one society, distinct from all other creatures. And were it not for the corruption and viciousness of degenerate men, there would be no need of any other; no necessity that men should separate from this great and natural community, and by positive agreements combine into smaller and divided associations.

The other power a man has in the state of nature is the power to punish the crimes committed against that law. Both these he gives up, when he joins in a private, if I may so call it, or particular political society, and incorporates into any commonwealth, separate from the rest of mankind.

§. 129. The first power, viz. of doing whatsoever he thought for the preservation of himself, and the rest of mankind, he gives up to be regulated by laws made by the society, so far forth as the preservation of himself, and the rest of that society shall require; which laws of the society in many things confine the liberty he had by the law of nature.

§. 130. Secondly, the power of punishing he wholly gives up, and engages his natural force, (which he might before employ in the execution of the law of nature, by his own single authority, as he thought fit) to assist the executive power of the society, as the law thereof shall require: for being now in a new state, wherein he is to enjoy many conveniences, from the labor, assistance, and society of others in the same community, as well as protection from its whole strength; he is to part also with as much of his natural liberty, in providing for himself, as the good, prosperity, and safety of the society shall require; which is not only necessary, but just, since the other members of the society do the like.

§. 131. But though men, when they enter into society, give up the equality, liberty, and executive power they had in the state of nature, into the hands of the society, to be so far disposed of by the legislative, as the good of the society shall require; yet it being only with an intention in everyone the better to preserve himself, his liberty and property; (for no rational creature can be supposed to change his condition with an intention to be worse) the power of the society, or legislative constituted by them, can never be supposed to extend farther, than the common good; but is obliged to secure everyone's property, by providing against those three defects above mentioned, that made the state of nature so unsafe and uneasy. And so whoever has the legislative or supreme power of any commonwealth, is bound to govern by established standing laws, promulgated and known to the people, and not by extemporary decrees; by indifferent and upright judges, who are to decide controversies by those laws; and to employ the force of the community at home, only in the execution of such laws, or abroad to prevent or redress foreign injuries, and secure the community from inroads and invasion. And all this to be directed to no other end, but the peace, safety, and public good of the people.

CHAPTER X
Of the Forms of a Commonwealth

§. 132. The majority having, as has been showed, upon men's first uniting into society, the whole power of the community naturally in them, may employ all that power in making laws for the community from time to time, and executing those laws by officers of their own appointing; and then the form of the government is a perfect democracy: or else may put the power of making laws into the hands of a few select men, and their heirs or successors; and then it is an oligarchy: or else into the hands of one man, and then it is a monarchy: if to him and his heirs, it is an hereditary monarchy: if to him only for life, but upon his death the power only of nominating a successor to return to them; an elective monarchy. And so accordingly of these the community may make compounded and mixed forms of government, as they think good. And if the legislative power be at first given by the majority to one or more persons only for their lives, or any limited time, and then the supreme power to revert to them again; when it is so reverted, the community may dispose of it again anew into what hands they please, and so constitute a new form of government: for the form of government depending upon the placing the supreme power, which is the legislative, it being impossible to conceive that an inferior power should prescribe to a superior, or any but the supreme make laws, according as the power of making laws is placed, such is the form of the commonwealth.

§. 133. By commonwealth, I must be understood all along to mean, not a democracy, or any form of government, but any independent community, which the Latins signified by the word *civitas*, to which the word which best answers in our language, is commonwealth, and most properly expresses such a society of men, which community or city in English does not; for there may be subordinate communities in a government; and city amongst us has a quite different notion from commonwealth: and therefore, to avoid ambiguity, I crave leave to use the word *commonwealth* in that sense, in which I find it used by King James the First[11]; and I take it to be its genuine signification; which if anybody dislike, I consent with him to change it for a better.

CHAPTER XI
Of the Extent of the Legislative Power

§. 134. The great end of men's entering into society, being the enjoyment of their properties in peace and safety, and the great instrument and means of that being the laws established in that society; the first and fundamental positive law of all commonwealths is the establishing of the legislative power; as the first and fundamental natural law, which is to govern even the legislative itself, is the preservation of the society, and (as far as will consist with the public good) of every person in it. This legislative is not only the supreme power of the commonwealth, but sacred and unalterable in the hands where the community have once placed it; nor can any edict of anybody else, in what form soever conceived, or by what power soever backed, have the force and obligation of a law, which has not its sanction from that legislative which the public has chosen and appointed: for without this the law could not have that, which is absolutely necessary to its being a law,° the consent of the society, over whom nobody can have a power to make laws, but by their own consent, and by authority received from them; and therefore all the obedience, which by the most solemn ties anyone can be obliged to pay, ultimately terminates in this supreme power, and is directed by those laws which it enacts: nor can any oaths to any foreign power whatsoever, or any domestic subordinate power, discharge any member of the society from his obedience to the legislative, acting pursuant to their trust; nor oblige him to any obedience contrary to the laws so enacted, or farther than they do allow; it being ridiculous to imagine one

11. King James I of England (1566–1625; reigned 1603–1625) was also King James VI of Scotland (reigned 1567–1625). He succeeded to the English throne following the death of Elizabeth I in 1603. In the early decades of the seventeenth century he wrote a number of treatises defending the power of kings.

can be tied ultimately to obey any power in the society, which is not the supreme.

(°*The lawful power of making laws to command whole politic societies of men, belonging so properly unto the same intire societies, that for any prince or potentate of what kind soever upon earth, to exercise the same of himself, and not by express commission immediately and personally received from God, or else by authority derived at the first from their consent, upon whose persons they impose laws, it is no better than meer tyranny. Laws they are not therefore which public approbation hath not made so. Hooker's Eccl. Pol. lib. 1. sect. 10. Of this point therefore we are to note, that since men naturally have no full and perfect power to command whole politic multitudes of men, therefore utterly without our consent, we could in such sort be at no mans commandment living. And to be commanded we do consent, when that society, whereof we be a part, hath at any time before consented, without revoking the same after by the like universal agreement. Laws therefore humane, of what kind so ever, are available by consent. Ibid.*)

§. 135. Though the legislative, whether placed in one or more, whether it be always in being, or only by intervals, though it be the supreme power in every commonwealth; yet:

First, it is not, nor can possibly be absolutely arbitrary over the lives and fortunes of the people: for it being but the joint power of every member of the society given up to that person, or assembly, which is legislator; it can be no more than those persons had in a state of nature before they entered into society, and gave up to the community: for nobody can transfer to another more power than he has in himself; and nobody has an absolute arbitrary power over himself, or over any other, to destroy his own life, or take away the life or property of another. A man, as has been proved, cannot subject himself to the arbitrary power of another; and having in the state of nature no arbitrary power over the life, liberty, or possession of another, but only so much as the law of nature gave him for the preservation of himself, and the rest of mankind; this is all he does, or can give up to the commonwealth, and by it to the legislative power, so that the legislative can have no more than this. Their power, in the utmost bounds of it, is limited to the public good of the society. It is a power, that has no other end but preservation, and therefore can never have a right to destroy, enslave, or designedly to impoverish the subjects.° The obligations of the law of nature cease not in society, but only in many cases are drawn closer, and have by human laws known penalties annexed to them, to enforce their observation. Thus the law of nature stands as an eternal rule to all men, legislators as well as others. The rules that they make for other men's actions, must, as well as their own and other men's actions, be conformable to the law of nature, i.e. to the will of God, of which that is a declaration, and the fundamental law of nature being the preservation of mankind, no human sanction can be good, or valid against it.

(°*Two foundations there are which bear up public societies; the one a natural inclination, whereby all men desire sociable life and fellowship; the other an order, expressly or secretly agreed upon, touching the manner of their union in living together: the latter is that which we call the law of a commonweal, the very soul of a politic body, the parts whereof are by law animated, held together, and set on work in such actions as the common good requireth. Laws politic, ordain'd for external order and regiment among men, are never framed as they should be, unless presuming the will of man to be inwardly obstinate, rebellious, and averse from all obedience to the sacred laws of his nature; in a word, unless presuming man to be, in regard of his depraved mind, little better than a wild beast, they do accordingly provide, notwithstanding, so to frame his outward actions, that they be no hindrance unto the common good, for which societies are instituted. Unless they do this, they are not perfect.* Hooker's *Eccl. Pol. lib.* 1. sect. 10.)

§. 136. Secondly, the legislative, or supreme authority, cannot assume to itself a power to rule by extemporary arbitrary decrees, but is bound to dispense justice, and decide the rights of the subject by promulgated standing laws, and known authorized judges:° for the law of nature being unwritten, and so nowhere to be found but in the minds of men, they who through passion or interest shall miscite, or misapply it, cannot so easily be convinced of their mistake where there is no established judge: and so it serves not, as it ought, to determine the rights, and fence the properties of those that live under it, especially where everyone is judge, interpreter, and executioner of it too, and that in his own case: and he that has right on his side, having ordinarily but his own single strength, has not force enough to defend himself from injuries, or to punish delinquents. To avoid these inconveniences, which disorder men's properties in the state of nature, men unite into societies, that they may have the united strength of the whole society to secure and defend their properties, and may have standing rules to bound it, by which everyone may know what is his. To this end it is that men give up all their natural power to the society which they enter into, and the community put the legislative power into such hands as they think fit, with this trust, that they shall be governed by declared laws, or else their peace, quiet, and property will still be at the same uncertainty, as it was in the state of nature.

(°*Humane laws are measures in respect of men whose actions they must direct, howbeit such measures they are as have also their higher rules to be measured by, which rules are two, the law of God, and the law of nature; so that laws humane must be made according to the general laws of nature, and without contradiction to any positive law of scripture, otherwise they are ill made.* Hooker's *Eccl. Pol. lib.* 3. sect. 9. *To constrain men to anything inconvenient doth seem unreasonable.* Ibid. l. i. sect. 10.)

§. 137. Absolute arbitrary power, or governing without settled standing laws, can neither of them consist with the ends of society and government, which men would not quit the freedom of the state of nature for, and tie themselves up under, were it not to preserve their lives, liberties and fortunes, and by stated rules of right and property to secure their peace and quiet. It cannot be supposed that they should intend, had they a power so to do, to give to any one, or more, an absolute arbitrary power over their persons and estates, and put a force into the magistrate's hand to execute his unlimited will arbitrarily upon them. This were to put themselves into a worse condition than the state of nature, wherein they had a liberty to defend their right against the injuries of others, and were upon equal terms of force to maintain it, whether invaded by a single man, or many in combination. Whereas by supposing they have given up themselves to the absolute arbitrary power and will of a legislator, they have disarmed themselves, and armed him, to make a prey of them when he pleases; he being in a much worse condition, who is exposed to the arbitrary power of one man, who has the command of 100,000, than he that is exposed to the arbitrary power of 100,000 single men; nobody being secure, that his will, who has such a command, is better than that of other men, though his force be 100,000 times stronger. And therefore, whatever form the commonwealth is under, the ruling power ought to govern by declared and received laws, and not by extemporary dictates and undetermined resolutions: for then mankind will be in a far worse condition than in the state of nature, if they shall have armed one, or a few men with the joint power of a multitude, to force them to obey at pleasure the exorbitant and unlimited decrees of their sudden thoughts, or unrestrained, and till that moment unknown wills, without having any measures set down which may guide and justify their actions: for all the power the government has, being only for the good of the society, as it ought not to be arbitrary and at pleasure, so it ought to be exercised by established and promulgated laws; that both the people may know their duty, and be safe and secure within the limits of the law; and the rulers too kept within their bounds, and not be tempted, by the power they have in their hands, to employ it to such purposes, and by such measures, as they would not have known, and own not willingly.

§. 138. Thirdly, the supreme power cannot take from any man any part of his property without his own consent: for the preservation of property being the end of government, and that for which men enter into society, it necessarily supposes and requires, that the people should have property, without which they must be supposed to lose that, by entering into society, which was the end for which they entered into it, too gross an absurdity for any man to own. Men therefore in society having property, they have such a right to the goods, which by the law of the community are theirs, that nobody has a right to take their substance or any part of it from them, without their own consent: without this they have no property at all. For I have truly no property in that, which another can by right take from me, when he pleases, against my consent. Hence it is a mistake to think, that the supreme or legislative power of any commonwealth, can do what it will, and dispose of the estates of the subject arbitrarily, or take any part of them at pleasure. This is not much to be feared in governments where the legislative consists, wholly or in part, in assemblies which are variable, whose members, upon the dissolution of the assembly, are subjects under the common laws of their country, equally with the rest. But in governments, where the legislative is in one lasting assembly always in being, or in one man, as in absolute monarchies, there is danger still, that they will think themselves to have a distinct interest from the rest of the community; and so will be apt to increase their own riches and power, by taking what they think fit from the people. For a man's property is not at all secure, though there be good and equitable laws to set the bounds of it between him and his fellow subjects, if he who commands those subjects have power to take from any private man, what part he pleases of his property, and use and dispose of it as he thinks good.

§. 139. But government, into whatsoever hands it is put, being, as I have before showed, entrusted with this condition, and for this end, that men might have and secure their properties, the prince, or senate, however it may have power to make laws, for the regulating of property between the subjects one amongst another, yet can never have a power to take to themselves the whole, or any part of the subject's property, without their own consent. For this would be in effect to leave them no property at all. And to let us see, that even absolute power, where it is necessary, is not arbitrary by being absolute, but is still limited by that reason, and confined to those ends, which required it in some cases to be absolute, we need look no farther than the common practice of martial discipline. For the preservation of the army, and in it of the whole commonwealth, requires an absolute obedience to the command of every superior officer, and it is justly death to disobey or dispute the most dangerous or unreasonable of them; but yet we see, that neither the sergeant, that could command a soldier to march up to the mouth of a cannon, or stand in a breach, where he is almost sure to perish, can command that soldier to give him one penny of his money; nor the general, that can condemn him to death for deserting his post, or for not obeying the most desperate orders, can yet, with all his absolute power of life and death, dispose of one farthing of that soldier's estate, or seize one jot of his goods; whom yet he can command anything, and hang for the least disobedience; because such a blind obedience is necessary to that end, for which the commander has his power, viz. the preservation of the rest; but the disposing of his goods has nothing to do with it.

§. 140. It is true, governments cannot be supported without great charge, and it is fit everyone who enjoys his share of the protection, should pay out of his estate his proportion for the maintenance of it. But still it must be with his own consent, i.e. the consent of the majority, giving it either by themselves, or their representatives chosen by them. For if anyone shall claim a power to lay and levy taxes on the people, by his own authority, and without such consent of the people, he thereby invades the fundamental law of property, and subverts the end of government. For what property have I in that, which another may by right take, when he pleases, to himself?

§. 141. Fourthly, the legislative cannot transfer the power of making laws to any other hands. For it being but a delegated power from the people, they who have it cannot pass it over to others. The people alone can appoint the form of the commonwealth, which is by constituting the legislative, and appointing in whose hands that shall be. And when the people have said, We will submit to rules, and be governed by laws made by such men, and in such forms, nobody else can say other men shall make laws for them; nor can the people be bound by any laws, but such as are enacted by those whom they have chosen, and authorized to make laws for them. The power of the legislative, being derived from the people by a positive voluntary grant and institution, can be no other than what that positive grant conveyed, which being only to make laws, and not to make legislators, the legislative can have no power to transfer their authority of making laws, and place it in other hands.

§. 142. These are the bounds which the trust, that is put in them by the society, and the law of God and nature, have set to the legislative power of every commonwealth, in all forms of government.

First, they are to govern by promulgated established laws, not to be varied in particular cases, but to have one rule for rich and poor, for the favorite at court, and the country man at plough.

Secondly, these laws also ought to be designed for no other end ultimately, but the good of the people.

Thirdly, they must not raise taxes on the property of the people, without the consent of the people, given by themselves, or their deputies. And this properly concerns only such governments where the legislative is always in being, or at least where the people have not reserved any part of the legislative to deputies, to be from time to time chosen by themselves.

Fourthly, the legislative neither must nor can transfer the power of making laws to anybody else, or place it anywhere, but where the people have.

CHAPTER XII
Of the Legislative, Executive, and Federative Power of the Commonwealth

§. 143. The legislative power is that, which has a right to direct how the force of the commonwealth shall be employed for preserving the community and the members of it. But because those laws which are constantly to be executed, and whose force is always to continue, may be made in a little time; therefore there is no need, that the legislative should be always in being, not having always business to do. And because it may be too great a temptation to human frailty, apt to grasp at power, for the same persons, who have the power of making laws, to have also in their hands the power to execute them, whereby they may exempt themselves from obedience to the laws they make, and suit the law, both in its making, and execution, to their own private advantage, and thereby come to have a distinct interest from the rest of the community, contrary to the end of society and government: therefore in well-ordered commonwealths, where the good of the whole is so considered, as it ought, the legislative power is put into the hands of diverse persons, who duly assembled, have by themselves, or jointly with others, a power to make laws, which when they have done, being separated again, they are themselves subject to the laws they have made; which is a new and near tie upon them, to take care, that they make them for the public good.

§. 144. But because the laws, that are at once, and in a short time made, have a constant and lasting force, and need a perpetual execution, or an attendance thereunto; therefore it is necessary there should be a power always in being, which should see to the execution of the laws that are made, and remain in force. And thus the legislative and executive power come often to be separated.

§. 145. There is another power in every commonwealth, which one may call natural, because it is that which answers to the power every man naturally had before he entered into society. For though in a commonwealth the members of it are distinct persons still in reference to one another, and as such are governed by the laws of the society; yet in reference to the rest of mankind, they make one body, which is, as every member of it before was, still in the state of nature with the rest of mankind. Hence it is, that the controversies that happen between any man of the society with those that are out of it, are managed by the public; and an injury done to a member of their body, engages the whole in the reparation of it. So that under this consideration, the whole community is one body in the state of nature, in respect of all other states or persons out of its community.

§. 146. This therefore contains the power of war and peace, leagues and alliances, and all the transactions, with all persons and communities without the commonwealth, and may be called federative, if anyone pleases. So the thing be understood, I am indifferent as to the name.

§. 147. These two powers, executive and federative, though they be really distinct in themselves, yet one comprehending the execution of the municipal laws of the society within itself, upon all that are parts of it; the other the management of the security and interest of the public without, with all those that it may receive benefit or damage from, yet they are always almost united. And though this federative power in the well or ill management of it be of great moment to the commonwealth, yet it is much less capable to be directed by antecedent, standing, positive laws, than the executive; and so must necessarily be left to the prudence and wisdom of those, whose hands it is in, to be managed for the public good: for the laws that concern subjects one amongst another, being to direct their actions, may well enough precede them. But what is to be done in reference to foreigners, depending much upon their actions, and the variation of designs and interests, must be left in great part to the prudence of those, who have this power committed to them, to be managed by the best of their skill, for the advantage of the commonwealth.

§. 148. Though, as I said, the executive and federative power of every community be really distinct in themselves, yet they are hardly to be separated, and placed at the same time, in the hands of distinct persons. For both of them requiring the force of the society for their exercise, it is almost impracticable to place the force of the commonwealth in distinct, and not subordinate hands; or that the executive and federative power should be placed in persons, that might act separately, whereby the force of the public would be under different commands: which would be apt some time or other to cause disorder and ruin.

CHAPTER XIII
Of the Subordination of the Powers of the Commonwealth

§. 149. Though in a constituted commonwealth, standing upon its own basis, and acting according to its own nature, that is, acting for the preservation of the community, there can be but one supreme power, which is the legislative, to which all the rest are and must be subordinate, yet the legislative being only a fiduciary power to act for certain ends, there remains still in the people a supreme power to remove or alter the legislative, when they find the legislative act contrary to the trust reposed in them. For all power given with trust for the attaining an end, being limited by that end, whenever that end is manifestly neglected, or opposed, the trust must necessarily be forfeited, and the power devolve into the hands of those that gave it, who may place it anew where they shall think best for their safety and security. And thus the community perpetually retains a supreme power of saving themselves from the attempts and designs of anybody, even of their legislators, whenever they shall be so foolish, or so wicked, as to lay and carry on designs against the liberties and properties of the subject. For no man or society of men, having a power to deliver up their preservation, or consequently the means of it, to the absolute will and arbitrary dominion of another; whenever anyone shall go about to bring them into such a slavish condition, they will always have a right to preserve, what they have not a power to part with; and to rid themselves of those, who invade this fundamental, sacred, and unalterable law of self-preservation, for which they entered into society. And thus the community may be said in this respect to be always the supreme power, but not as considered under any form of government, because this power of the people can never take place till the government be dissolved.

§. 150. In all cases, while the government subsists, the legislative is the supreme power. For what can give laws to another, must needs be superior to him: and since the legislative is no otherwise legislative of the society, but by the right it has to make laws for all the parts, and for every member of the society, prescribing rules to their actions, and giving power of execution, where they are transgressed, the legislative must needs be the supreme, and all other powers, in any members or parts of the society, derived from and subordinate to it.

§. 151. In some commonwealths, where the legislative is not always in being, and the executive is vested in a single person, who has also a share in the legislative; there that single person in a very tolerable sense may also be called supreme, not that he has in himself all the supreme power, which is that of law making: but because he has in him the supreme execution, from whom all inferior magistrates derive all their several subordinate powers, or at least the greatest part of them: having also no legislative superior to him, there being no law to be made without his consent, which cannot be expected should ever subject him to the other part of the legislative, he is properly enough in this sense supreme. But yet it is to be observed, that though oaths of allegiance and fealty are taken to him, it is not to him as supreme legislator, but as supreme executor of the law, made by a joint power of him with others; allegiance being nothing but an obedience according to law, which when he violates, he has no right to obedience, nor can claim it otherwise than as the public person vested with the power of the law, and so is to be considered as the image, phantom, or representative of the commonwealth, acted by the will of the society, declared in its laws; and thus he has no will, no power, but that of the law. But when he quits this representation, this public will, and acts by his own private will, he degrades himself, and is but a single private person without power, and without will, that has any right to obedience; the members owing no obedience but to the public will of the society.

§. 152. The executive power, placed anywhere but in a person that has also a share in the legislative, is visibly subordinate and accountable to it, and may be at pleasure changed and displaced; so that it is not the supreme executive power, that is exempt from subordination, but the supreme executive power vested in one, who having a share in the legislative, has no distinct superior legislative to be subordinate and accountable to, farther than he himself shall join and consent: so that he is no more subordinate than he himself shall think fit, which one may certainly conclude will be but very little. Of other ministerial and subordinate powers in a commonwealth, we need not speak, they being so multiplied with infinite variety, in the different customs and constitutions of distinct commonwealths, that it is impossible to give a particular account of them all. Only thus much, which is necessary to our present purpose, we may take notice of concerning them, that they have no manner of authority, any of them, beyond what is by positive grant and commission delegated to them, and are all of them accountable to some other power in the commonwealth.

§. 153. It is not necessary, no nor so much as convenient, that the legislative should be always in being; but absolutely necessary that the executive power should, because there is not always need of new laws to be made, but always need of execution of the laws that are made. When the legislative has put the execution of the laws they make into other hands, they have a power still to resume it out of those hands, when they find cause, and to punish for any maladministration against the laws. The same holds also in regard of the federative power, that and the executive being both ministerial and subordinate to the legislative, which, as has been showed, in a constituted commonwealth is the supreme. The legislative also in this case being supposed to consist of several persons, (for if it be a single person, it cannot but be always in being, and so will, as supreme, naturally have the supreme executive power, together with the legislative) may assemble, and exercise their legislature, at the times that either their original constitution, or their own adjournment, appoints, or when they please; if neither of these has appointed any time, or there be no other way prescribed to convoke them. For the supreme power being placed in them by the people, it is always in them, and they may exercise it when they please, unless by their original constitution they are limited to certain seasons, or by an act of their supreme power they have adjourned to a certain time; and when that time comes, they have a right to assemble and act again.

§. 154. If the legislative, or any part of it, be made up of representatives chosen for that time by the people, which afterwards return into the ordinary state of subjects, and have no share in the legislature but upon a new choice, this power of choosing must also be exercised by the people, either at certain appointed seasons, or else when they are summoned to it; and in this latter case the power of convoking the legislative is ordinarily placed in the executive, and has one of these two limitations in respect of time: that either the original constitution requires their assembling and acting at certain intervals, and then the executive power does nothing but ministerially issue directions for their electing and assembling, according to due forms: or else it is left to his prudence to call them by new elections, when the occasions or exigencies of the public require the amendment of old, or making of new laws, or the redress or prevention of any inconveniences, that lie on, or threaten the people.

§. 155. It may be demanded here, What if the executive power, being possessed of the force of the commonwealth, shall make use of that force to hinder the meeting and acting of the legislative, when the original constitution, or the public exigencies require it? I say, using force upon the people without authority, and contrary to the trust put in him that does so, is a state of war with the people, who have a right to reinstate their legislative in the exercise of their power. For having erected a legislative, with an intent they should exercise the power of making laws, either at certain set times, or when there is need of it, when they are hindered by any force from what is so necessary to the society, and wherein the safety and preservation of the people consists, the people have a right to remove it by force. In all states and conditions, the true remedy of force without authority, is to oppose force to it. The use of force without authority, always puts him that uses it into a state of war, as the aggressor, and renders him liable to be treated accordingly.

§. 156. The power of assembling and dismissing the legislative, placed in the executive, gives not the executive a superiority over it, but is a fiduciary trust placed in him, for the safety of the people, in a case where the uncertainty and variableness of human affairs could not bear a steady fixed rule. For it not being possible, that the first framers of the government should, by any foresight, be so much masters of future events, as to be able to prefix so just periods of return and duration to the assemblies of the legislative, in all times to come, that might exactly answer all the exigencies of the commonwealth; the best remedy could be found for this defect, was to trust this to the prudence of one who was always to be present, and whose business it was to watch over the public good. Constant frequent meetings of the legislative, and long continuations of their assemblies, without necessary occasion, could not but be burdensome to the people, and must necessarily in time produce more dangerous inconveniences, and yet the quick turn of affairs might be sometimes such as to need their present help: any delay of their convening might endanger the public; and sometimes too their business might be so great, that the limited time of their sitting might be too short for their work, and rob the public of that benefit which could be had only from their mature deliberation. What then could be done in this case to prevent the community from being exposed some time or other to eminent hazard, on one side or the other, by fixed intervals and periods, set to the meeting and acting of the legislative, but to entrust it to the prudence of some, who being present, and acquainted with the state of public affairs, might make use of this prerogative for the public good? And where else could this be so well placed as in his hands, who was entrusted with the execution of the laws for the same end? Thus supposing the regulation of times for the assembling and sitting of the legislative, not settled by the original constitution, it naturally fell into the hands of the executive, not as an arbitrary power depending on his good pleasure, but with this trust always to have it exercised only for the public weal, as the occurrences of times and change of affairs might require. Whether settled periods of their convening, or a liberty left to the prince for convoking the legislative, or perhaps a mixture of both, has the least inconvenience attending it, it is not my business here to inquire, but only to show, that though the executive power may have the prerogative of convoking and dissolving such conventions of the legislative, yet it is not thereby superior to it.

§. 157. Things of this world are in so constant a flux that nothing remains long in the same state. Thus people, riches, trade, power, change their stations, flourishing mighty cities come to ruin, and prove in times neglected desolate corners, while other unfrequented places grow into populous countries, filled with wealth and inhabitants. But things not always changing equally, and private interest often keeping up customs and privileges, when the reasons of them are ceased, it often comes to pass, that in governments, where part of the legislative consists of representatives chosen by the people, that in tract of time this representation becomes very unequal and disproportionate to the reasons it was at first established upon. To what gross absurdities the following of custom, when reason has left it, may lead, we may be satisfied, when we see the bare name of a town, of which there remains not so much as the ruins, where scarce so much housing as a sheepcote, or more inhabitants than a shepherd is to be found, sends as many representatives to the grand assembly of law-makers, as a whole county numerous in people, and powerful in riches. This strangers stand amazed at, and everyone must confess needs a remedy. Though most think it hard to find one, because the constitution of the legislative being the original and supreme act of the society, antecedent to all positive laws in it, and depending wholly on the people, no inferior power can alter it. And therefore the people, when the legislative is once constituted, having, in such a government as we have been speaking of, no power to act as long as the government stands; this inconvenience is thought incapable of a remedy.

§. 158. *Salus populi suprema lex*,[12] is certainly so just and fundamental a rule, that he, who sincerely follows it, cannot dangerously err. If therefore the executive, who has the power of convoking the legislative, observing rather the true proportion, than fashion of representation, regulates, not by old custom, but true reason, the number of members, in all places that have a right to be distinctly represented, which no part of the people however incorporated can pretend to, but in proportion to the assistance which it affords to the public, it cannot be judged to have set up a new legislative, but to have restored the old and true one, and to have rectified the disorders which succession of time had insensibly, as well as inevitably introduced. For it being the interest as well as intention of the people, to have a fair and equal representative; whoever brings it nearest to that, is an undoubted friend to, and establisher of the government, and cannot miss the consent and approbation of the community; prerogative being nothing but a power, in the hands of the prince, to provide for the public good, in such cases, which depending upon unforeseen and uncertain occurrences, certain and unalterable laws could not safely direct, whatsoever shall be done manifestly for the good of the people, and the establishing the government upon its true foundations, is, and always will be, just prerogative. The power of erecting new corporations, and therewith new representatives, carries with it a supposition, that in time the measures of representation might vary, and those places have a just right to be represented which before had none; and by the same reason, those cease to have a right, and be too inconsiderable for such a privilege, which before had it. It is not a change from the present state, which perhaps corruption or decay has introduced, that makes an inroad upon the government, but the tendency of it to injure or oppress the people, and to set up one part or party, with a distinction from, and an unequal subjection of the rest. Whatsoever cannot but be acknowledged to be of advantage to the society, and people in general, upon just and lasting measures, will always, when done, justify itself; and whenever the

12. The Latin phrase meaning "Let the good of the people be the supreme law" was first popularized by Cicero (106–43 BCE) in his dialogue *De legibus*.

people shall choose their representatives upon just and undeniably equal measures, suitable to the original frame of the government, it cannot be doubted to be the will and act of the society, whoever permitted or caused them so to do.

CHAPTER XIV
Of Prerogative

§. 159. Where the legislative and executive power are in distinct hands, (as they are in all moderated monarchies, and well-framed governments) there the good of the society requires, that several things should be left to the discretion of him that has the executive power. For the legislators not being able to foresee, and provide by laws, for all that may be useful to the community, the executor of the laws having the power in his hands, has by the common law of nature a right to make use of it for the good of the society, in many cases, where the municipal law has given no direction, till the legislative can conveniently be assembled to provide for it. Many things there are, which the law can by no means provide for, and those must necessarily be left to the discretion of him that has the executive power in his hands, to be ordered by him as the public good and advantage shall require: nay, it is fit that the laws themselves should in some cases give way to the executive power, or rather to this fundamental law of nature and government, viz. That as much as may be, all the members of the society are to be preserved. For since many accidents may happen, wherein a strict and rigid observation of the laws may do harm; (as not to pull down an innocent man's house to stop the fire, when the next to it is burning) and a man may come sometimes within the reach of the law, which makes no distinction of persons, by an action that may deserve reward and pardon; it is fit the ruler should have a power, in many cases, to mitigate the severity of the law, and pardon some offenders. For the end of government being the preservation of all, as much as may be, even the guilty are to be spared, where it can prove no prejudice to the innocent.

§. 160. This power to act according to discretion, for the public good, without the prescription of the law, and sometimes even against it, is that which is called prerogative. For since in some governments the law-making power is not always in being, and is usually too numerous, and so too slow, for the dispatch requisite to execution; and because also it is impossible to foresee, and so by laws to provide for, all accidents and necessities that may concern the public, or to make such laws as will do no harm, if they are executed with an inflexible rigor, on all occasions, and upon all persons that may come in their way, therefore there is a latitude left to the executive power, to do many things of choice which the laws do not prescribe.

§. 161. This power, while employed for the benefit of the community, and suitably to the trust and ends of the government, is undoubted prerogative, and never is questioned. For the people are very seldom or never scrupulous or nice in the point; they are far from examining prerogative, while it is in any tolerable degree employed for the use it was meant, that is, for the good of the people, and not manifestly against it: but if there comes to be a question between the executive power and the people, about a thing claimed as a prerogative; the tendency of the exercise of such prerogative to the good or hurt of the people, will easily decide that question.

§. 162. It is easy to conceive, that in the infancy of governments, when commonwealths differed little from families in number of people, they differed from them too but little in number of laws: and the governors, being as the fathers of them, watching over them for their good, the government was almost all prerogative. A few established laws served the turn, and the discretion and care of the ruler supplied the rest. But when mistake or flattery prevailed with weak princes to make use of this power for private ends of their own, and not for the public good, the people were fain by express laws to get prerogative determined in those points wherein they found disadvantage from it: and thus declared limitations of prerogative were by the people found necessary in cases which they and their ancestors had left, in the utmost latitude, to the wisdom of those princes who made no other but a right use of it, that is, for the good of their people.

§. 163. And therefore they have a very wrong notion of government, who say, that the people have encroached upon the prerogative, when they have got any part of it to be defined by positive laws. For in so doing they have not pulled from the prince anything that of right belonged to him, but only declared, that that power which they indefinitely left in his or his ancestor's hands, to be exercised for their good, was not a thing which they intended him when he used it otherwise. For the end of government being the good of the community, whatsoever alterations are made in it, tending to that end, cannot be an encroachment upon anybody, since nobody in government can have a right tending to any other end. And those only are encroachments which prejudice or hinder the public good. Those who say otherwise, speak as if the prince had a distinct and separate interest from the good of the community, and was not made for it; the root and source from which spring almost all those evils and disorders which happen in kingly governments. And indeed, if that be so, the people under his government are not a society of rational creatures, entered into a community for their mutual good; they are not such as have set rulers over themselves, to guard, and promote that good; but are to be looked on as a herd of inferior creatures under the dominion of a master, who keeps them and works them for his own pleasure or profit. If men were so void of reason, and brutish, as to enter into society upon such terms, prerogative might indeed be, what some men would have it, an arbitrary power to do things hurtful to the people.

§. 164. But since a rational creature cannot be supposed when free to put himself into subjection to another for his own harm: (though, where he finds a good and wise ruler, he may not perhaps think it either necessary or useful to set precise bounds to his power in all things) prerogative can be nothing but the people's permitting their rulers to do several things, of their own free choice, where the law was silent, and sometimes too against the direct letter of the law, for the public good; and their acquiescing in it when so done. For as a good prince, who is mindful of the trust put into his hands, and careful of the good of his people, cannot have too much prerogative, that is, power to do good; so a weak and ill prince, who would claim that power which his predecessors exercised without the direction of the law, as a prerogative belonging to him by right of his office, which he may exercise at his pleasure, to make or promote an interest distinct from that of the public, gives the people an occasion to claim their right, and limit that power, which, while it was exercised for their good, they were content should be tacitly allowed.

§. 165. And therefore he that will look into the history of England, will find that prerogative was always largest in the hands of our wisest and best princes, because the people, observing the whole tendency of their actions to be the public good, contested not what was done without law to that end; or, if any human frailty or mistake (for princes are but men, made as others) appeared in some small declinations from that end; yet it was visible, the main of their conduct tended to nothing but the care of the public. The people therefore, finding reason to be satisfied with these princes, whenever they acted without, or contrary to the letter of the law, acquiesced in what they did, and, without the least complaint, let them enlarge their prerogative as they pleased, judging rightly, that they did nothing herein to the prejudice of their laws, since they acted conformable to the foundation and end of all laws, the public good.

§. 166. Such god-like princes indeed had some title to arbitrary power by that argument, that would prove absolute monarchy the best government, as that which God himself governs the universe by; because such kings partake of his wisdom and goodness. Upon this is founded that saying, That the reigns of good princes have been always most dangerous to the liberties of their people. For when their successors, managing the government with different thoughts, would draw the actions of those good rulers into precedent, and make them the standard of their prerogative, as if what had been done only for the good of the people was a right in them to do, for the harm of the people, if they so pleased; it has often occasioned contest, and sometimes public disorders, before the people could recover their original right, and get that to be declared not to be prerogative, which truly was never so: since it is impossible that anybody in the society should ever have a right to do the people harm; though it be very possible, and reasonable, that the people should not go about to set any bounds to the prerogative of those kings, or rulers, who themselves transgressed not the bounds of the public good. For prerogative is nothing but the power of doing public good without a rule.

§. 167. The power of calling parliaments in England, as to precise time, place, and duration, is certainly a prerogative of the king, but still with this trust, that it shall be made use of for the good of the nation, as the exigencies of the times, and variety of occasions, shall require. For it being impossible to foresee which should always be the fittest place for them to assemble in, and what the best season; the choice of these was left with the executive power, as might be most subservient to the public good, and best suit the ends of parliaments.

§. 168. The old question will be asked in this matter of prerogative, But who shall be judge when this power is made a right use of? I answer: between an executive power in being, with such a prerogative, and a legislative that depends upon his will for their convening, there can be no judge on earth: as there can be none between the legislative and the people, should either the executive, or the legislative, when they have got the power in their hands, design, or go about to enslave or destroy them. The people have no other remedy in this, as in all other cases where they have no judge on earth, but to appeal to heaven. For the rulers, in such attempts, exercising a power the people never put into their hands, (who can never be supposed to consent that anybody should rule over them for their harm) do that which they have not a right to do. And where the body of the people, or any single man, is deprived of their right, or is under the exercise of a power without right, and have no appeal on earth, then they have a liberty to appeal to heaven, whenever they judge the cause of sufficient moment. And therefore, though the people cannot be judge, so as to have, by the constitution of that society, any superior power, to determine and give effective sentence in the case; yet they have, by a law antecedent and paramount to all positive laws of men, reserved that ultimate determination to themselves which belongs to all mankind, where there lies no appeal on earth, viz. to judge, whether they have just cause to make their appeal to heaven. And this judgment they cannot part with, it being out of a man's power so to submit himself to another, as to give him a liberty to destroy him; God and nature never allowing a man so to abandon himself, as to neglect his own preservation: and since he cannot take away his own life, neither can he give another power to take it. Nor let anyone think, this lays a perpetual foundation for disorder; for this operates not, till the inconvenience is so great, that the majority feel it, and are weary of it, and find a necessity to have it amended. But this the executive power, or wise princes, never need come in the danger of: and it is the thing, of all others, they have most need to avoid, as of all others the most perilous.

CHAPTER XV
Of Paternal, Political, and Despotical Power,
Considered Together

§. 169. Though I have had occasion to speak of these separately before, yet the great mistakes of late about government, having, as I suppose, arisen from confounding these distinct powers one with another, it may not, perhaps, be amiss to consider them here together.

§. 170. First, then, Paternal or parental power is nothing but that which parents have over their children, to govern them for the children's good, till they come to the use of reason, or a state of knowledge, wherein they may be supposed capable to understand that rule, whether it be the law of nature, or the municipal law of their country, they are to govern themselves by: capable, I say, to know it, as well as several others, who live as freemen under that law. The affection and tenderness which God has planted in the breast of parents toward their children, makes it evident, that this is not intended to be a severe arbitrary government, but only for the help, instruction, and preservation of their offspring. But happen it as it will, there is, as I have proved, no reason why it should be thought to extend to life and death, at any time, over their children, more than over anybody else; neither can there be any pretence why this parental power should keep the child, when grown to a man, in subjection to the will of his parents, any farther than having received life and education from his parents, obliges him to respect, honor, gratitude, assistance and support, all his life, to both father and mother. And thus, it is true, the paternal is a natural government, but not at all extending itself to the ends and jurisdictions of that which is political. The power of the father does not reach at all to the property of the child, which is only in his own disposing.

§. 171. Secondly, Political power is that power, which every man having in the state of nature, has given up into the hands of the society, and therein to the governors, whom the society has set over itself, with this express or tacit trust, that it shall be employed for their good, and the preservation of their property: now this power, which every man has in the state of nature, and which he parts with to the society in all such cases where the society can secure him, is to use such means, for the preserving of his own property, as he thinks good, and nature allows him; and to punish the breach of the law of nature in others, so as (according to the best of his reason) may most conduce to the preservation of himself, and the rest of mankind. So that the end and measure of this power, when in every man's hands in the state of nature, being the preservation of all of his society, that is, all mankind in general, it can have no other end or measure, when in the hands of the magistrate, but to preserve the members of that society in their lives, liberties, and possessions; and so cannot be an absolute, arbitrary power over their lives and fortunes, which are as much as possible to be preserved; but a power to make laws, and annex such penalties to them, as may tend to the preservation of the whole, by cutting off those parts, and those only, which are so corrupt, that they threaten the sound and healthy, without which no severity is lawful. And this power has its original only from compact and agreement, and the mutual consent of those who make up the community.

§. 172. Thirdly, Despotical power is an absolute, arbitrary power one man has over another, to take away his life, whenever he pleases. This is a power, which neither nature gives, for it has made no such distinction between one man and another; nor compact can convey, for man not having such an arbitrary power over his own life, cannot give another man such a power over it; but it is the effect only of forfeiture, which the aggressor makes of his own life, when he puts himself into the state of war with another: for having quitted reason, which God has given to be the rule between man and man, and the common bond whereby humankind is united into one fellowship and society; and having renounced the way of peace which that teaches, and made use of the force of war, to compass his unjust ends upon another, where he has no right; and so revolting from his own kind to that of beasts, by making force, which is theirs, to be his rule of right, he renders himself liable to be destroyed by the injured person, and the rest of mankind, that will join with him in the execution of justice, as any other wild beast, or noxious brute, with whom mankind can have neither society nor security. And thus captives, taken in a just and lawful war, and such only, are subject to a despotical power, which, as it arises not from compact, so neither is it capable of any, but is the state of war continued: for what compact can be made with a man that is not master of his own life? What condition can he perform? And if he be once allowed to be master of his own life, the despotical, arbitrary power of his master ceases. He that is master of himself, and his own life, has a right too to the means of preserving it, so that as soon as compact enters, slavery ceases, and he so far quits his absolute power, and puts an end to the state of war, who enters into conditions with his captive.

§. 173. Nature gives the first of these, viz. paternal power to parents for the benefit of their children during their minority, to supply their want of ability, and understanding how to manage their property. (By property I must be understood here, as in other places, to mean that property which men have in their persons as well as goods.) Voluntary agreement gives the second, viz. political power to governors for the benefit of their subjects, to secure them in the possession and use of their properties. And forfeiture gives the third despotical power to lords for their own benefit, over those who are stripped of all property.

§. 174. He, that shall consider the distinct rise and extent, and the different ends of these several powers, will plainly see, that paternal power comes as far short of that of the magistrate, as despotical exceeds it; and that absolute dominion, however placed, is so far from being one kind of civil society, that it is as inconsistent with it, as slavery is with property. Paternal power is only where minority makes the child incapable to manage his property; political, where men have property in their own disposal; and despotical over such as have no property at all.

CHAPTER XVI
Of Conquest

§. 175. Though governments can originally have no other rise than that before mentioned, nor polities be founded on anything but the consent of the people; yet such have been the disorders ambition has filled the world with, that in the noise of war, which makes so great a part of the history of mankind, this consent is little taken notice of: and therefore many have mistaken the force of arms for the consent of the people, and reckon conquest as one of the originals of government. But conquest is as far from setting up any government, as demolishing a house is from building a new one in the place. Indeed, it often makes way for a new frame of a commonwealth, by destroying the former; but, without the consent of the people, can never erect a new one.

§. 176. That the aggressor, who puts himself into the state of war with another, and unjustly invades another man's right, can, by such an unjust war, never come to have a right over the conquered, will be easily agreed by all men, who will not think, that robbers and pirates have a right of empire over whomsoever they have force enough to master; or that men are bound by promises, which unlawful force extorts from them. Should a robber break into my house, and with a dagger at my throat make me seal deeds to convey my estate to him, would this give him any title? Just such a title, by his sword, has an unjust conqueror, who forces me into submission. The injury and the crime is equal, whether committed by the wearer of a crown, or some petty villain. The title of the offender, and the number of his followers, make no difference in the offence, unless it be to aggravate it. The only difference is, great robbers punish little ones, to keep them in their obedience, but the great ones are rewarded with laurels and triumphs because they are too big for the weak hands of justice in this world, and have the power in their own possession, which should punish offenders. What is my remedy against a robber, that so broke into my house? Appeal to the law for justice. But perhaps justice is denied, or I am crippled and cannot stir, robbed and have not the means to do it. If God has taken away all means of seeking remedy, there is nothing left but patience. But my son, when able, may seek the relief of the law, which I am denied: he or his son may renew his appeal, till he recovers his right. But the conquered, or their children, have no court, no arbitrator on earth to appeal to. Then they may appeal, as Jephtha did, to heaven, and repeat their appeal till they have recovered the native right of their ancestors, which was, to have such a legislative over them, as the majority should approve, and freely acquiesce in. If it be objected: This would cause endless trouble; I answer, no more than justice does, where she lies open to all that appeal to her. He that troubles his neighbor without a cause, is punished for it by the justice of the court he appeals to. And he that appeals to heaven must be sure he has right on his side; and a right too that is worth the trouble and cost of the appeal, as he will answer at a tribunal that cannot be deceived, and will be sure to retribute to everyone according to the mischiefs he has created to his fellow subjects; that is, any part of mankind. From whence it is plain, that he that conquers in an unjust war can thereby have no title to the subjection and obedience of the conquered.

§. 177. But supposing victory favors the right side, let us consider a conqueror in a lawful war, and see what power he gets, and over whom.

First, it is plain he gets no power by his conquest over those that conquered with him. They that fought on his side cannot suffer by the conquest, but must at least be as much freemen as they were before. And most commonly they serve upon terms, and on condition to share with their leader, and enjoy a part of the spoil, and other advantages that attend the conquering sword; or at least have a part of the subdued country bestowed upon them. And the conquering people are not, I hope, to be slaves by conquest, and wear their laurels only to show they are sacrifices to their leader's triumph. They that found absolute monarchy upon the title of the sword, make their heroes, who are the founders of such monarchies, arrant Draw-can-sirs,[13] and forget they had any officers and soldiers that fought on their side in the battles they won, or assisted them in the subduing, or shared in possessing, the countries they mastered. We are told by some, that the English monarchy is founded in the Norman Conquest,[14] and that our princes have thereby a title to absolute dominion: which if it were true, (as by the history it appears otherwise) and that William had a right to make war on this island; yet his dominion by conquest could reach no farther than to the Saxons and Britons, that were then inhabitants of this country. The Normans that came with him, and helped to conquer, and all descended from them, are freemen, and no subjects by conquest; let that give what dominion it will. And if I, or anybody else, shall claim freedom, as derived from them, it will be very hard to prove the contrary: and it is plain, the law, that has made no distinction between the one and the other, intends not there should be any difference in their freedom or privileges.

§. 178. But supposing, which seldom happens, that the conquerors and conquered never incorporate into one people, under the same laws and freedom. Let us see next what power a lawful conqueror has over the subdued; and that I say is purely despotical. He has an absolute power over the lives of those who by an unjust war have forfeited them; but not over the lives or fortunes of those who engaged not in the war, nor over the possessions even of those who were actually engaged in it.

§. 179. Secondly, I say then the conqueror gets no power but only over those who have actually assisted, concurred, or consented to that unjust force that is used against him. For the people having given to their governors no power to do an unjust thing, such as is to make an unjust war, (for they never had such a power in themselves) they ought not to be charged as guilty of the violence and injustice that is committed in an unjust war, any farther than they actually abet it; no more than they are to be thought guilty

13. These are blustering, bullying braggarts who show no mercy to their opponents.

14. The victory of Norman invaders under the command of William I over Harold, the last Saxon king of England, after the Battle of Hastings, in 1066.

of any violence or oppression their governors should use upon the people themselves, or any part of their fellow subjects, they having empowered them no more to the one than to the other. Conquerors, it is true, seldom trouble themselves to make the distinction, but they willingly permit the confusion of war to sweep all together; but yet this alters not the right: for the conqueror's power over the lives of the conquered, being only because they have used force to do, or maintain an injustice, he can have that power only over those who have concurred in that force; all the rest are innocent; and he has no more title over the people of that country, who have done him no injury, and so have made no forfeiture of their lives, than he has over any other, who, without any injuries or provocations, have lived upon fair terms with him.

§. 180. Thirdly, the power a conqueror gets over those he overcomes in a just war, is perfectly despotical: he has an absolute power over the lives of those, who, by putting themselves in a state of war, have forfeited them; but he has not thereby a right and title to their possessions. This I doubt not, but at first sight will seem a strange doctrine, it being so quite contrary to the practice of the world; there being nothing more familiar in speaking of the dominion of countries, than to say such a one conquered it. As if conquest, without any more ado, conveyed a right of possession. But when we consider, that the practice of the strong and powerful, how universal soever it may be, is seldom the rule of right, however it be one part of the subjection of the conquered, not to argue against the conditions cut out to them by the conquering sword.

§. 181. Though in all war there be usually a complication of force and damage, and the aggressor seldom fails to harm the estate, when he uses force against the persons of those he makes war upon; yet it is the use of force only that puts a man into the state of war. For whether by force he begins the injury, or else having quietly, and by fraud, done the injury, he refuses to make reparation, and by force maintains it, (which is the same thing, as at first to have done it by force) it is the unjust use of force that makes the war. For he that breaks open my house, and violently turns me out of doors; or having peaceably got in, by force keeps me out, does in effect the same thing; supposing we are in such a state, that we have no common judge on earth, whom I may appeal to, and to whom we are both obliged to submit: for of such I am now speaking. It is the unjust use of force then, that puts a man into the state of war with another; and thereby he that is guilty of it makes a forfeiture of his life. For quitting reason, which is the rule given between man and man, and using force, the way of beasts, he becomes liable to be destroyed by him he uses force against, as any savage ravenous beast, that is dangerous to his being.

§. 182. But because the miscarriages of the father are no faults of the children, and they may be rational and peaceable, notwithstanding the brutishness and injustice of the father; the father, by his miscarriages and violence, can forfeit but his own life, but involves not his children in his guilt or destruction. His goods, which nature, that wills the preservation of all mankind as much as is possible, has made to belong to the children to keep them from perishing, do still continue to belong to his children. For supposing them not to have joined in the war, either through infancy, absence, or choice, they have done nothing to forfeit them: nor has the conqueror any right to take them away, by the bare title of having subdued him that by force attempted his destruction; though perhaps he may have some right to them, to repair the damages he has sustained by the war, and the defense of his own right; which how far it reaches to the possessions of the conquered, we shall see by and by. So that he that by conquest has a right over a man's person to destroy him if he pleases, has not thereby a right over his estate to possess and enjoy it: for it is the brutal force the aggressor has used, that gives his adversary a right to take away his life, and destroy him if he pleases, as a noxious creature; but it is damage sustained that alone gives him title to another man's goods: for though I may kill a thief that sets on me in the highway, yet I may not (which seems less) take away his money, and let him go: this would be robbery on my side. His force, and the state of war he put himself in, made him forfeit his life, but gave me no title to his goods. The right then of conquest extends only to the lives of those who joined in the war, not to their estates, but only in order to make reparation for the damages received, and the charges of the war, and that too with reservation of the right of the innocent wife and children.

§. 183. Let the conqueror have as much justice on his side, as could be supposed, he has no right to seize more than the vanquished could forfeit: his life is at the victor's mercy; and his service and goods he may appropriate, to make himself reparation; but he cannot take the goods of his wife and children; they too had a title to the goods he enjoyed, and their shares in the estate he possessed. For example, I in the state of nature (and all commonwealths are in the state of nature one with another) have injured another man, and refusing to give satisfaction, it comes to a state of war, wherein my defending by force what I had gotten unjustly, makes me the aggressor. I am conquered: my life, it is true, as forfeit, is at mercy, but not my wife's and children's. They made not the war, nor assisted in it. I could not forfeit their lives; they were not mine to forfeit. My wife had a share in my estate; that neither could I forfeit. And my children also, being born of me, had a right to be maintained out of my labor or substance. Here then is the case: the conqueror has a title to reparation for damages received, and the children have a title to their father's estate for their subsistence: for as to the wife's share, whether her own labor, or compact, gave her a title to it, it is plain, her husband could not forfeit what was hers. What must be done in the case? I answer; the fundamental law of nature being, that all, as much as may be, should be preserved, it follows, that if there be not enough fully to satisfy both, viz. for the conqueror's losses, and children's maintenance, he that has, and to spare, must remit something of his full satisfaction, and give way to the pressing and preferable title of those who are in danger to perish without it.

§. 184. But supposing the charge and damages of the war are to be made up to the conqueror, to the utmost farthing, and that the children of the vanquished, spoiled of all their father's goods, are to be left to starve and perish: yet the satisfying of what shall, on this score, be due to the conqueror, will scarce give him a title to any country he shall conquer. For the damages of war can scarce amount to the value of any considerable tract of land, in any part of the world, where all the land is possessed, and none lies waste. And if I have not taken away the conqueror's land, which, being vanquished, it is impossible I should; scarce any other spoil I have done him can amount to the value of mine, supposing it equally cultivated, and of an extent any way coming near what I had over-run of his. The destruction of a year's product or two (for it seldom reaches four or five) is the utmost spoil that usually can be done. For as to money, and such riches and treasure taken away, these are none of nature's goods, they have but a fantastical imaginary value: nature has put no such upon them: they are of no more account by her standard, than the *wampompeke* of the Americans to an European prince, or the silver money of Europe would have been formerly to an American. And five years product is not worth the perpetual inheritance of land, where all is possessed, and none remains waste, to be taken up by him that is [dispossessed][15]: which will be easily granted, if one do but take away the imaginary value of money, the disproportion being more than between five and five hundred; though, at the same time, half a year's product is more worth than the inheritance, where there being more land than the inhabitants possess and make use of, anyone has liberty to make use of the waste: but there conquerors take little care to possess themselves of the lands of the vanquished. No damage therefore, that men in the state of nature (as all princes and governments are in reference to one another) suffer from one another, can give a conqueror power to dispossess the posterity of the vanquished, and turn them out of that inheritance, which ought to be the possession of them and their descendants to all generations. The conqueror indeed will be apt to think himself master: and it is the very condition of the subdued not to be able to dispute their right. But if that be all, it gives no other title than what bare force gives to the stronger over the weaker: and, by this reason, he that is strongest will have a right to whatever he pleases to seize on.

§. 185. Over those then that joined with him in the war, and over those of the subdued country that opposed him not, and the posterity even of those that did, the conqueror, even in a just war, has, by his conquest, no right of dominion: they are free from any subjection to him, and if their former government be dissolved, they are at liberty to begin and erect another to themselves.

§. 186. The conqueror, it is true, usually, by the force he has over them, compels them, with a sword at their breasts, to stoop to

15. See note at I: 160.

his conditions, and submit to such a government as he pleases to afford them; but the enquiry is, what right he has to do so? If it be said, they submit by their own consent, then this allows their own consent to be necessary to give the conqueror a title to rule over them. It remains only to be considered, whether promises extorted by force, without right, can be thought consent, and how far they bind. To which I shall say, they bind not at all; because whatsoever another gets from me by force, I still retain the right of, and he is obliged presently to restore. He that forces my horse from me, ought presently to restore him, and I have still a right to retake him. By the same reason, he that forced a promise from me, ought presently to restore it, i.e. quit me of the obligation of it; or I may resume it myself, i.e. choose whether I will perform it. For the law of nature laying an obligation on me only by the rules she prescribes, cannot oblige me by the violation of her rules: such is the extorting anything from me by force. Nor does it at all alter the case to say, I gave my promise, no more than it excuses the force, and passes the right, when I put my hand in my pocket, and deliver my purse myself to a thief, who demands it with a pistol at my breast.

§. 187. From all which it follows, that the government of a conqueror, imposed by force on the subdued, against whom he had no right of war, or who joined not in the war against him, where he had right, has no obligation upon them.

§. 188. But let us suppose, that all the men of that community, being all members of the same body politic, may be taken to have joined in that unjust war wherein they are subdued, and so their lives are at the mercy of the conqueror.

§. 189. I say this concerns not their children who are in their minority, for since a father has not, in himself, a power over the life or liberty of his child, no act of his can possibly forfeit it. So that the children, whatever may have happened to the fathers, are freemen, and the absolute power of the conqueror reaches no farther than the persons of the men that were subdued by him, and dies with them: and should he govern them as slaves, subjected to his absolute arbitrary power, he has no such right of dominion over their children. He can have no power over them but by their own consent, whatever he may drive them to say or do; and he has no lawful authority, while force, and not choice, compels them to submission.

§. 190. Every man is born with a double right: first, a right of freedom to his person, which no other man has a power over, but the free disposal of it lies in himself. Secondly, a right, before any other man, to inherit with his brethren his father's goods.

§. 191. By the first of these, a man is naturally free from subjection to any government, though he be born in a place under its jurisdiction; but if he disclaim the lawful government of the country he was born in, he must also quit the right that belonged to him by the laws of it, and the possessions there descending to him from his ancestors, if it were a government made by their consent.

§. 192. By the second, the inhabitants of any country, who are descended, and derive a title to their estates from those who are subdued, and had a government forced upon them against their free consents, retain a right to the possession of their ancestors, though they consent not freely to the government, whose hard conditions were by force imposed on the possessors of that country. For the first conqueror never having had a title to the land of that country, the people who are the descendants of, or claim under those who were forced to submit to the yoke of a government by constraint, have always a right to shake it off, and free themselves from the usurpation or tyranny which the sword has brought in upon them, till their rulers put them under such a frame of government as they willingly and of choice consent to. Who doubts but the Grecian Christians, descendants of the ancient possessors of that country, may justly cast off the Turkish yoke, which they have so long groaned under, whenever they have an opportunity to do it? For no government can have a right to obedience from a people who have not freely consented to it; which they can never be supposed to do, till either they are put in a full state of liberty to choose their government and governors, or at least till they have such standing laws, to which they have by themselves or their representatives given their free consent, and also till they are allowed their due property, which is so to be proprietors of what they have, that nobody can take away any part of it without their own consent, without which, men under any government are not in the state of freemen, but are direct slaves under the force of war.

§. 193. But granting that the conqueror in a just war has a right to the estates, as well as power over the persons, of the conquered; which, it is plain, he has not: nothing of absolute power will follow from hence, in the continuance of the government. Because the descendants of these being all freemen, if he grants them estates and possessions to inhabit his country, (without which it would be worth nothing) whatsoever he grants them, they have, so far as it is granted, property in. The nature whereof is, that without a man's own consent it cannot be taken from him.

§. 194. Their persons are free by a native right, and their properties, be they more or less, are their own, and at their own dispose, and not at his; or else it is no property. Supposing the conqueror gives to one man a thousand acres, to him and his heirs forever; to another he lets a thousand acres for his life, under the rent of 50£ or 500£ per annum. Has not the one of these a right to his thousand acres forever, and the other, during his life, paying the said rent? And has not the tenant for life a property in all that he gets over and above his rent, by his labor and industry during the said term, supposing it be double the rent? Can anyone say, the king, or conqueror, after his grant, may by his power of conqueror take away all, or part of the land from the heirs of one, or from the other during his life, he paying the rent? Or can he take away from either the goods or money they have got upon the said land, at his pleasure? If he can, then all free and voluntary contracts cease, and are void in the world; there needs nothing to dissolve them at any time, but power enough: and all the grants and promises of men in power are but mockery and collusion. For can there be anything more ridiculous than to say, I give you and yours this forever, and that in the surest and most solemn way of conveyance can be devised: and yet it is to be understood, that I have right, if I please, to take it away from you again tomorrow?

§. 195. I will not dispute now whether princes are exempt from the laws of their country; but this I am sure, they owe subjection to the laws of God and nature. Nobody, no power, can exempt them from the obligations of that eternal law. Those are so great, and so strong, in the case of promises, that omnipotency itself can be tied by them. Grants, promises, and oaths, are bonds that hold the Almighty: whatever some flatterers say to princes of the world, who all together, with all their people joined to them, are, in comparison of the great God, but as a drop of the bucket, or a dust on the balance, inconsiderable nothing!

§. 196. The short of the case in conquest is this: the conqueror, if he have a just cause, has a despotical right over the persons of all, that actually aided, and concurred in the war against him, and a right to make up his damage and cost out of their labor and estates, so he injure not the right of any other. Over the rest of the people, if there were any that consented not to the war, and over the children of the captives themselves, or the possessions of either, he has no power; and so can have, by virtue of conquest, no lawful title himself to dominion over them, or derive it to his posterity; but is an aggressor, if he attempts upon their properties, and thereby puts himself in a state of war against them, and has no better a right of principality, he, nor any of his successors, than Hingar, or Hubba, the Danes, had here in England; or Spartacus,[16] had he conquered Italy, would have had; which is to have their yoke cast off, as soon as God shall give those under their subjection courage and opportunity to do it. Thus, notwithstanding whatever title the kings of Assyria had over Judah, by the sword, God assisted Hezekiah to throw off the dominion of that conquering empire. *And the lord was with Hezekiah, and he prospered; wherefore he went forth, and he rebelled against the king of Assyria, and served him not,* 2 Kings 18. 7. Whence it is plain, that shaking off a power, which force, and not right, has set over anyone, though it has the name of rebellion, yet is no offence before God, but is that which he allows and countenances, though even promises and covenants, when obtained by force, have intervened: for it is very probable, to anyone that reads the story of Ahaz and Hezekiah attentively, that the Assyrians subdued Ahaz, and deposed him, and made Hezekiah king in his father's lifetime; and that Hezekiah by agreement had done him homage, and paid him tribute all this time.

16. Hyngwar and Ubba were Viking chieftains who led the Danish invasions of England in the ninth century. Spartacus (111–71 BCE) was a Thracian gladiator who led a major slave rebellion against the Roman Republic.

CHAPTER XVII
Of Usurpation

§. 197. As conquest may be called a foreign usurpation, so usurpation is a kind of domestic conquest, with this difference, that an usurper can never have right on his side, it being no usurpation, but where one is got into the possession of what another has right to. This, so far as it is usurpation, is a change only of persons, but not of the forms and rules of the government: for if the usurper extends his power beyond what of right belonged to the lawful princes, or governors of the commonwealth, it is tyranny added to usurpation.

§. 198. In all lawful governments, the designation of the persons, who are to bear rule, is as natural and necessary a part as the form of the government itself, and is that which had its establishment originally from the people. Hence all commonwealths, with the form of government established, have rules also of appointing those who are to have any share in the public authority, and settled methods of conveying the right to them. For the anarchy is much alike, to have no form of government at all; or to agree that it shall be monarchical, but to appoint no way to know or design the person that shall have the power, and be the monarch. Whoever gets into the exercise of any part of the power, by other ways than what the laws of the community have prescribed, has no right to be obeyed, though the form of the commonwealth be still preserved; since he is not the person the laws have appointed, and consequently not the person the people have consented to. Nor can such an usurper, or any deriving from him, ever have a title, till the people are both at liberty to consent, and have actually consented to allow, and confirm in him the power he has till then usurped.

CHAPTER XVIII
Of Tyranny

§. 199. As usurpation is the exercise of power, which another has a right to; so tyranny is the exercise of power beyond right, which nobody can have a right to. And this is making use of the power anyone has in his hands, not for the good of those who are under it, but for his own private separate advantage. When the governor, however entitled, makes not the law, but his will, the rule; and his commands and actions are not directed to the preservation of the properties of his people, but the satisfaction of his own ambition, revenge, covetousness, or any other irregular passion.

§. 200. If one can doubt this to be truth, or reason, because it comes from the obscure hand of a subject, I hope the authority of a king will make it pass with him. King James the First, in his speech to the parliament, 1603, tells them thus,

I will ever prefer the weal of the publick, and of the whole commonwealth, in making of good laws and constitutions, to any particular and private ends of mine. Thinking ever the wealth and weal of the commonwealth to be my greatest weal and worldly felicity; a point wherein a lawful king doth directly differ from a tyrant. For I do acknowledge, that the special and greatest point of difference that is between a rightful king and an usurping tyrant, is this, that whereas the proud and ambitious tyrant doth think his kingdom and people are only ordained for satisfaction of his desires and unreasonable appetites; the righteous and just king doth by the contrary acknowledge himself to be ordained for the procuring of the wealth and property of his people.

And again, in his speech to the parliament, 1609, he has these words:

The king binds himself by a double oath, to the observation of the fundamental laws of his kingdom. Tacitly, as by being a king, and so bound to protect as well the people, as the laws of his kingdom, and expressly, by his oath at his coronation; so as every just king, in a setled kingdom, is bound to observe that paction made to his people, by his laws, in framing his government agreeable thereunto, according to that paction which God made with Noah after the deluge. Hereafter, seed-time and harvest, and cold and heat, and summer and winter, and day and night, shall not cease while the earth remaineth. And therefore a king governing in a setled kingdom, leaves to be a king, and degenerates into a tyrant, as soon as he leaves off to rule according to his laws.

And a little after,

*Therefore all kings that are not tyrants, or perjured, will be glad
to bound themselves within the limits of their laws; and they that
persuade them the contrary, are vipers, and pests both against them
and the commonwealth.*

Thus that learned king, who well understood the notion of
things, makes the difference between a king and a tyrant to consist
only in this, that one makes the laws the bounds of his power, and
the good of the public, the end of his government; the other makes
all give way to his own will and appetite.

§. 201. It is a mistake, to think this fault is proper only to monarchies; other forms of government are liable to it, as well as that. For
wherever the power, that is put in any hands for the government of
the people, and the preservation of their properties, is applied to
other ends, and made use of to impoverish, harass, or subdue them
to the arbitrary and irregular commands of those that have it; there
it presently becomes tyranny, whether those that thus use it are
one or many. Thus we read of the thirty tyrants at Athens, as well as
one at Syracuse; and the intolerable dominion of the *Decemviri* at
Rome was nothing better.

§. 202. Wherever law ends, tyranny begins, if the law be transgressed to another's harm. And whosoever in authority exceeds
the power given him by the law, and makes use of the force he has
under his command, to compass that upon the subject, which the
law allows not, ceases in that to be a magistrate; and, acting without
authority, may be opposed, as any other man, who by force invades
the right of another. This is acknowledged in subordinate magistrates. He that has authority to seize my person in the street, may
be opposed as a thief and a robber, if he endeavors to break into my
house to execute a writ, notwithstanding that I know he has such a
warrant, and such a legal authority, as will empower him to arrest
me abroad. And why this should not hold in the highest, as well as
in the most inferior magistrate, I would gladly be informed. Is it
reasonable, that the eldest brother, because he has the greatest part
of his father's estate, should thereby have a right to take away any
of his younger brother's portions? Or that a rich man, who possessed a whole country, should from thence have a right to seize,
when he pleased, the cottage and garden of his poor neighbor? The

being rightfully possessed of great power and riches, exceedingly beyond the greatest part of the sons of Adam, is so far from being an excuse, much less a reason, for rapine and oppression, which the endamaging another without authority is, that it is a great aggravation of it. For the exceeding the bounds of authority is no more a right in a great, than a petty officer; no more justifiable in a king than a constable; but is so much the worse in him, in that he has more trust put in him, has already a much greater share than the rest of his brethren, and is supposed, from the advantages of his education, employment, and counsellors, to be more knowing in the measures of right and wrong.

§. 203. May the commands then of a prince be opposed? May he be resisted as often as anyone shall find himself aggrieved, and but imagine he has not right done him? This will unhinge and over-turn all polities, and, instead of government and order, leave nothing but anarchy and confusion.

§. 204. To this I answer, that force is to be opposed to nothing, but to unjust and unlawful force; whoever makes any opposition in any other case, draws on himself a just condemnation both from God and man; and so no such danger or confusion will follow, as is often suggested. For,

§. 205. First, as, in some countries, the person of the prince by the law is sacred; and so, whatever he commands or does, his person is still free from all question or violence, not liable to force, or any judicial censure or condemnation. But yet opposition may be made to the illegal acts of any inferior officer, or other commissioned by him; unless he will, by actually putting himself into a state of war with his people, dissolve the government, and leave them to that defense which belongs to everyone in the state of nature. For of such things who can tell what the end will be? And a neighbor kingdom has shown the world an odd example. In all other cases the sacredness of the person exempts him from all inconveniences, whereby he is secure, while the government stands, from all violence and harm whatsoever; than which there cannot be a wiser constitution. For the harm he can do in his own person not being likely to happen often, nor to extend itself far; nor being able by his single strength to subvert the laws, nor oppress the body of the people, should any prince have so much weakness, and ill nature as to be willing to do it, the inconvenience of some particular mischiefs, that may happen sometimes, when a heady prince comes to the throne, are well recompensed by the peace of the public, and security of the government, in the person of the chief magistrate, thus set out of the reach of danger: it being safer for the body, that some few private men should be sometimes in danger to suffer, than that the head of the republic should be easily, and upon slight occasions, exposed.

§. 206. Secondly, but this privilege, belonging only to the king's person, hinders not, but they may be questioned, opposed, and resisted, who use unjust force, though they pretend a commission from him, which the law authorizes not. As is plain in the case of him that has the king's writ to arrest a man, which is a full commission from the king; and yet he that has it cannot break open a man's house to do it, nor execute this command of the king upon certain days, nor in certain places, though this commission have no such exception in it; but they are the limitations of the law, which if anyone transgress, the king's commission excuses him not. For the king's authority being given him only by the law, he cannot empower anyone to act against the law, or justify him, by his commission, in so doing. The commission, or command of any magistrate, where he has no authority, being as void and insignificant, as that of any private man. The difference between the one and the other, being that the magistrate has some authority so far, and to such ends, and the private man has none at all: for it is not the commission, but the authority, that gives the right of acting; and against the laws there can be no authority. But, notwithstanding such resistance, the king's person and authority are still both secured, and so no danger to governor or government.

§. 207. Thirdly, supposing a government wherein the person of the chief magistrate is not thus sacred; yet this doctrine of the lawfulness of resisting all unlawful exercises of his power, will not upon every slight occasion endanger him, or embroil the government. For where the injured party may be relieved, and his damages repaired by appeal to the law, there can be no pretence for force, which is only to be used where a man is intercepted from appealing to the law. For nothing is to be accounted hostile force, but where it leaves not the remedy of such an appeal. And it is such force alone that puts him that uses it into a state of war, and makes it lawful to resist him. A man with a sword in his hand demands my purse in the highway, when perhaps I have not twelve pence in my pocket: this man I may lawfully kill. To another I deliver 100£ to hold only while I alight, which he refuses to restore me, when I am got up again, but draws his sword to defend the possession of it by force, if I endeavor to retake it. The mischief this man does me is a hundred, or possibly a thousand times more than the other perhaps intended me (whom I killed before he really did me any); and yet I might lawfully kill the one, and cannot so much as hurt the other lawfully. The reason whereof is plain; because the one using force, which threatened my life, I could not have time to appeal to the law to secure it: and when it was gone, it was too late to appeal. The law could not restore life to my dead carcass: the loss was irreparable; which to prevent, the law of nature gave me a right to destroy him, who had put himself into a state of war with me, and threatened my destruction. But in the other case, my life not being in danger, I may have the benefit of appealing to the law, and have reparation for my 100£ that way.

§. 208. Fourthly, but if the unlawful acts done by the magistrate be maintained (by the power he has got), and the remedy which is due by law, be by the same power obstructed; yet the right of resisting, even in such manifest acts of tyranny, will not suddenly, or on slight occasions, disturb the government: for if it reach no farther than some private men's cases, though they have a right to defend themselves, and to recover by force what by unlawful force is taken from them; yet the right to do so will not easily engage them in a contest, wherein they are sure to perish; it being as impossible for one, or a few oppressed men to disturb the government, where the body of the people do not think themselves concerned in it, as for a raving mad man, or heady malcontent to overturn a well-settled state; the people being as little apt to follow the one, as the other.

§. 209. But if either these illegal acts have extended to the majority of the people; or if the mischief and oppression has lighted only on some few, but in such cases, as the precedent, and consequences seem to threaten all, and they are persuaded in their consciences, that their laws, and with them their estates, liberties, and lives are in danger, and perhaps their religion too, how they will be hindered from resisting illegal force, used against them, I cannot tell. This is an inconvenience, I confess, that attends all governments whatsoever, when the governors have brought it to this pass, to be generally suspected of their people; the most dangerous state which they can possibly put themselves in, wherein they are the less to be pitied, because it is so easy to be avoided; it being as impossible for a governor, if he really means the good of his people, and the preservation of them, and their laws together, not to make them see and feel it, as it is for the father of a family, not to let his children see he loves, and takes care of them.

§. 210. But if all the world shall observe pretences of one kind, and actions of another; arts used to elude the law, and the trust of prerogative (which is an arbitrary power in some things left in the prince's hand to do good, not harm to the people) employed contrary to the end for which it was given: if the people shall find the ministers and subordinate magistrates chosen suitable to such ends, and favored, or laid by, proportionably as they promote or oppose them: if they see several experiments made of arbitrary power, and that religion underhand favored, (though publicly proclaimed against) which is readiest to introduce it; and the operators in it supported, as much as may be; and when that cannot be done, yet approved still, and liked the better: if a long train of actings show the councils all tending that way, how can a man any more hinder himself from being persuaded in his own mind, which way things are going; or from casting about how to save himself, than he could from believing the captain of the ship he was in, was carrying him, and the rest of the company, to Algiers, when he found him always steering that course, though cross winds, leaks in his ship, and want of men and provisions did often force him to turn his course another way for some time, which he steadily returned to again, as soon as the wind, weather, and other circumstances would let him?

CHAPTER XIX
Of the Dissolution of Government

§. 211. He that will with any clearness speak of the dissolution of government, ought in the first place to distinguish between the dissolution of the society and the dissolution of the government. That which makes the community, and brings men out of the loose state of nature, into one politic society, is the agreement which everyone has with the rest to incorporate, and act as one body, and so be one distinct commonwealth. The usual, and almost only way whereby this union is dissolved, is the inroad of foreign force making a conquest upon them. For in that case, (not being able to maintain and support themselves, as one entire and independent body) the union belonging to that body which consisted therein, must necessarily cease, and so everyone return to the state he was in before, with a liberty to shift for himself, and provide for his own safety, as he thinks fit, in some other society. Whenever the society is dissolved, it is certain the government of that society cannot remain. Thus conqueror's swords often cut up governments by the roots, and mangle societies to pieces, separating the subdued or scattered multitude from the protection of, and dependence on, that society which ought to have preserved them from violence. The world is too well instructed in, and too forward to allow of this way of dissolving of governments, to need any more to be said of it: and there wants not much argument to prove, that where the society is dissolved, the government cannot remain; that being as impossible, as for the frame of an house to subsist when the materials of it are scattered and dissipated by a whirl wind, or jumbled into a confused heap by an earthquake.

§. 212. Besides this overturning from without, governments are dissolved from within.

First, when the legislative is altered. Civil society being a state of peace, amongst those who are of it, from whom the state of war is excluded by the umpirage, which they have provided in their legislative, for the ending all differences that may arise amongst any of them, it is in their legislative, that the members of a commonwealth are united, and combined together into one coherent living body. This is the soul that gives form, life, and unity, to the commonwealth: from hence the several members have their mutual influence, sympathy, and connexion: and therefore, when the legislative is broken, or dissolved, dissolution and death follows. For the essence and union of the society consisting in having one will, the legislative, when once established by the majority, has the declaring, and as it were keeping of that will. The constitution of the legislative is the first and fundamental act of society, whereby provision is made for the continuation of their union, under the direction of persons, and bonds of laws, made by persons authorized thereunto, by the consent and appointment of the people, without which no one man, or number of men, amongst them, can have authority of making laws that shall be binding to the rest. When any one, or more, shall take upon them to make laws, whom the people have not appointed so to do, they make laws without authority, which the people are not therefore bound to obey; by which means they come again to be out of subjection, and may constitute to themselves a new legislative, as they think best, being in full liberty to resist the force of those, who without authority would impose anything upon them. Everyone is at the disposure of his own will, when those who had, by the delegation of the society, the declaring of the public will, are excluded from it, and others usurp the place, who have no such authority or delegation.

§. 213. This being usually brought about by such in the commonwealth who misuse the power they have: it is hard to consider it aright, and know at whose door to lay it, without knowing the form of government in which it happens. Let us suppose then the legislative placed in the concurrence of three distinct persons:

(1) A single hereditary person, having the constant, supreme, executive power, and with it the power of convoking and dissolving the other two within certain periods of time.

(2) An assembly of hereditary nobility.

(3) An assembly of representatives chosen, *pro tempore*, by the people. Such a form of government supposed, it is evident,

§. 214. First, that when such a single person, or prince, sets up his own arbitrary will in place of the laws, which are the will of the society, declared by the legislative, then the legislative is changed.

For that being in effect the legislative, whose rules and laws are put in execution, and required to be obeyed; when other laws are set up, and other rules pretended, and enforced, than what the legislative, constituted by the society, have enacted, it is plain that the legislative is changed. Whoever introduces new laws, not being thereunto authorized by the fundamental appointment of the society, or subverts the old, disowns and overturns the power by which they were made, and so sets up a new legislative.

§. 215. Secondly, when the prince hinders the legislative from assembling in its due time, or from acting freely, pursuant to those ends for which it was constituted, the legislative is altered. For it is not a certain number of men, no, nor their meeting, unless they have also freedom of debating, and leisure of perfecting, what is for the good of the society, wherein the legislative consists: when these are taken away or altered, so as to deprive the society of the due exercise of their power, the legislative is truly altered. For it is not names that constitute governments, but the use and exercise of those powers that were intended to accompany them; so that he, who takes away the freedom, or hinders the acting of the legislative in its due seasons, in effect takes away the legislative, and puts an end to the government.

§. 216. Thirdly, when, by the arbitrary power of the prince, the electors, or ways of election, are altered, without the consent, and contrary to the common interest of the people, there also the legislative is altered. For if others, than those whom the society has authorized thereunto, do choose, or in another way than what the society has prescribed, those chosen are not the legislative appointed by the people.

§. 217. Fourthly, the delivery also of the people into the subjection of a foreign power, either by the prince, or by the legislative, is certainly a change of the legislative, and so a dissolution of the government. For the end why people entered into society being to be preserved one entire, free, independent society, to be governed by its own laws; this is lost, whenever they are given up into the power of another.

§. 218. Why in such a constitution as this, the dissolution of the government in these cases is to be imputed to the prince, is evident; because he, having the force, treasure and offices of the state to employ, and often persuading himself, or being flattered by others, that as supreme magistrate he is incapable of control; he alone is in a condition to make great advances toward such changes, under pretence of lawful authority, and has it in his hands to terrify or suppress opposers, as factious, seditious, and enemies to the government: whereas no other part of the legislative, or people, is capable by themselves to attempt any alteration of the legislative, without open and visible rebellion, apt enough to be taken notice of, which, when it prevails, produces effects very little different from foreign conquest. Besides, the prince in such a form of government, having the power of dissolving the other parts of the legislative, and thereby rendering them private persons, they can never in opposition to him, or without his concurrence, alter the legislative by a law, his consent being necessary to give any of their decrees that sanction. But yet, so far as the other parts of the legislative any way contribute to any attempt upon the government, and do either promote, or not, what lies in them, hinder such designs, they are guilty, and partake in this, which is certainly the greatest crime which men can partake of one toward another.

§. 219. There is one way more whereby such a government may be dissolved, and that is, when he who has the supreme executive power, neglects and abandons that charge, so that the laws already made can no longer be put in execution. This is demonstratively to reduce all to anarchy, and so effectually to dissolve the government. For laws not being made for themselves, but to be, by their execution, the bonds of the society, to keep every part of the body politic in its due place and function, when that totally ceases, the government visibly ceases, and the people become a confused multitude, without order or connection. Where there is no longer the administration of justice, for the securing of men's rights, nor any remaining power within the community to direct the force, or provide for the necessities of the public, there certainly is no government left. Where the laws cannot be executed, it is all one as if there were no laws, and a government without laws is, I suppose, a mystery in politics, inconceivable to human capacity, and inconsistent with human society.

§. 220. In these and the like cases, when the government is dissolved, the people are at liberty to provide for themselves, by erecting a new legislative, differing from the other, by the change of persons, or form, or both, as they shall find it most for their safety and good. For the society can never, by the fault of another, lose the native and original right it has to preserve itself, which can only be done by a settled legislative, and a fair and impartial execution of the laws made by it. But the state of mankind is not so miserable that they are not capable of using this remedy, till it be too late to look for any. To tell people they may provide for themselves, by erecting a new legislative, when by oppression, artifice, or being delivered over to a foreign power, their old one is gone, is only to tell them, they may expect relief when it is too late, and the evil is past cure. This is in effect no more than to bid them first be slaves, and then to take care of their liberty; and when their chains are on, tell them, they may act like freemen. This, if barely so, is rather mockery than relief; and men can never be secure from tyranny, if there be no means to escape it till they are perfectly under it: and therefore it is, that they have not only a right to get out of it, but to prevent it.

§. 221. There is therefore, secondly, another way whereby governments are dissolved, and that is, when the legislative, or the prince, either of them, act contrary to their trust.

First, the legislative acts against the trust reposed in them, when they endeavor to invade the property of the subject, and to make themselves, or any part of the community, masters, or arbitrary disposers of the lives, liberties, or fortunes of the people.

§. 222. The reason why men enter into society, is the preservation of their property; and the end why they choose and authorize a legislative, is, that there may be laws made, and rules set, as guards and fences to the properties of all the members of the society, to limit the power, and moderate the dominion, of every part and member of the society. For since it can never be supposed to be the will of the society, that the legislative should have a power to destroy that which everyone designs to secure, by entering into

society, and for which the people submitted themselves to legislators of their own making; whenever the legislators endeavor to
take away, and destroy the property of the people, or to reduce
them to slavery under arbitrary power, they put themselves into a
state of war with the people, who are thereupon absolved from any
farther obedience, and are left to the common refuge, which God
has provided for all men, against force and violence. Whensoever
therefore the legislative shall transgress this fundamental rule of
society; and either by ambition, fear, folly or corruption, endeavor
to grasp themselves, or put into the hands of any other, an absolute
power over the lives, liberties, and estates of the people; by this
breach of trust they forfeit the power the people had put into their
hands for quite contrary ends, and it devolves to the people, who
have a right to resume their original liberty, and, by the establishment of a new legislative, (such as they shall think fit) provide for
their own safety and security, which is the end for which they are
in society. What I have said here, concerning the legislative in general, holds true also concerning the supreme executor, who having
a double trust put in him, both to have a part in the legislative,
and the supreme execution of the law, acts against both, when he
goes about to set up his own arbitrary will as the law of the society.
He acts also contrary to his trust, when he either employs the
force, treasure, and offices of the society, to corrupt the representatives, and gain them to his purposes; or openly pre-engages the
electors, and prescribes to their choice, such, whom he has, by
solicitations, threats, promises, or otherwise, won to his designs;
and employs them to bring in such, who have promised beforehand what to vote, and what to enact. Thus to regulate candidates
and electors, and new-model the ways of election, what is it but to
cut up the government by the roots, and poison the very fountain
of public security? For the people having reserved to themselves
the choice of their representatives, as the fence to their properties,
could do it for no other end, but that they might always be freely
chosen, and so chosen, freely act, and advise, as the necessity of the
commonwealth, and the public good should, upon examination,
and mature debate, be judged to require. This, those who give their
votes before they hear the debate, and have weighed the reasons on
all sides, are not capable of doing. To prepare such an assembly as
this, and endeavor to set up the declared abettors of his own will,

for the true representatives of the people, and the law-makers of the society, is certainly as great a breach of trust, and as perfect a declaration of a design to subvert the government, as is possible to be met with. To which, if one shall add rewards and punishments visibly employed to the same end, and all the arts of perverted law made use of, to take off and destroy all that stand in the way of such a design, and will not comply and consent to betray the liberties of their country, it will be past doubt what is doing. What power they ought to have in the society, who thus employ it contrary to the trust went along with it in its first institution, is easy to determine; and one cannot but see, that he, who has once attempted any such thing as this, cannot any longer be trusted.

§. 223. To this perhaps it will be said, that the people being ignorant, and always discontented, to lay the foundation of government in the unsteady opinion and uncertain humor of the people, is to expose it to certain ruin; and no government will be able long to subsist, if the people may set up a new legislative, whenever they take offence at the old one. To this I answer, Quite the contrary. People are not so easily got out of their old forms, as some are apt to suggest. They are hardly to be prevailed with to amend the acknowledged faults in the frame they have been accustomed to. And if there be any original defects, or adventitious ones introduced by time, or corruption; it is not an easy thing to get them changed, even when all the world sees there is an opportunity for it. This slowness and aversion in the people to quit their old constitutions, has, in the many revolutions which have been seen in this kingdom, in this and former ages, still kept us to, or, after some interval of fruitless attempts, still brought us back again to our old legislative of king, lords and commons: and whatever provocations have made the crown be taken from some of our princes' heads, they never carried the people so far as to place it in another line.

§. 224. But it will be said, this hypothesis lays a ferment for frequent rebellion. To which I answer,

First, no more than any other hypothesis. For when the people are made miserable, and find themselves exposed to the ill usage of arbitrary power, cry up their governors, as much as you will, for sons of Jupiter let them be sacred and divine, descended, or authorized from heaven; give them out for whom or what you please, the same will happen. The people generally ill treated, and contrary to right, will be ready upon any occasion to ease themselves of a burden that sits heavy upon them. They will wish and seek for the opportunity, which in the change, weakness and accidents of human affairs, seldom delays long to offer itself. He must have lived but a little while in the world, who has not seen examples of this in his time; and he must have read very little, who cannot produce examples of it in all sorts of governments in the world.

§. 225. Secondly, I answer, such revolutions happen not upon every little mismanagement in public affairs. Great mistakes in the ruling part, many wrong and inconvenient laws, and all the slips of human frailty, will be born by the people without mutiny or murmur. But if a long train of abuses, prevarications and artifices, all tending the same way, make the design visible to the people, and they cannot but feel what they lie under, and see whither they are going; it is not to be wondered, that they should then rouse themselves, and endeavor to put the rule into such hands which may secure to them the ends for which government was at first erected; and without which, ancient names, and specious forms, are so far from being better, that they are much worse, than the state of nature, or pure anarchy; the inconveniences being all as great and as near, but the remedy farther off and more difficult.

§. 226. Thirdly, I answer, that this doctrine of a power in the people of providing for their safety anew, by a new legislative, when their legislators have acted contrary to their trust, by invading their property, is the best fence against rebellion, and the most probable means to hinder it. For rebellion being an opposition, not to persons, but authority, which is founded only in the constitutions and laws of the government; those, whoever they be, who by force break through, and by force justify their violation of them, are truly and properly rebels: for when men, by entering into society and civil government, have excluded force, and introduced laws for the preservation of property, peace, and unity amongst themselves, those who set up force again in opposition to the laws, do *rebellare*, that is, bring back again the state of war, and are properly rebels: which they who are in power, (by the pretence they have to authority, the temptation of force they have in their hands, and the flattery of those about them) being likeliest to do; the most proper way to prevent the evil, is to show them the danger and injustice of it, who are under the greatest temptation to run into it.

§. 227. In both the aforementioned cases, when either the legislative is changed, or the legislators act contrary to the end for which they were constituted; those who are guilty are guilty of rebellion. For if anyone by force takes away the established legislative of any society, and the laws by them made, pursuant to their trust, he thereby takes away the umpirage, which everyone had consented to, for a peaceable decision of all their controversies, and a bar to the state of war amongst them. They, who remove, or change the legislative, take away this decisive power, which nobody can have, but by the appointment and consent of the people; and so destroying the authority which the people did, and nobody else can set up, and introducing a power which the people has not authorized, they actually introduce a state of war, which is that of force without authority: and thus, by removing the legislative established by the society (in whose decisions the people acquiesced and united, as to that of their own will) they untie the knot, and expose the people anew to the state of war. And if those, who by force take away the legislative, are rebels, the legislators themselves, as has been shown, can be no less esteemed so; when they, who were set up for the protection, and preservation of the people, their liberties and properties, shall by force invade and endeavor to take them away; and so they putting themselves into a state of war with those who made them the protectors and guardians of their peace, are properly, and with the greatest aggravation, *rebellantes*, rebels.

§. 228. But if they, who say it lays a foundation for rebellion, mean that it may occasion civil wars, or intestine broils, to tell the people they are absolved from obedience when illegal attempts are made upon their liberties or properties, and may oppose the unlawful violence of those who were their magistrates, when they invade their properties contrary to the trust put in them; and that therefore this doctrine is not to be allowed, being so destructive to the peace of the world. They may as well say, upon the same ground, that honest men may not oppose robbers or pirates, because this may occasion disorder or bloodshed. If any mischief comes in such cases, it is not to be charged upon him who defends his own right, but on him that invades his neighbors. If the innocent honest man must quietly quit all he has, for peace sake, to him who will lay violent hands upon it, I desire it may be considered, what a kind of peace there will be in the world, which consists only in violence and rapine; and which is to be maintained only for the benefit of robbers and oppressors. Who would not think it an admirable peace between the mighty and the mean, when the lamb, without resistance, yielded his throat to be torn by the imperious wolf? Polyphemus' den[17] gives us a perfect pattern of such a peace, and such a government, wherein Ulysses and his companions had nothing to do, but quietly to suffer themselves to be devoured. And no doubt Ulysses, who was a prudent man, preached up passive obedience, and exhorted them to a quiet submission, by representing to them of what concernment peace was to mankind; and by showing the inconveniences might happen, if they should offer to resist Polyphemus, who had now the power over them.

§. 229. The end of government is the good of mankind, and which is best for mankind, that the people should be always exposed to the boundless will of tyranny, or that the rulers should be sometimes liable to be opposed, when they grow exorbitant in the use of their power, and employ it for the destruction, and not the preservation of the properties of their people?

§. 230. Nor let anyone say, that mischief can arise from hence, as often as it shall please a busy head, or turbulent spirit, to desire the alteration of the government. It is true, such men may stir, whenever they please; but it will be only to their own just ruin and perdition. For till the mischief be grown general, and the ill designs of the rulers become visible, or their attempts sensible to the greater part, the people, who are more disposed to suffer than right themselves by resistance, are not apt to stir. The examples of particular injustice, or oppression of here and there an unfortunate man, moves them not. But if they universally have a persuasion,

---

17.   Polyphemus is one of the Cyclops described in Homer's *Odyssey*. After seeing some of his crew eaten by Polyphemus, the wily Odysseus (Ulysses) tricked him into allowing most of his men to escape the brutal Cyclops' cave.

grounded upon manifest evidence, that designs are carrying on against their liberties, and the general course and tendency of things cannot but give them strong suspicions of the evil intention of their governors, who is to be blamed for it? Who can help it, if they, who might avoid it, bring themselves into this suspicion? Are the people to be blamed, if they have the sense of rational creatures, and can think of things no otherwise than as they find and feel them? And is it not rather their fault, who put things into such a posture, that they would not have them thought to be as they are? I grant, that the pride, ambition, and turbulency of private men have sometimes caused great disorders in commonwealths, and factions have been fatal to states and kingdoms. But whether the mischief has oftener begun in the people's wantonness, and a desire to cast off the lawful authority of their rulers, or in the ruler's insolence, and endeavors to get and exercise an arbitrary power over their people; whether oppression, or disobedience, gave the first rise to the disorder, I leave it to impartial history to determine. This I am sure, whoever, either ruler or subject, by force goes about to invade the rights of either prince or people, and lays the foundation for overturning the constitution and frame of any just government, is guilty of the greatest crime, I think, a man is capable of, being to answer for all those mischiefs of blood, rapine, and desolation, which the breaking to pieces of governments bring on a country. And he who does it, is justly to be esteemed the common enemy and pest of mankind, and is to be treated accordingly.

§. 231. That subjects or foreigners, attempting by force on the properties of any people, may be resisted with force, is agreed on all hands. But that magistrates, doing the same thing, may be resisted, has of late been denied: as if those who had the greatest privileges and advantages by the law, had thereby a power to break those laws, by which alone they were set in a better place than their brethren: whereas their offence is thereby the greater, both as being ungrateful for the greater share they have by the law, and breaking also that trust, which is put into their hands by their brethren.

§. 232. Whosoever uses force without right, as everyone does in society, who does it without law, puts himself into a state of war with those against whom he so uses it; and in that state all former ties are cancelled, all other rights cease, and everyone has a right to defend himself, and to resist the aggressor. This is so evident, that Barclay[18] himself, that great assertor of the power and sacredness of kings, is forced to confess, that it is lawful for the people, in some cases, to resist their king; and that too in a chapter, wherein he pretends to show, that the divine law shuts up the people from all manner of rebellion. Whereby it is evident even by his own doctrine that, since they may in some cases resist, all resisting of princes is not rebellion. His words are these. *Quod siquis dicat, Ergone populus tyrannicae crudelitati & furori jugulum semper praebebit? Ergone multitudo civitates suas famae, ferro, & flammâ vastari, seque, conjuges, & liberos fortunae ludibrio & tyranni libidini exponi, inque omnia vitae pericula omnesque miserias & molestias à Rege deduci patientur? Num illis quod omni animantium generi est à naturâ tributum, denegari debet, ut sc. vim vi repellant, seseq; ab injuriâ, tueantur? Huic breviter responsum sit, Populo universo non negari defensionem, quae juris naturalis est, neque ultionem quae praeter naturam est adversus Regem concedi debere. Quapropter si Rex non in singulares tantum personas aliquot privatum odium exerceat, sed corpus etiam Reipublicae, cujus ipse caput est, i.e. totum populum, vel insignem aliquam ejus partem immani & intolerandâ saevitiâ seu tyrannide divexet; populo, quidem hoc casu resistendi ac tuendi se ab injuriâ potestas competit, sed tuendi se tantum, non enim in principem invadendi: & restituendae injuriae illatae, non recedendi à debitâ reverentiâ propter acceptam injuriam. Praesentem denique impetum propulsandi non vim praeteritam ulciscendi jus habet. Horum enim alterum à naturâ est, ut vitam scilicet corpusque tueamur. Alterum vero contra naturam, ut inferior de superiori supplicium sumat. Quod itaque populus malum, antequam factum sit, impedire potest, ne fiat, id postquam factum est, in Regem authorem sceleris vindicare non potest: Populus igitur hoc ampliùs quam privatus quispiam habet: Quod huic, vel ipsis adversariis judicibus, excepto Buchanano, nullum nisi in patientia remedium superest. Cùm ille si intolerabilis tyrannus est (modicum enim ferre omnino debet) resistere cum reverentiâ possit,* Barclay, *contra Monarchom.* 1. iii. c. 8.

---

18. For William Barclay, see the note at I: 4.

In English thus:

§. 233. *But if anyone should ask, Must the people then always lay themselves open to the cruelty and rage of tyranny? Must they see their cities pillaged, and laid in ashes, their wives and children exposed to the tyrant's lust and fury, and themselves and families reduced by their king to ruin, and all the miseries of want and oppression, and yet sit still? Must men alone be debarred the common privilege of opposing force with force, which nature allows so freely to all other creatures for their preservation from injury? I answer: Self-defence is a part of the law of nature; nor can it be denied the community, even against the king himself: but to revenge themselves upon him, must by no means be allowed them; it being not agreeable to that law. Wherefore if the king shall show an hatred, not only to some particular persons, but sets himself against the body of the common-wealth, whereof he is the head, and shall, with intolerable ill usage, cruelly tyrannize over the whole, or a considerable part of the people, in this case the people have a right to resist and defend themselves from injury: but it must be with this caution, that they only defend themselves, but do not attack their prince: they may repair the damages received, but must not for any provocation exceed the bounds of due reverence and respect. They may repulse the present attempt, but must not revenge past violences: for it is natural for us to defend life and limb, but that an inferior should punish a superior, is against nature. The mischief which is designed them, the people may prevent before it be done; but when it is done, they must not revenge it on the king, though author of the villainy. This therefore is the privilege of the people in general, above what any private person has; that particular men are allowed by our adversaries themselves (Buchanan*[19] *only excepted) to have no other remedy but patience; but the body of the people may with respect resist intolerable tyranny; for when it is but moderate, they ought to endure it.*

§. 234. Thus far that great advocate of monarchical power allows of resistance.

§. 235. It is true he has annexed two limitations to it, to no purpose:

---

19.   George Buchanan (1506–1582) was a Scottish thinker who believed that supreme political power derived from the people; he also developed a theory of popular resistance to tyranny.

First, he says, it must be with reverence.

Secondly, it must be without retribution, or punishment; and the reason he gives is, because an inferior cannot punish a superior. First, how to resist force without striking again, or how to strike with reverence, will need some skill to make intelligible. He that shall oppose an assault only with a shield to receive the blows, or in any more respectful posture, without a sword in his hand, to abate the confidence and force of the assailant, will quickly be at an end of his resistance, and will find such a defense serve only to draw on himself the worse usage. This is as ridiculous a way of resisting, as Juvenal[20] thought it of fighting; *ubi tu pulsas, ego vapulo tantum*. And the success of the combat will be unavoidably the same he there describes it:

> ———*Libertas pauperis haec est:*
> *Pulsatus rogat, et pugnis concisus, adorat,*
> *Ut liceat paucis cum dentibus inde reverti.*

This will always be the event of such an imaginary resistance, where men may not strike again. He therefore who may resist, must be allowed to strike. And then let our author, or anybody else, join a knock on the head, or a cut on the face, with as much reverence and respect as he thinks fit. He that can reconcile blows and reverence, may, for aught I know, desire for his pains, a civil, respectful cudgeling wherever he can meet with it.

Secondly, as to his second, an inferior cannot punish a superior; that is true, generally speaking, while he is his superior. But to resist force with force, being the state of war that levels the parties, cancels all former relation of reverence, respect, and superiority: and then the odds that remains, is, that he, who opposes the unjust aggressor, has this superiority over him, that he has a right, when he prevails, to punish the offender, both for the breach of the peace, and all the evils that followed upon it. Barclay therefore, in another place, more coherently to himself, denies it to be lawful to

---

20. Decimus Iunius Iuvenalis, or Juvenal (b. first century CE, d. second century) was a Roman poet famed for his *Satires*, of which the first Latin passage is: "I writhe with the blows you put upon me." The second passage is: "This is a poor man's freedom: / the more he is beaten, the more he implores, / and he prostates himself as he goes down in the struggle so that he may come back a little with his teeth."

resist a king in any case. But he there assigns two cases, whereby a king may un-king himself. His words are,

Quid ergo, nulline casus incidere possunt quibus populo sese erigere atque in Regem impotentius dominantem arma capere & invadere jure suo suâque authoritate liceat? Nulli certe quamdiu Rex manet. Semper enim ex divinis id obstat, Regem honorificato; & qui potestati resistit, Dei ordinationi resisit: *Non aliàs igitur in eum populo potestas est quam si id committat propter quod ipso jure rex esse desinat. Tunc enim se ipse principatu exuit atque in privatis constituit liber: Hoc modo populus & superior efficitur, reverso ad eum sc. jure illo quod ante regem inauguratum in interregno habuit. At sunt paucorum generum commissa ejusmodi quae hunc effectum pariunt. At ego cum plurima animo perlustrem, duo tantum invenio, duos, inquam, casus quibus rex ipso facto ex Rege non regem se facit & omni honore & dignitate regali atque in subditos potestate destituit; quorum etiam meminit Winzerus. Horum unus est, Si regnum disperdat, quemadmodum de Nerone fertur, quod is nempe senatum populumque Romanum, atque adeo urbem ipsam ferro flammaque vastare, ac novas sibi sedes quaerere decrevisset. Et de Caligula, quod palam denunciarit se neque civem neque principem senatui amplius fore, inque animo habuerit interempto utriusque ordinis Electissimo quoque Alexandriam commigrare, ac ut populum uno ictu interimeret, unam ei cervicem optavit. Talia cum rex aliquis meditatur & molitur serio, omnem regnandi curam & animum ilico abjicit, ac proinde imperium in subditos amittit, ut dominus servi pro derelicto habiti, dominium.*

§. 236. *Alter casus est, Si rex in alicujus clientelam se contulit, ac regnum quod liberum à majoribus & populo traditum accepit, alienae ditioni mancipavit. Nam tunc quamvis forte non eâ mente id agit populo plane ut incommodet: Tamen quia quod praecipuum est regiae dignitatis amisit, ut summus scilicet in regno secundum Deum sit, & solo Deo inferior, atque populum etiam totum ignorantem vel invitum, cujus libertatem sartam & tectam conservare debuit, in alterius gentis ditionem & potestatem dedidit; hâc velut quadam regni ab alienatione effecit, ut nec quod ipse in regno imperium habuit retineat, nec in eum cui collatum voluit, juris quicquam transferat; atque ita eo facto liberum jam & suae potestatis populum*

relinquit, cujus rei exemplum unum annales Scotici suppeditant.
Barclay, *contra Monarchom.* 1. iii. c. 16.[21]

Which in English runs thus:

§. 237. *What then, can there no case happen wherein the people may of right, and by their own authority, help themselves, take arms, and set upon their king, imperiously domineering over them? None at all, while he remains a king.* Honour the king, and he that resists the power, resists the ordinance of God; *are divine oracles that will never permit it. The people therefore can never come by a power over him, unless he does something that makes him cease to be a king: for then he divests himself of his crown and dignity, and returns to the state of a private man, and the people become free and superior, the power which they had in the interregnum, before they crowned him king, devolving to them again. But there are but few miscarriages which bring the matter to this state. After considering it well on all sides, I can find but two. Two cases there are, I say, whereby a king, ipso facto, becomes no king, and loses all power and regal authority over his people; which are also taken notice of by Winzerus.*[22]

The first is, if he endeavour to overturn the government, that is, if he have a purpose and design to ruin the kingdom and common-wealth, as it is recorded of Nero, that he resolved to cut off the sen-ate and people of Rome, lay the city waste with fire and sword, and then remove to some other place. And of Caligula,[23] *that he openly declared, that he would be no longer a head to the people or senate, and that he had it in his thoughts to cut off the worthiest men of both ranks, and then retire to Alexandria: and he wished that the people had but one neck, that he might dispatch them all at a blow. Such designs as these, when any king harbours in his thoughts, and seri-ously promotes, he immediately gives up all care and thought of the commonwealth; and consequently forfeits the power of governing his*

---

21. The full title of the work by William Barclay (1546–1608) to which Locke refers is *De Regno et Regali Potestati adversus Buchananum, Brutum Boucherium et reliquos Monarchomachos* (1600).

22. Probably Ninian Winzet (1519–1592), who was a Scottish defender of the sacred character of royal power.

23. Caligula (12–41 CE) was a Roman emperor known to posterity as a cruel, sadistic, and vicious tyrant.

subjects, as a master does the dominion over his slaves whom he has abandoned.

§. 238. *The other case is, When a king makes himself the dependent of another, and subjects his kingdom which his ancestors left him, and the people put free into his hands, to the dominion of another: for however perhaps it may not be his intention to prejudice the people; yet because he has hereby lost the principal part of regal dignity, viz. to be next and immediately under God, supreme in his kingdom; and also because he betrayed or forced his people, whose liberty he ought to have carefully preserved, into the power and dominion of a foreign nation. By this, as it were, alienation of his kingdom, he himself loses the power he had in it before, without transferring any the least right to those on whom he would have bestowed it; and so by this act sets the people free, and leaves them at their own disposal. One example of this is to be found in the Scotch Annals.*

§. 239. In these cases Barclay, the great champion of absolute monarchy, is forced to allow, that a king may be *resisted*, and *ceases to be a king*. That is, in short, not to multiply cases, in whatsoever he has *no authority*, there he is no *king*, and may be *resisted: for wheresoever the authority ceases, the king ceases too*, and becomes like other men who have no authority. And these two cases he instances in, differ little from those above mentioned, to be destructive to governments, only that he has omitted the principle from which his doctrine flows: and that is, the breach of trust, in not preserving the form of government agreed on, and in not intending the end of government itself, which is the public good and preservation of property. When a king has dethroned himself, and put himself in a state of war with his people, what shall hinder them from prosecuting him who is no king, as they would any other man, who has put himself into a state of war with them, Barclay, and those of his opinion, would do well to tell us. This farther I desire may be taken notice of out of Barclay, that he says, *The mischief that is designed them, the people may prevent before it be done*: whereby he allows *resistance* when tyranny is but in design. *Such designs as these* (says he) *when any king harbours in his thoughts and seriously promotes, he immediately gives up all care and thought of the commonwealth*; so that, according to him, the neglect of the public good is to be taken as an evidence of such design, or at least for a sufficient cause of resistance. And the reason of all, he gives in these words, *because he betrayed or forced his people, whose liberty he ought carefully to have preserved.* What he adds, *into the power and dominion of a foreign nation*, signifies nothing, the fault and forfeiture lying in the loss of their *liberty*, which he *ought to have preserved*, and not in any distinction of the persons to whose dominion they were subjected. The people's right is equally invaded, and their liberty lost, whether they are made slaves to any of their own, or a foreign nation; and in this lies the injury, and against this only have they the right of defense. And there are instances to be found in all countries, which show, that it is not the change of nations in the persons of their governors, but the change of government, that gives the offence. Bilson,[24] a bishop of our church, and a great stickler for the power and prerogative of princes, does, if I mistake not, in his *treatise of Christian subjection*, acknowledge, *that princes may forfeit their power*, and their title to the obedience of their subjects; and if there needed authority in a case where reason is so plain, I could send my reader to Bracton, Fortescue, and the author of the *Mirrour*,[25] and others, writers that cannot be suspected to be ignorant of our government, or enemies to it. But I thought Hooker alone might be enough to satisfy those men, who relying on him for their ecclesiastical polity, are by a strange fate carried to deny those principles upon which he builds it. Whether they are herein made the tools of more cunning workmen, to pull down their own fabric, they were best look. This I am sure, their civil policy is so new, so dangerous, and so destructive to both rulers and people, that as former ages never could bear the broaching of it; so it may be hoped, those to come, redeemed from the impositions of these Egyptian under-taskmasters, will abhor the memory of such servile flatterers, who, while it seemed to serve their turn, resolved all

24.   Thomas Bilson (1547–1616) was an Anglican bishop who supported the right of kings but allowed for some limits on the exercise of royal power.

25.   Sir John Fortescue (1394–1480) and Sir Henry de Bracton (1210–1268) were English jurists who, because they argued that the power of the monarch is limited by law, were seen as authorities in the constitutionalist reading of English political history that opposed divine rightists, such as Filmer, Sibthorpe, and Manwaring. The "author of the *Mirrour*" is likely Andrew Horn (1275–1328), who wrote a fourteenth-century English law text titled *The Mirrour of Justice*.

government into absolute tyranny, and would have all men born to, what their mean souls fitted them for, slavery.

§. 240. Here, it is like, the common question will be made, Who shall be judge, whether the prince or legislative act contrary to their trust? This, perhaps, ill-affected and factious men may spread amongst the people, when the prince only makes use of his due prerogative. To this I reply, The people shall be judge; for who shall be judge whether his trustee or deputy acts well, and according to the trust reposed in him, but he who deputes him, and must, by having deputed him, have still a power to discard him, when he fails in his trust? If this be reasonable in particular cases of private men, why should it be otherwise in that of the greatest moment, where the welfare of millions is concerned, and also where the evil, if not prevented, is greater, and the redress very difficult, dear, and dangerous?

§. 241. But farther, this question, (Who shall be judge?) cannot mean, that there is no judge at all. For where there is no judicature on earth, to decide controversies amongst men, God in heaven is judge: He alone, it is true, is judge of the right. But every man is judge for himself, as in all other cases, so in this, whether another has put himself into a state of war with him, and whether he should appeal to the Supreme Judge, as Jephtha did.

§. 242. If a controversy arise between a prince and some of the people, in a matter where the law is silent, or doubtful, and the thing be of great consequence, I should think the proper umpire, in such a case, should be the body of the people. For in cases where the prince has a trust reposed in him, and is dispensed from the common ordinary rules of the law; there, if any men find themselves aggrieved, and think the prince acts contrary to, or beyond that trust, who so proper to judge as the body of the people, (who, at first, lodged that trust in him) how far they meant it should extend? But if the prince, or whoever they be in the administration, decline that way of determination, the appeal then lies nowhere but to heaven. Force between either persons, who have no known superior on earth, or which permits no appeal to a judge on earth, being properly a state of war, wherein the appeal lies only to heaven, and in that state the injured party must judge for himself, when he will think fit to make use of that appeal, and put himself upon it.

§. 243. To conclude, The power that every individual gave the society, when he entered into it, can never revert to the individuals again, as long as the society lasts, but will always remain in the community; because without this there can be no community, no commonwealth, which is contrary to the original agreement: so also when the society has placed the legislative in any assembly of men, to continue in them and their successors, with direction and authority for providing such successors, the legislative can never revert to the people while that government lasts: because having provided a legislative with power to continue forever, they have given up their political power to the legislative, and cannot resume it. But if they have set limits to the duration of their legislative, and made this supreme power in any person, or assembly, only temporary: or else, when by the miscarriages of those in authority, it is forfeited; upon the forfeiture of their rulers, or at the determination of the time set, it reverts to the society, and the people have a right to act as supreme, and continue the legislative in themselves; or erect a new form, or under the old form place it in new hands, as they think good.

FINIS

THEMATIC INDEX

In this index Roman numerals refer to either the *First* or the *Second Treatise*, and the Arabic numerals that follow indicate the sections in the specified treatise.